Multinational Companies and Exploitation of Women in Developing Countries

Multinational Companies and Exploitation of Women in Developing Countries

P Kumar

MD Publications Pvt Ltd
New Delhi
www.mdppl.com

Published by :

MD Publications Pvt Ltd
"MD House", 11, Darya Ganj,
New Delhi-110 002
Phone : +91-11-45355555
E-mail : contact@mdppl.com
Website : www.mdppl.com

ISBN : 978-81-7533-279-9

Published and Printed by Mr. Pranav Gupta on behalf of MD Publications Pvt Ltd at Printext, New Delhi.

Preface

Since the 1960s, multinationals have scattered factories across the globe as export-oriented industrialization-touted by the United Nations Development Organization (UNIDO), the World Bank, and the International Monetary Fund-has become the favored strategy for Third World development. Third World countries roll out the red carpet for foreign investors and become "export platforms" producing goods for the world market. In return, "host governments" are promised jobs, technology, and foreign exchange.

Since multinationals go overseas to reduce labor costs, women are the natural choice for assembly jobs. Wage-earning opportunities for women are limited and women are considered only supplementary income earners for their families. Management uses that secondary status to pay women less than men and justify layoffs during slow periods, claiming that women don't need to work and will probably quit to get married anyway. Women are the preferred workforce for other reasons. Multinationals want a workforce that is docile, easily manipulated, and willing to do boring, repetitive assembly work. Women, they claim, are the perfect employees, with their "natural patience" and "manual dexterity." Multinationals prefer single women with no children and no plans to have any. Pregnancy tests are routinely given to potential employees to avoid the issue of maternity benefits.

The majority of the new female workforce is young, between 16 and 25 years old. As one management consultant explains, "When seniority rises, wages rise"; so the companies prefer to train a fresh group of teenagers rather than give experienced women higher pay. The youngest workers, usually under 23 years old, are found in electronics and textile factories where keen eyesight and dexterity are essential. A second, older group of women work in industries like food processing where nimble fingers and perfect vision are not required. Multinationals can get away with worse conditions in these factories because the women generally can't find jobs elsewhere.

The sex wage difference reflects female subordination and the sexual division of labor in indigenous society, particularly the constraints of the female/mother role which results in the short job tenure, low seniority, and hence low average wages of women workers. In these as in other predominantly female occupations, women quit when they marry and have children. Neither the national nor the sex wage difference is the specific responsibility of these multinationals, though they take advantage of and in some cases may even reinforce them.

A widely accepted criticism of multinationals argues that the wages paid in multinational export factories are so low that they are insufficient to cover in some cases even the minimum physical subsistence of workers employed in very intensive tasks, so they become quickly "exhausted." But the evidence in the literature itself shows that not only do the vast majority of workers cover their own physical subsistence and basic needs of food, housing, clothing and transportation, they have enough left over for small luxuries, savings, and contributions to their families.

I am very grateful to Mr. Pranav Gupta, Director of MD Publications Pvt Ltd, New Delhi, for his kind cooperation and support for this book.

P Kumar

CONTENTS

1

Implications for Women's Work and Struggles

This chapter attempts to redirect our understanding of moral relations from the boundaries of religious or legal doctrine to the field of discourse and micro level politics. Too often external criteria, such as religious codes or state laws, are used to determine and evaluate what is appropriate or inappropriate social behavior. Placing such a heavy emphasis on these centralized positions of power, however, ignores the more subtle and multiple forms of power relations that are involved in guiding and changing people's conduct and activity. In this chapter, I emphasize the role of moral discourse as a technique of power in shaping social and economic relations and in directing the action of people by circumscribing arenas of obedience and duty.

Specifically, my research in rural Turkey highlights how everyday moral discourses and practices incite, undermine, and authorize women's and men's relations, as well as mediate economic transformation. In the spheres of social class, work, and gender relations, moral discourses are shown as both instruments and effects of power, as well as points of resistance. In this way, the first section of this chapter conceptualizes morality within a genealogical frame of reference, emphasizing the connections and relations between people by locating the power struggles of these relations.

The second section highlights how moral discourses at both the national and local level negotiate economic development and influence gender and work dynamics. In the context of the northwestern region of Turkey, I analyze how the availability and moral value of migrant (male) wage labor altered landlord-peasant relations and introduced a series of new developments and challenges in women's work responsibilities. This section also elaborates on contemporary relations in the community, including the process of the feminization of subsistence agriculture, the regulation of women's work and activities through a masculinist moral discourse, and the everyday forms of resistance by women.

In the Middle East, conceptions of morality customarily hold that Qur'anic moral/legal codes are directly correlated with everyday "reality". Likewise, and within the Turkish context, some scholars deduce certain forms of social behavior, such as polygamy and inheritance, gender, family, or property relations, from the Qur'an. However, while Qur'anic law and rhetoric are powerful tools for understanding certain social and political environments, as a master narrative they cannot always provide a sufficient account of patterns of social behavior, especially variable patterns of gender relations. As Najmabadi states, "There is a tendency toward an essentialist conception of Islam, reducing Islam to a given set of doctrines, with a given set of edicts on women, and attributing the current practices and ideology of Islamic movements to the implementation of these doctrines."

In other words, religious or legal perspectives defer to the authority of the text or adopt authoritarian dogma as explanations of social relations. Such totalizing strategies are unable to fully explain or recognize the complexity, contradictions, and transformations of gender relations. It is therefore important to document other less formal techniques that influence and shape gender and work dynamics. In moving away from positing official Islam as the basis for understanding moral action and belief, it is essential to highlight a more genealogical approach to morality. Differing from legalistic approaches, a genealogical approach to morality involves researching or tracing the connections and relations between people by locating the power struggles of these relations.

This methodological approach acknowledges that there is a difference between people's accounts of their connections to others and the social struggles within which these discourses emerge in the first place. In other words, the moral discourses people use to connect themselves to (or disconnect themselves from) others, do not fully disclose the nature of the underlying relationship between discourses and power contests. Everyday moral rhetoric (i.e., that one should do this or that; that one ought to act in such and such a way; that things ought to be like this, etc.) only marks the site of contested relations; it does not specify the character of the power struggles (or the forms of resistance) that underscore them.

Therefore, it is the role of the analyst to discover the nature of the power struggles and to recognize that there are diverse techniques through which the actions and judgments of individuals and groups can be linked to political processes. Simply to translate how people understand their relations with others, what they judge as appropriate and inappropriate, good or bad, right or wrong, would be to understand these claims only as rationalizations and defenses of their way of life. In so doing, however, there is always the potential problem of being caught up in the reasoning certain groups give for why they think and act the way they do. It is often the case, for example, that scholars take people's purposes, interests, or intentions as the origin of the discourse, without examining the discourse's internal relations and the generative aspects of the relationships to which it speaks.

In an effort to avoid functional or teleological explanations for "the ways things are or should be," it is essential to separate the alleged purpose of morality (what moral discourse says it does) from its origin (power relation). In this regard, I show how moral claims, rather than preserving, defending, or protecting something, emerge from a form of power that attempts to guide people's possibility of conduct in the present or in the future. In this way, I present morality as a form of regulation. Instead of simply analyzing moral relations as devoid of social conflict, this methodological technique conceptually distinguishes the discursive from the non-discursive or moral discourse from everyday power struggles. Such an approach permits a sociological analysis of the northwestern community of Sakli's moral economy and an excavation of patterns and exercises of power.

In what follows, I illustrate how moral discourses at both the national and local levels are critical for understanding social regulation and power relations, especially in the way in which they mediate development regimes and shape gender and work dynamics. Recent advances in information technology, coupled with deregulation and market liberalization worldwide, have fueled an unprecedented surge in the growth of multinational corporations (MNCs). While some regard them as ruthless exploiters, others view them as benign engines of prosperity. But today's multinationals bear little resemblance to their forebears. They are reinventing themselves in diverse ways that confound the assumptions of critics and advocates alike.

Globalization Has Made MNCs More "Footloose" Than Ever Partly true. There is a widespread perception that multinational corporations will rush to relocate in response to changing economic conditions. Yet there are compelling reasons for many MNCS tO stay put or, at the very least, to shift the location of their operations at a gradual pace. Some multinationals often find themselves "locked" into emerging hot-spot "clusters" of related assets and specialized infrastructure-such as Silicon Valley for microprocessors, Tsukuba City for miniaturization, and London for foreign exchange. Increasingly, such clusters can even be found in developing countries such as India, where Bangalore has become a hub for the software industry. These immobile resources are comprised of a dense network of specialized, often small, independent enterprises that supply crucial inputs and are difficult to replicate elsewhere. Leading MNCs must interact with these clusters if they are to gain and retain access to the latest thinking.

Another reason why MNCs are reluctant to uproot their operations is that they depend upon the skills of specialized teams of local workers. Volkswagen, for example, is using its Resende plant in Brazil as a lead site for experimenting with ways to change the assembly process. Multinationals that have become dependent on such "intelligent systems" can continue to attract investors by maintaining and strengthening these human assets, not by walking away.

MNCs Are, First and Foremost, Creatures of Their Home Countries. Not always. Most people assume that the home country always gets first priority whenever MNCs have to make hard choices: If faced with a downturn in the market, multinationals will close facilities abroad to protect those at home. Yet Japanese MNCs have strived to remain competitive by developing lower-cost capacity in facilities abroad. In doing so, corporate executives have played a role in "hollowing out" Japan's economy and have broken with generations of tradition that put national interest above all else. Moreover, corporations now place higher priority on the innovation process - regardless of where that process is centered - than on outdated notions of home country. Some MNCs have developed world product mandates that farm out management authority and research-and-development leadership to foreign units.

Tokyo is "home" to IBM's personal computers, while Taiwan is "home" to Philips' computer monitors. Indeed, there is now widespread unease that MNCs are becoming truly "stateless," acting in the interests of shareholders who are themselves becoming globally dispersed. These concerns are amplified by the growing trend among major corporations to promote foreign nationals to top management positions. Some French and German companies even use English as the lingua franca for their management communications globally.

ALL MULTINATIONALS ARE LARGE CORPORATIONS

No. It is easy to get that impression, since giant MNCs dominate the news. The top 100 multinationals own nearly $2 trillion of assets outside their home countries, a quarter of the world's stock of all foreign direct investment (FDI). And the recent wave of megamergers has made many large multinationals even larger. But a closer look at the marketplace reveals that the surge in MNC growth is also being driven by myriad newcomers, many of whom are actually quite small. Most of the estimated 45,000 firms that operate internationally employ fewer than 250 people. It is commonplace to find service companies that maintain fewer than 100 employees operating across more than 15 countries. For years the traditional wisdom among multinational corporations was that bigger is better. Large MNCs could lower their production costs by producing massive volumes to serve global markets. By achieving such "economies of scale," they gained a crucial advantage over their competitors.

In today's turbulent markets, however, size does not always matter. Big banks have been merging across borders to make themselves even bigger, but their success rates have been dismal. In the oil and gas industry, traditional leaders such as Exxon and Shell now face serious challenges from smaller upstarts that have carved out industry niches in exploration or lubricants. The success of Enron in transforming itself from a sleepy, domestic-pipeline operator in Texas to an international force in gas and power generation shows how potent this new challenge can be. New competitors are emphasizing the power of intangible resources such as intellectual property and a flexible organizational structure that allows firms to respond better to their customers' diverse needs.

These emerging multinationals are beginning to develop and link together expert teams within the corporation in ways that resemble the activities of the hot-spot clusters that lie outside the corporation. In contrast to traditional economic models of competition, these companies have found that economies of scale can best be achieved at the corporate level rather than the production level. The message is clear to the major incumbents: transform or die. At a time when size and market shares are growing in importance for some MNCs, for others the value of incumbency has never been less.

MNC MARKETS ARE IMPENETRABLE TO RIVAL COMPANIES

No. Multinational leaders such as General Electric and Shell took many years to build their empires, helping create the impression that growth is slow and dependent on physical assets (such as sprawling factories) to erect high barriers to the entry of new competitors. But what about Microsoft (software), Cisco (computers), Fresenius (dialysis treatment), Enron (energy), Ispat Steel, and many other firms that have built billion-dollar international businesses in just a few years? They have relied on human skills to promote growth and remain competitive. These multinationals possess organizational hierarchies that are ideally suited to the creation and deployment of human resources and intangible assets such as patents or brands. By combining these attributes with a reputation for reliability, these new specialists have taken business away from much larger incumbents.

Innovations in strategy are at the heart of today's rapid internationalization. For example, it took India's Ispat Steel only 10 years to become one of the top 10 steel makers in the world. Ispat Steel challenged the old business model - based on achieving economies of scale through giant production units - by building a global network of small-scale steel plants. Along the way, it replaced trade with local production. Ispat added further corporate-level strength by transferring across borders lessons learned in any one plant about promoting greater efficiency. In other industries, new technology is transforming supply possibilities.

Mass customization allows a customer to get precisely what he or she wants, anywhere in the world. A person can walk into a bicycle shop in the United States, specify the preferred design and components have the bicycle built to order overseas, and ride it home from the shop within weeks. Similarly, British women have been experimenting with computer-assisted equipment that allows them to specify the perfect fit for their jeans, which are cut and sewn in Latin America. Creating the necessary flexibility in the supply chain to achieve these new performance demands is a challenge that many incumbent MNCS are finding difficult to meet.

Competition is no longer solely about richly endowed firms battling against poorer ones: It is also a contest to develop strategies and learn new skills. Competition now needs to be thought of in terms of the intensity of managers' imagination. The message of today's competitive environment is that David can beat Goliath and does so with increasing frequency.

ONLY SOME INDUSTRIES ARE GOING GLOBAL

Not anymore. A few years ago, the conventional wisdom held that many industries were impervious to globalization, particularly those in the service sector. Yet today we find MNCs in office cleaning (International Service Systems in Denmark), dialysis treatment clinics (Fresenius in Germany), and fresh-food retailing. There are international operators in real estate, law, and even simple services such as taxis and hairdressing. In the absence of protective regulations, no sector in any country can be confident that it will never be confronted by foreign competitors.

None of these developments suggest that all firms must go global. But to survive even local businesses can (and must) adopt global standards. A firm can be world-class in behavior without being global in its asset disposition, provided it has a global perspective, a global information base, and the necessary imagination to strive for continuous improvement and adapt to shifting circumstances. For example, there are many fast-growing businesses in India - such as the luggage company VIP - that have achieved world-class status in operational efficiency and technical proficiency and that are run by entrepreneurs who relentlessly travel the world in search of fresh inspiration. These firms may well be some of tomorrow's MNCs, leveraging the advantages that they have already created at home. In many industries, the greatest challenge to purely local businesses comes from their immediate neighbors, firms that have been faster to seize the opportunities afforded by the information revolution and liberalization.

MNCS ARE BIGGER THAN THEIR ASSETS

True. The reach and influence of multinationals, large and small, is far greater than the official statistics suggest. Policymakers can, therefore, seriously underestimate the extent to which national economies have become intertwined with others. There are at least two sources for this misconception: the way in which cross-border investments are estimated and the manner in which the "boundary" of a firm is defined. The official figures for the flow of FDI - the historical cost-accounting basis for the asset base of multinational corporations - show an annual flow of nearly $400 billion.

The United Nations, however, has recently begun to question these figures and has estimated that if one includes the capital mobilized by local borrowings and the equity shares of partners, the "real" figure is closer to $1.4 trillion per year. In other words, a corporation's "presence" in a country goes beyond the assets that it chooses to locate there. The influence of a multinational can also be gauged by its effect on local suppliers as it creates new demand and sets new standards of quality. All these elements are part of a world where the local production of MNCs in overseas markets now greatly exceeds the sum of world trade. The resulting deep integration of national economies is growing so fast that any suggestion in developed economies that the domestic-policy agenda can be isolated from the global economy seems antediluvian.

Perhaps even more seriously, the explosion of strategic alliances among firms is transforming the competitive landscape. One estimate is that more than 20,000 alliances have been formed within the last two years alone. How, then, should one now think about where economic power is located? As one executive observed some years ago: "The electronics business in Europe is not the same as the European electronics business." Competition is no longer defined solely by the ownership of assets; it is also a matter of who is in league with whom.

The airline industry in its post-deregulation phase, for example, is coalescing around several global alliances: One such partnership is the Star Alliance, with Lufthansa and United

Airlines as central players. These groups hope to gain advantages from shared ticketing, loyalty programs (such as frequent flyer miles), and even the occasional use of shared equipment. Public policy has yet to come to grips with the salient issue that ownership is not the same as control, and that the real power of the MNCs lies in their ability to exert control far beyond their legal "boundaries." New rules are needed, probably on an international basis, to ensure that this new "group-to-group" competition is adequately supervised to avoid abuses of power.

MNCS ARE INHERENTLY EXPLOITATIVE

Yes and no. Advocacy groups often portray multinationals as globetrotting sweatshop operators, indifferent polluters, and systematic tax evaders. But for many industries, labor costs are not the determining factor in deciding where to locate. Remember the debate over the North American Free Trade Agreement and presidential candidate Ross Perot's warning of a "giant sucking sound?" If low wages were the primary criteria, then U.S. businesses would have leapfrogged over Mexico and relocated in Haiti. Labor costs in many segments of consumer electronics are less than 5 percent of the total cost (although in other segments and industries, such as textiles, wage rate differentials can be significant). Overall, wages are only one part of the productivity and quality equation.

That said, exploitation remains a problem. But how much of this is a function of business in general, rather than MNCs in particular? Smaller, local firms often can be much more exploitative than foreigners. Multinationals typically pay at or above the going wage and provide superior training. But even if most MNCS are well intentioned, they suffer from a credibility gap. The very fact that they can, and sometimes do, leave the host country contradicts their implicit commitment to provide economic security through "good" employment. Many management teams underestimate this reality. Perhaps unwittingly, MNCS can fuel public concern by being culturally insensitive, not honoring promises made by their predecessors, and being inconsistent in other aspects of their "social contract" with local society. With regard to the environment, international big business is both the creator of pollution and the only resource available for its cleanup.

The MNCs' record on pollution pales in comparison with those of many local businesses and state-owned enterprises: Look at the environmental damage in the former Soviet Union and Eastern Europe, not to mention today's mess in China. By whose standards should performance be judged? Should local businesses in Eastern Europe adhere to local standards while MNCs operating there are held to more stringent international standards? Who is really going to be able to implement the Kyoto Protocol on Climate Change - local governments faced with strong domestic opposition or MNCs that can be held accountable through international regulations? It should not be forgotten that the Montreal Protocol on Substances that Deplete the Ozone Layer owes much of its success to the active participation of MNCs that possessed both the incentive to write workable regulations and the technical expertise to define what was possible. But multinationals also need to accept their obligation, as Shell has recently done, to engage much more extensively in the public debate about environmental-policy options.

The issue of tax evasion continues to generate acrimonious debate, despite guidelines produced by the Organisation for Economic Cooperation and Development. Multinational corporations protest that they pay their taxes responsibly. For example, the U.S. Chamber of Commerce in Bangkok claimed a few years ago that MNCs paid 70 percent of Thailand's corporate taxes, implying considerable tax evasion by the locals. But even this seemingly simple claim was clouded by the intricate workings of the local tax code.

Some state governments in the United States, such as California's, have sought to tax MNCs based on a proportion of their worldwide income, regardless of the profitability of their local operations. The underlying motive of such legislation is to preempt possible tax evasion through transfer price practices - whereby multinationals overprice and under price components shipped among various affiliates in an attempt to shift income from high- to low-tax venues. Corporate reaction to broad taxation has been predictably negative. What is the benchmark for fairness? The debate will most likely continue as an arcane technical subject, leaving public opinion unaltered in its negative perception.

Investments by MNCs are good; Investments by International Money Managers are bad. Not necessarily. Foreign direct investment by multinational corporations has a long-term effect and is not always mobile. Foreign portfolio investment (FPI) is mostly volatile money that can go away overnight - and often does, as demonstrated by the 1998 panic over emerging markets. Although spending plans for FDI are being cut back, few firms are rushing to the exit. Therefore, FDI might be more stable than FPI, but there have been periods of volatility. In the 1970s, when Malaysia announced plans for highly discriminatory ethnic controls as part of that country's New Economic Policy, many MNCs concluded that the government had abandoned its favorable investment climate. Accordingly, they cut back on capital spending, closed some plants, and moved money offshore. Such instances, however, have become rare: Most governments want to welcome foreigners, not scare them away.

Another popular misconception is that, since foreign direct investment and foreign portfolio investment have both boomed in the 1990s, they are somehow related. The drivers behind them, however, are different. Foreign portfolio investment is a story of deregulation and the changing attitudes of investors. There are new opportunities to invest in emerging markets that used to be closed. Moreover, the perceived risk of investing abroad has declined as better information has become available. Whereas the principal objective of FPI is to maximize the return to the investor, FDI has a more complex set of motivations. One such motivation is resource seeking - gaining access either to natural resources (an oil field or copper mine) or man-made resources (skilled labor or the technologies within a cluster).

There are also marker-seeking investors who hope to gain a foothold in an expanding local market. And there are efficiency-seeking investors who believe that a series of investments linked across borders can lower total system costs below what could be achieved in one territory alone. These objectives cannot be attained overnight and the costs of quitting are usually high. Consequently, most FDI activity has been concentrated in relatively few countries, leaving the poorest countries unable to benefit from the MNCs' resources and abilities to create new industries.

MNCS ARE CREATIONS OF WEALTHY COUNTRIES

Not anymore. Historically this has been the case, with the United Kingdom and United States in leading positions. But many of the newcomers are based in developing countries. For example, Taiwan is now home to many MNCs, such as computer companies Acer and Mitac that have secured high world market shares in many niche products - most notably, handy scanners (96 percent) and the PC mouse (63 percent).

Many developing-country firms that deal in natural resources, such as Petrobras in Brazil and Kuwait Oil, have expanded abroad to control more of the chain of supply and get closer to consumers. For instance, Petroleos de Venezuela owns Citgo, a leading chain of gas stations in the United States. Many new forms of multinationals are emerging - such as the family empires of the overseas Chinese - that add further variety to the stew of organizational forms now represented by the multinationals. Governments in some of the smaller countries now find that they must contend with both host-and home-country influences in their negotiations with MNCS.

MNCS ARE BEYOND GOVERNMENT CONTROL

Absolutely not. The relationship between governments and multinationals is characterized by a complex distribution of benefits. Multinational corporations increasingly demand the "freedom" they need to optimize their operations across borders, with the goal of lowering their total costs and continuously upgrading quality. Their key bargaining chip in dealing with host governments is that they have the option not to invest. But once multinationals enter a country, they are, to some degree, locked in by the commitments that they have made to develop local operations and provide job training. Multinationals need access to local skills and other resources such as hot-spot clusters. Host governments need MNCS to act as agents in building competitiveness and trade.

Instead of engaging in adversarial bargaining about the distribution of wealth, both sides have a strong incentive to work on building partnerships that create wealth in the first place. The growth of "welcome-mat" investment incentives - tax breaks, investments grants, sometimes even preferential access to capital and guarantees of exclusive market rights - is one indicator of the sea change in government thinking. Governments would do well to employ officials who not only understand the economics of traditional market structures but also the managerial forces that change those structures. In addition, more vigorous intergovernmental collaboration is needed to strengthen institutions such as the World Trade Organization.

Policymakers urgently need a new mindset if they are to maintain a reasonable equity in the balance of power among states, firms, and consumers. Just as domestic banks require regulatory institutions that restrain their speculative instincts, MNCs require regulatory mechanisms that check their instincts to put profit above all else. The challenge is to maintain fairness without sabotaging the innovation engine that drives both new and old MNCs and creates new wealth. Consumers and governments can no longer rely exclusively on market mechanisms to rein in multinationals, nor can they blindly trust executives in the boardroom to do the "right thing."

DEVELOPMENT REGIMES AND SOCIAL CHANGE

Many rural development regimes, including policies and state subsidies geared to bring about market expansion, industrial employment, or production for profit, are often based upon the explicit or implicit moral assumption that the standard for evaluating "the good life" is Western society. The question of how rural peoples attain "the good life," is usually answered in terms of their incorporation in market or commercialized production or, more generally, as state citizens or subjects embodying this moral character. Ultimately, for rural transformation to occur, changes are expected to take place at various social, cultural, and political levels, and in development discourses it is often assumed that these changes bring about benefits to local regions, nation states, and the international market system.

A common and overly economistic argument is that development regimes are primarily responsible for transforming rural societies and village traditions (i.e., large kin networks as sources of insurance and labor pools based on family kin, class, or neighborhood). However, such views envision and promote "rural communities" as static, rule-bound entities, ignoring the exercise of moral beliefs by rural peoples in the context of social change and power struggles. Local political and cultural settings play a vital role in mediating development regimes because rural peoples who begin to leave subsistence agriculture, to start cash cropping or selling their farm products for world markets, or to engage in wage labor relations, do so in ways that are shaped and influenced by moral discourses. This is not meant to suggest that moral relations resist economic development or preserve and protect anything (i.e., tradition, family unity, community, etc.).

Far from adhering to such functional matters, it is precisely moral subjects that respond to material and economic conditions in ways that cannot be considered permanent or traditional but rather are considered to be transformative. Moral judgments, that "one ought to do this or that," are beliefs interpreted as choice or duty, and direct the action of people by restricting them to spheres of conformity and responsibility- with such regulation inevitably permeating various development processes and social relations. For these reasons, I wish to present a view of power relations that moves away from a centralized position of force (i.e., state, Islam, etc.) that controls and structures the field of possible actions, to one which focuses on a multiplicity of force relations that brings about change and guides people's activities.

In addressing such issues, the following discussion provides a brief background into the historical character and processes of development regimes in rural Turkey generally, and in the northwestern community of Sakli specifically. Since the formation of the Turkish Republic in 1923, various attempts have been made to change political, economic, and cultural landscapes in the countryside. These changes have contributed, in part, to the formation of moral subjects and to the development of new gender divisions of labor. In particular, the role of the Turkish state in initiating rural transformation has broadly defined how people "should" behave and what they "should" deem good or bad. Central to Ataturk's political regime of modernization beginning in the early 1920s, state policies and plans played a primary role in improving the country's position in exports, increasing production to generate a large agricultural surplus, nationalizing coal mining operations, and taking over main railways, utilities, transportation, and port facilities.

This modernization regime was geared to foster a demand for industrial work, wage laborers, and export and internal markets. It also imposed the standards of fashion (e.g., outlawing the fez and replacing it with the Western hat), the use of language (e.g., displacing the Arabic alphabet with the Latin alphabet), the organization of work schedules (e.g., replacing the Islamic lunar calendar with the Gregorian calendar), and introduced several new civil laws abolishing polygamy, equalizing property inheritance for men and women, and regulating divorce, marriage, and child custody procedures.

All of these social and cultural changes were done in the name of "modernity": a process that attempted not only to mobilize and discipline populations but also to morally regulate and create subjects that would comply to certain ways of modern thinking, acting, and behaving. State-initiated development during this early modern period sought to transform rural agrarian relations through the abolition of afar (crop tax) in 1925, the introduction of state subsidies for agricultural production in 1926, and the acceleration of state-supported capitalist development, especially after World War II. However, it is difficult to claim that state-initiated regimes alone are responsible for governing and transforming rural life.

To do so would be to ignore the multiplicity of social forces involved in the regulation of groups, communities, and populations. In contrast to such a totalizing view of power, a micro level analysis permits us to better understand local economies of power and the manner in which these intercede economic processes. It also enables us at the same time, to identify how certain groups become linked to regional or national economic development while others remain peripheral to it. In what follows, I will show how capitalist expansion and the demand for rural migrant labor in Turkey articulate with landlord-peasant moral relations and gender divisions of labor in the northwestern community of Sakli.

Sakli is a mountainous rural community in the province of Zonguldak. Under Ottoman rule and long before the formation of the Turkish republic in 1923, the village was inhabited by a few subsistence farming families. Over two centuries ago, three families from the Bolu region of Turkey established an agalik or landlord system in Sakli- a system of social and economic relations common to various parts of Turkey up until World War II. Under this system, local villagers, including women, men, and children, were compelled to work as sharecroppers for these village landlords who controlled all of the land in the area, owned over 250 sheep, and employed village shepherds, servants, barbers, and garden keepers. Until the 1920s (and to a lesser extent until the late 1950s), agricultural production was largely under agalik control.

The vast inequality in the ownership and regulation of land enabled Sakli landlords, and landlords from other regions, to dominate social, economic, and moral relations. In fact, during the Kemalist regime, some 2.5 million small and impoverished peasant families in Turkey were under the rule of wealthy landowning families. Gender and class divisions of labor in subsistence production characterized this early modern period. Peasant women, men, and children worked the land for their own consumption needs as well as for village landlords. During field preparation and planting, both men and women participated but each performed separate tasks. Men generally led the oxen in the ploughing of fields and women and young children followed behind, removing rocks and planting seeds.

Other tasks associated with field work, such as the cooking for kin in the field, was the domain of women, while the delivering of food and produce to landlords was the domain of men. Furthermore, the division of labor in agriculture was highly class specific in that peasant women and men were the ones responsible for farm production, whereas village landlords were responsible for distributing the produce back to the peasants, minus their share. During this time period, social class conflicts characterized community relations and local politics. The agalik system was responsible for maintaining a well-trained and compliant farming population. Since peasants did not own any land, landlords forced them to clear the forest for land, to seed, to harvest, and to transport the produce back to the landlords' manors. In addition to this economic domination, landlords also attempted to regulate the peasantry through moral means.

Villagers were expected to ask the landlord's approval of their daughter's or son's marriage partner. Even the appropriate bride-price payment was negotiated between the groom's father and the landlord. Often, villagers could not afford to pay the bride-price and relied on the landlord to help them financially. In addition, villagers were compelled to pay part of the bride-price money (usually half) to the landlord upon the marriage of their children. In their attempt to preserve the agalik system, landlords approved only marriages between those families that were compliant and forbade marriages with households with whom they had conflicts. Due to their domination, landlords were in a position to create a sense of moral obligation among the peasantry by defining the parameters of appropriate interaction between landlords and peasants and between males and females.

Noncompliance with landlord expectations could result in villagers being beaten, sexually assaulted, killed, and/or having their homesteads razed. As one elderly woman said, "yediler bizi" (literally, "they ate us"), "they took everything from us." As a notable moral expression in Sakli, the verb "to eat" (yemek) means to spend or to consume and villagers commonly use it to describe their state of exploitation and other forms of injustice. Peasants rebelled against this oppressive system in numerous ways, especially during the late 1920s and early 1930s. In some situations, couples formed marriages without the consent of the landlords. A type of marriage known as kiz kaçirma (literally, "girl kidnapping" or elopement) emerged to curb landlord control and to avoid the landlord's marriage tax.

A villager could accomplish this by "carrying away" a woman to a cleric (imam). In other cases, some peasants reacted to the demands of the agalik system by clearing small plots of land from the forest without the landlord's consent. This enabled them, if they did not get caught, to increase their harvest without increasing the share owed to landlords. Others simply stole from the landlord's granary what they thought was rightfully theirs, while some resorted to magical spells (muska) in an effort to gain control over the landlords. The landlords, for their part, developed countermeasures of their own. By controlling the distribution of goods, the landlords made it difficult for peasant families to steal or hide produce. They closely surveilled the peasantry during the harvesting season and often employed other villagers as spies to report on those who did not comply.

By the late 1930s (through to the 1970s), the state's role in expanding industrial development, in economic investment, and in the intensifying of economic relations with the West provided employment for many male peasants. Farmers from Sakli and surrounding areas seasonally migrated to the nearby city of Zonguldak for work in the coal mining industry. Facilitated by the state's Second Five Year Plan to implement industrial development, Zonguldak witnessed the establishment of heavy industry based on raw materials, the improvement of transportation facilities, and the construction of a modern port for the export of steel and coal. With the growing demand for wage labor in the Zonguldak area, the stronghold of the agalik system in Sakli was clearly reduced. Specifically, this period witnessed the first decline in sharecropping practices, the emergence of land rental arrangements between landlords and peasants, and the ability of peasants to purchase small pieces of land for subsistence purposes.

The decline in landlord domination, however, stems from factors other than the male peasantry simply being pulled externally from sharecropping into migrant work. Sakli peasants came to consider the value of migrant labor in moral terms, enabling many of them to mitigate landlord domination. Peasants did not regard the "value" of work in the context of what it earns in the market. Rather, the meaning of migrant work came to be viewed in terms of its value in changing previous relations of domination and subordination that is, overcoming landlord domination, surveillance, and brutality. The introduction of wage or migrant labor therefore served the political purpose of reducing landlord control over the peasantry. This bears similarity to how the advent of tractors, the availability of increased credit, and the emigration of peasants to urban areas after World War II contributed to a decline in sharecropping arrangements in other parts of Turkey.

Processes of capitalist expansion also brought about new changes to other areas of rural Turkey. Especially after World War II, many of Turkey's rural economies underwent enormous shifts, partly due to the introduction of local industry and wage labor, state-facilitated cash crop production, irrigation systems, fertilizers, or farm technology. However, and more specific to the theme at hand, is the manner in which local economies and populations mediate development efforts and the effects of this mediation on understanding micro levels of power and gender relations. The following section discusses the contemporary situation of women's lives and work processes in the community of Sakli.

Based on this research, I will show how complex interrelationships exist between social transformation and the moral discourses deployed to circumscribe arenas of obedience and duty for those regulated by it (especially women) and the sites of resistance it engenders. The empirical basis of this discussion stems from several research methods employed during my one year of field work conducted in Turkey. Data is drawn, in part, from a village wide household survey, in-depth interviews and oral histories with women and men, informal group discussions, and participant observation. My personal involvement with women's activities in the farm fields and in the homes has enabled me to draw upon the women's experiences and struggles, giving greater depth to the intricacies of power operating in their lives.

WOMEN'S WORK AND FORMS OF RESISTANCE IN SAKLI

In Sakli (population 567), and in the region generally, local residents identify themselves as Sunni Islamic, reckon descent in patrilineal terms, support arranged marriages and virilocal residence, and live mainly in three- to four-generational households. Their major economic activities include labor-intensive subsistence agriculture, together with household reproductive labor and seasonal male migrant work. Land distribution among farming households is fairly even, but great variations do still exist between landlords and villagers in terms of land ownership.

With the historical development and value of migrant work and subsequent changes in landlord-peasant relations, a "feminization" of subsistence agriculture and a "masculinization" of cash relations can be identified in Sakli today. In a situation quite different from that seen in the earlier period, most men have virtually withdrawn from labor-intensive agriculture. Usually one or two male household members (a husband or a young married or unmarried son) now work as seasonal migrants, while other household members take responsibility for the bulk of agricultural work.

Women and young girls, in fact, do most of the agricultural work, including the labor-intensive operations of ploughing, hoeing, planting, weeding, and the caring and feeding of animals. Even the labor-intensive harvesting of wheat and corn is mainly undertaken by women. When men do participate in agriculture, their involvement is generally restricted to performing tasks during the peak ploughing and harvesting seasons, working in mechanized activities (in some clearing, ploughing, and threshing operations), and supervising the labor process. Likewise, young boys (especially those under 12) also participate in agricultural work, as well as help their male kin rebuild houses or barns, and paint and upgrade fences. Overall, men predominate in mechanized agriculture, restoration work, commercial transactions, and migrant labor.

It is considered unmanly, however, for a male to do what is now considered traditional female work- the mundane and time-consuming work of labor intensive farming and gardening. Within village households, there is also a marked gender division of labor. Women and young girls perform all of the major cooking, most of the child care, and virtually all of the work associated with other household demands when not working in the fields or tending to gardens, women and girls spend their time making goods for trousseaus and preparing for upcoming marriages and other festive ceremonies. In contrast, men and boys engage in a minimal amount of household-related work. They do, however, take weekly trips to the town market to purchase fresh fruit and other food and will for short periods of time supervise their own young children or siblings.

When not working as seasonal migrants or laboring during the peak farming season, men (along with some young boys) spend many of their days or evenings in the local coffee shop. This is a location only males frequent, since it is considered socially unacceptable for women and girls to be in the company of unrelated men. The availability of wage and migrant labor, however, not only brought about a remarkable alteration in the gender division of labor but also new moral views concerning the status and perception of men's and women's work. With seasonal migration accelerating until the 1970s, the overwhelming majority of village households today have (or have had) predominately male members who work as wage laborers outside of the community.

While this wage labor is viewed by villagers in highly valued moral terms, as previously discussed, the same cannot be said for the work that women do in subsistence agriculture. Prized by women as traditionally significant and essential to agricultural production, labor-intensive farm tasks are currently viewed by men as work inherently suited to women. In fact, younger and older men do not consider women's work as embodying much skill or expertise. Often when men talk about those who work with agricultural machines, they refer to the skill and experience that this type of work requires, contrasting it with the lack of skill involved in labor-intensive agriculture. As one male peasant says, our women work in the fields and this is the work that they are accustomed to. Our daughters, too, are there with them and they learn how to work the land. Men don't do much work in the fields the way they did before...Yes, I sometimes help my brother with his harvest and work the threshing machine with him and deliver the wheat to the flour mill, but this is more difficult than just working in the fields...Women can't do that kind of work.

The moral judgment that women are not suited to a particular kind of work only attempts to circumscribe arenas of duty and obligation for women, not fully disclosing the underlying power contests between men and women or the fact that the primary target of masculinist power has been the subjugation of women. The fact that women's attitudes toward agricultural labor are different from men's reveals their location in the battleground of power networks. Women claim that it takes a great deal of training to become a good farmer and many older women express their desire someday to have a physically strong (kuvvetli) daughter-in-law (gelin) to teach and take over their farming chores. As in other parts of rural Turkey, and unlike the situation in earlier periods, older married women in Sakli gain more social status and respect when they withdraw from agricultural work and become more restricted to performing tasks inside the home.

This newly acquired status is, however, an effect of power since it derives from the devaluation of women's farm work by wage-earning male kin. Other new cultural changes have been generated in this local community. One important development has to do with the emergence of a new discourse, referred to as "tradition" (adet), which defines the permitted and forbidden by linking current social relations to those of the past. However, the contemporary meaning of tradition in Sakli does not simply refer to ways of acting and behaving that derive from conventionally established practice or from the sanctity of age-old rules and powers. Tradition has been transformed from the way it operated under the landlord-peasant regime to its present exercise, as a technique of power, administered under different economic and gender conditions.

Prior to the onset of seasonal male out-migration, village life was envisioned in slave-like terms, since much of what the peasants did was done under the watchful eye of village landlords. During this time period, there was little conception of a well-established peasant tradition since the landlord regime regulated and influenced the major aspects of social ties and relations, including property and distribution networks, work ethics and labor processes, marriage negotiations, arrangements, and bride-price payments. As one older peasant woman said, "We served and worked for them [landlords] and then, later, we worked for half of the yield. This work had to be done under any circumstances, even if there was a death in the family. We even had to carry their drinking water.

With the way it was, our life was really in their hands." The sentiments expressed here speak to a way of life that was very much ordered and governed by a landlord tradition of sorts, where peasant voices and social preferences were just beginning to alter relations of power. Nevertheless, the discursive emergence of tradition today builds from, yet breaks with, the distributions of power associated with the landlord-peasant tradition. The current discourses of adet reveal not only an exaggeration of the links to the past (or the "original") but also the transmission and production of new power relations.

Especially after the slow decline of the landlord-peasant regime and the availability of male migrant work, the importance of tradition became a specific point of discussion in Sakli because relations of power (particularly between men and women) started to establish it as a possible object of investigation.

During the initial period when a large proportion of male peasants seasonally migrated to urban centers for work, one of the most significant developments emerged when the practices of adet became tied to a moral concern over village women. With the seasonal absence of men, the moral behavior of women was called into question by men and it was at this point that women's activities came under closer scrutiny and were subject to new forms of moral regulation. The discourse of tradition is an especially dense transfer point for uncovering relations of power between men and women and for guiding people's possibilities of conduct in the sphere of gendered activities.

Male villagers, in particular, speak about their tradition in a gendered fashion, emphasizing women's roles in household and subsistence agriculture and men's roles outside the household and in migrant work. Even some older women see it as their obligation to carry on this tradition, attaching much prestige and status to their roles as wives, mothers, or daughters. As one married woman said, "It is our tradition for women to look after their husbands and their children...We are proud to work the land the way we do ...yes it is hard work and long hours, but what else can we do...Our sons work hard too and when they marry, their wives will do what we do now. This is how it is in our village."

This discourse on tradition is cloaked in positive and functional terms, and while it is made to seem as if "things have always been such and such a way," its most profound effect is that it masks its success in organizing and imposing constraints upon women's lives. In providing a way to render community life amenable to certain kinds of actions, the discourse on tradition serves as a point of support for the idea that women are the main transmitters of tradition and village values. Because of their reproductive capacity and their confined location within the village, women's roles as workers or citizens are not as important as their perceived roles as wives and especially as mothers.

Their responsibilities of caring for and socializing young children are viewed by both women and men as morally superior to those of the urban world, where women dress and travel openly, working in public places alongside male strangers. In their attempt to strive toward traditional ideals, women in Sakli take on the bulk of agricultural work, household maintenance, and child-rearing duties and are responsible for training future daughters-in-law for home and farm labor. They are also involved in morally training sons and male kin toward a life of migrant work, expecting daughters to marry migrant laborers over male farmers. In fact, the women's responsibility for labor-intensive subsistence production is taken as if it is a safeguard of family tradition, even though families themselves are characterized by paternal authority, gendered property and inheritance, virilocality, and power relations, and by separable, often competing, interests, rights, and responsibilities. Therefore, the deployment of traditional values is an effect of power since it confines women to certain social spaces and enmeshes them in relations viewed as traditional.

Aside from being an effect of power, traditional discourse also becomes "naturalized" or "normalized" as it is used to act upon people's lives and to provide a way to make the domain in question (gender, family, work) susceptible to evaluation, criticism, and intervention. This is particularly the case when the discourse of tradition is employed as an instrument of power, most especially by men, to explain women's inability to travel by themselves from one village to another, to speak to unrelated men, or to engage in wage labor. It is thought that women should be shielded from unknown or untrustworthy men, since these men have the potential to take sexual advantage of them and cause much shame to husbands and male kin and to village tradition. Even when women enter the forest to cut, collect, and carry wood, they are thought to be in need of surveillance so as to protect village tradition.

As one young married man said, "Kadin yalniz gitmez, yaninda birisi lazim: ya erkek kardei, ya kocasi, ya da kom°usu" ("A woman cannot go [to the forest] alone as someone must be with her: either her brother, husband, or neighbor"). More specifically, the discourse on tradition permeates the nondiscursive domains of travel and movement by constituting them as gender specific. That is, women are expected to work and visit within the geographical boundaries of the village, travel in groups rather than by themselves, and speak with more deference to others in public than men do in similar circumstances (such as among strangers or people physically near but morally remote). In contrast, most men travel both within and outside of the village, engage in both wage and nonwage work, and participate in a variety of urban consumption practices that are socially prohibited to women.

Making use of moral values, together with their mechanisms of discipline, is an important cultural strategy for regulating women's movement in other areas of rural Turkey as well. Morvaridi's study of economic and cultural development in northeast Turkey, for example, highlights how certain moral sentiments attempt to seclude and subordinate women, by regulating their dress, mobility, and interactions with community members. In his words, "Only when accompanied by a male member of her household can a woman move outside the village. An unaccompanied woman caught talking in public to a man from the village would find it difficult to marry, as she is seen as dishonoring her family".

Likewise, Sirman highlights the interrelations of state, village, and gender in a western Turkish village, illustrating how men (as household heads and providers) represent the politics of the state within the village, and how women remain under their moral rule. This kind of moral regulation has the potential to subsume women, in this case, into systems of governance by making them "subjects" to these meanings and seducing them to believe in its goals, and to speak and act its claims. And, when they come to believe in these moral values and to identify themselves as agents protecting or enhancing a group or tradition (as in Sakli), then moral discourses serve as clever disguises and subtle expressions of the forces of domination.

In order to understand local community politics and its links to rural transformation, we must take seriously the significance of cultural strategies, such as the uses to which morality is put. For it is morality, as a micro economy of knowledge and power, that explains why development or social change is not simply a matter of state initiation, technological diffusion, market rationalization, or capitalist penetration. In other words, and as I have shown above, there is a relationship between moral regulation and other forms of economic processes. However, while micro level forms of power in Sakli attempt to morally regulate women's work and behavior, they should not be thought of as having a totalizing effect that resolves all differences and contradictions through a masculinist or traditional discourse.

Post-structural analysts of power remind us that we are not entirely encapsulated by a prevailing discourse. Discourses can be both instruments and effects of power, as well as points of resistance. How both women and men are involved in supporting the existing system of power through the deployment and naturalization of tradition illustrated below is that women, as one of the most marginal groups, also resist these forms of moral regulation and, in this way, we cannot ignore their attempt to overcome the totalizing incentives of a dominant and often masculinist morality. It is essential, therefore, to document how women themselves engage in acts of resistance to prevailing discourses. In what follows, I will briefly describe two main forms of resistance undertaken by women, showing how these intersect with the techniques of power or moral regulation outlined above.

Sakli women engage in a variety of resistance efforts that work against the dominating effects of traditional discourse. The first arena of resistance, one I have described elsewhere, is one in which women attempt to overcome their perceived subordinate status as household and farm workers through the use of magic. Women use magic (büyü or muska) as a way to change daily working conditions and demands within their virilocal households, alter conflictual relations with family members and local residents, and subvert moral expectations surrounding arranged marriages, spousal sexual demands, and home and child-care duties.

This form of resistance indicates one way power is exercised by women through a range of spiritual strategies that attempt to transform traditional relations and aspirations. Muska not only exposes the contradictions of women's lives but it also creates an avenue from which they can disembody themselves from the confines of moral regulation. In this regard, muska has the potential to transform, reverse, or undermine forms of moral regulation because it seeks to change all sorts of power relations by arresting their strength, such as when women arrange to have spells cast upon husbands who demand too much from them or upon in-laws who restrict their social mobility. Within power domains- such as those between women and men- there is resistance, and the use of magic permits women the possibility to mobilize themselves and others and to control certain types of behavior and expectations.

Furthermore, women's engagement in magic (in comparison to men's) is considered by most men to possess less transformative qualities, thus revealing how power struggles culminate in the production of new knowledge around women's activities. A second and widespread form of resistance is the manner in which women engage in clandestine activities to ensure that incoming brides meet women's own needs as well as their household's. One of the most popular ways that married women attempt to control future working relations within their households is by exerting their influence over their sons' choice of spouse. Women, and their informal networks, are extremely active in bride searches, in that they try to seek out women with whom they can get along. This works to their advantage, especially when they find a bride who is reputed to be a hard worker, looks physically strong, and has the potential to take responsibility for a large segment of farm and household tasks.

These women also play an important role in occasionally preventing their daughters from marrying men arranged for them by older, male kin. In such cases, women and their female friends search actively for any information on a prospective groom and his family that would raise doubts about his suitability including any immoral activities affiliated with a household or its members. Furthermore, contemporary young women occasionally resist arranged marriages by eloping with another man, a traditional activity that was once a form of resistance to landlord taxation still referred to as kiz kaçirma. Overall, these practices reveal that women can resist the decisions of their husbands or fathers in marriage arrangements and negotiations and, as such, can influence changes in their status, and in some cases, alterations in their work and household schedules.

The acts that just described are not exhaustive of all female sites of resistance to traditional discourses in Sakli. Women have also been known to resist prevailing standards of appropriate femininity by secretly engaging in extramarital relations, selling homemade goods to local townspeople for cash, and traveling to areas outside the village. No matter what the extent of these forms of resistance, they indeed demonstrate sites of struggle and power relations and have implications for the way in which they operate through women's work and status in the community. Moreover, these resistance efforts provide a context out of which women can pluralize meaning by breaking presumably established constructs which influences their social, economic, and political domains.

Contrary to the view that new economic efforts completely transform old forms of community relations and domination, processes of cultural change in this community mediate development regimes. This chapter has illustrated that the moral values associated with male migrant work were central in overcoming landlord-peasant relations, creating new gendered fields, and in producing modern perceptions and judgments of work and responsibility. Together and in line with these changes demonstrates how the emergence and discursive invention of tradition plays a role in guiding people's possibilities of conduct and in regulating more directly women's work activities. While the exercise of this form of moral regulation masks its success in confining women's movement and work patterns, it also culminates as a point of resistance by women through their informal participation in magic and marriage practices.

Instead of conceptualizing moral relations as strictly rule-bound or as devoid of conflict, this chapter has revealed that the genealogy of these relations necessarily draws from, and impinges upon, a multiplicity of power regimes and resistance efforts. In the context of Sakli, the transition from subsistence production to varied forms of work and relations also becomes part of a transition to a new and different disciplinary society (where people discipline themselves in distinctive ways from each other and from the past). What is interesting about these processes is that we can identify how unique social relations unfold for various gender and work dynamics, and how the forces of development articulate with local cultural meanings and disciplinary techniques.

What is to be understood by disciplinary techniques, such as the uses to which morality is put, is not that individuals or groups who become part of them become more obedient, but rather that an increasingly invigilated process of adjustment is sought after by those who attempt to transform others in the field of social activities and through the play of power relations. A relationship of power is a mode of action that does not act directly and immediately on others; instead, it acts upon their actions, in the present or the future, and consists of guiding people's possibilities of conduct, including the manner in which they may be regulated and the forms of resistance they may embrace. Therefore, in any hierarchically ordered society, power is not simply centralized (in the state, in Islam, or in the global economy), but dispersed in a multiplicity of sites, continuously directing people's potentiality of comportment. This is why the analysis, elaboration, and the bringing into question of moral regulation is at the heart of understanding local rural transformation.

2

The Gender and Generational Hierarchies

Methodological Aspects

One of the main problems currently confronting those who reflect on the social dimensions of change in the context of international development stems from the fact that relevant models and theories were conceived for understanding structural processes referred to, by some, as macro sociological. When the particular situation of women and children within these processes of change constitutes one's main interest, as it does mine, these theoretical models appear to have no direct significance. The same problem presents itself with approaches that focus to a greater extent on individuals and actors: They seem to lose all meaning when we attempt to understand the structural integration of the latter. The discussion presented here deals with the methodological alternatives available for studies that take into account all of the dimensions of social change in general, and of social relations between various significant social categories.

Throughout this discussion two main influences will be apparent: that of feminist thought and that of political economy in anthropology, as described by William Roseberry in an important article published in 1988 in which he shows to what extent Marxist anthropology of the 1970s has undergone a mutation, making it more sensitive to the practices of daily life. This chapter comprises three main parts.

The La Cocha region is located in the Colombian Andes, more precisely in the province of Narino. The contact with the people of this region to evaluate a small development project funded since 1985 by the Canadian International Development Agency (CIDA) through one of its executing agencies, the Société de dévelopement international Desjardins (SDID). One aspect of the project was the creation of small income-generating projects for women, mainly raising guinea pigs and dairy cows, and secondarily growing blackberries and fish farming. The approach generally referred to as "women and development" therefore constituted the context for the research project to carry out in the region, funded by the Social Sciences and Humanities Research Council of Canada (SSHRC). Some of our findings have been published in Côté, Labrecque, Lopez Arellano, and Ménard.

The La Cocha region derives its name from a lake also known as Lake Guamuez. At 14 km long and 3 to 5 km wide, La Cocha is one of the largest lakes in Colombia. Located at an altitude slightly under 3,000 meters, the lake drains an area covering approximately 22,500 hectares. The source of the Guamuez River is south of the lake and joins the Putumayo River, which is itself a tributary of the Amazon River. The climate is cool (average of 14U+00BO C) and rainy (200 mm per month). The land is hilly and the vegetation is lush, although the virgin forest has been decimated and replaced by second growth forest. The slopes around the lake have been eroded, and occasionally there are landslides. Seventeen hamlets (or veredas), whose houses are quite dispersed, surround the lake.

The population, mostly from other regions of the province of Narino, was about 4,500 in 1984. The slopes around the lake were settled only about fifty years ago by peasants who were expelled from communities devastated by minifundismo and political violence. Although they define themselves as farmers, the inhabitants of La Cocha practice a wide range of activities, some of which, for example the making of charcoal, are as important as agriculture, with men, women, and children all actively involved in its production. While certain tasks are exclusively carried out by adult men, all social categories of the population are acquainted with all of the production processes.

The La Cocha peasantry is integrated into wider commercial networks through local merchants in a context of clientele relations that could be qualified as "classical." Merchants provide the people with subsistence items in exchange, most often, for their charcoal production. In fact, there is a hierarchy of intermediaries between the communities, the nearest town, and the capital, Pasto. In the communities, there are peasants who usually have a means of transportation (a small motorboat) and some cash and who can act as intermediaries for the less fortunate. In an environment that is characterized by an absence of roads, the control over transportation can constitute the basis for a certain accumulation. Since the price of charcoal tends to remain stagnant while that of consumer goods continually rises, the vast majority of peasant families have been indebted for years to the merchants in town or in the city, who are in fact moneylenders, or in the local language, gamonales.

Several governmental or Para governmental entities are present in La Cocha, some of whom deal with the protection and development of the environment. The La Cocha region in fact constitutes a significant tourist resource for the country. The Colombian state is represented in every hamlet by the Junta de Accion Comunal, an entity that was set up in the context of a rise in guerrilla activity in the 1970s in order to better control the population. The president of the junta has very limited power, but nonetheless constitutes the first link in the administrative chain. The people of La Cocha share several cultural traits distinctive to the Andean region. Since there have never been any ethnographic studies of the region, it is difficult to say to what extent the people, while not indigenous, have integrated certain aspects of the heritage of the native Indians of the neighboring valley of Sibundoy.

Several elements of indigenous material culture can be observed, such as brewing chicha, a fermented drink made of corn. Certain beliefs and representations that are not directly related to native culture as such, but rather to the blend that ensued from the confrontation between dominant colonial society and native peoples over the past centuries, also persist. Of the traits that have their origin in the broader Andean culture and that are practices of the people of La Cocha, the minga is a good example. It consists of occasional community work carried out to solve practical problems such as making trails, draining riverbanks, or building a school or a chapel.

Because it constitutes an obvious opportunity for mobilizing people and is part of the cultural background of the population, the minga has been used by various political and community groups for a variety of purposes. It is currently one of the main tools used by the Association for Peasant Development. This association was the SDID's partner in its development work in the region. Through its promotion of income-generating projects for women from the mid-1980s on, it contributed to spreading a particular conception of social change, which explains why it occupies a special place in this research.

One of the initial questions of the La Cocha research concerned the changes likely to take place within the division of labor and their effects on gender relations. However, given the relatively limited time between the initiation of income-generating projects and the beginning of our research, the difficulty in measuring the changes and bearing witness to their effects very quickly became apparent. This methodological difficulty prompted me to broaden the research beyond the study of development projects and to reflect on the anthropological approach to change and its relevance to understanding gender relations.

Having realized that La Cocha constituted one of the rare recently colonized regions of the Andes, I expanded the definition of development in order to take into account the changes that had taken place since the beginning of the settlement, about fifty years ago. This made it possible to incorporate all of the socioeconomic and political measures the population had been subject to, particularly in the context of integrated rural development policies in Colombia. Pinpointing these measures in the structural arena and identifying their general effects on Colombian peasant communities was relatively easy due to paradigms developed on the basis of political economy both by Colombian researchers and by foreign researchers interested in Colombia.

Difficulties in interpretation arose when I attempted to focus on the specific dynamic of development and social change in the immediate study region, as well as on the integration of the various categories, particularly women, within the population. It must be admitted that the approaches and models used for studying development and social change in general are more concerned with the social structure than with individuals and their daily lives. As feminists have demonstrated, concentrating on the study of structure rather than on that of daily life or individuals has detrimental consequences for social categories such as women who are particularly invisible within structures. The question that arose out of this research is therefore the following: How, in a study on social change, can we take into account structures and daily life while acknowledging the complexity of social relations, in particular, those involving women?

Thus formulated, the question appears to be resolved through a combined study of both macro sociological and micro sociological factors. Since the mid-1980s, while political economy approaches have become somewhat less popular, and we have been witness to a "return of the social actor," it is considered good form to propose a structural study of the socioeconomic context followed by an ethnographic study of the community. One of the methodological problems of this approach lies in the fact that the dimensions and categories selected for the analysis of each of these arenas, that is, the structure and the daily life of individuals, do not coincide. Such studies generally show that social changes in the areas of structure and daily life have their own separate dynamics that meet only during special, spectacular moments such as revolutions or concrete protest movements. Social change is still generally viewed as a mechanical variation of enumerable features.

However, thanks to researchers like Georges Balandier, for instance, we know that social change is far from being mechanical and that its study cannot be limited to such special moments. He considers social change to be a complex phenomenon with multiple dimensions. Its study must simultaneously take into account a great number of factors. Among these factors, social relations certainly constitute a valuable object of analysis. It is therefore less a question of studying social change in a way that takes into account structures, daily life, and individuals, but rather that considers the continuity between structures and individuals. From a methodological point of view, the problem is one of studying social processes without reifying them and interpreting them in an effort to finally understand the dynamic of social change. We can then, along with the people concerned, help orient social change in a given direction.

In light of the few descriptive elements provided above on the region and taking into account the preceding critical remarks, the objective of the next section is to share some elements of the methodological approach used in the research in La Cocha and in the analysis of the findings. Beyond the specific case of this region, I would like to emphasize the interest of an approach to social change based on the study of social relations rather than on that of the structure, of daily life, or of individuals as such, By focusing on social relations, research is better able to reveal the dynamic of the multiple connections between the various arenas of social life.

More specifically, we need an approach that recognizes that social relations, most notably gender and generational relations, cross the whole social fabric, thus connecting the structure, daily life, and individuals. In the following section, the discussion will focus on the notion of hierarchy, enabling us to deal with social relations in all their dimensions. We could, of course, examine several types of hierarchies. However, we will limit the discussion to gender and generational hierarchies because they are both based on physical differences. While corresponding intimately to the global structure of society, these hierarchies influence the daily practice of all individuals without exception. Examining these hierarchies constitutes a basic step for those who wish to understand social change as a dynamic process connecting the structure with individuals. The argument I will develop, based on the contributions of feminist scholars, is that it is equally as important to study the relationships between categories as it is to study the categories themselves.

HIERARCHIES AND SOCIAL RELATIONS

In the study of gender and generational relations, the use of the word hierarchy seems to impose itself. However, in social anthropology, the contribution of Louis Dumont obliges us to move beyond the common meaning of the term and to contemplate its multiple dimensions. In its most simple form, hierarchy can be considered a relationship between two adjacent levels of experience. In the case of gender relations, Dumont states that the fact of being a man or of being a woman corresponds to these "two adjacent levels of experience." From a certain point of view, there is therefore identity. Experience, placed in its historic and social context, shows however that one category has been incorporated into the other. Thus, the category "Woman" is included in the general category "Man." From another point of view there is also difference.

The two adjacent levels of experience are, in fact, different levels. As Dumont says: "Thus the hierarchical relationship or incorporation can be analyzed in simple logical terms whose contradiction is avoided by implementing two different levels". The notion of hierarchy therefore constitutes an interesting contribution to the study of social relations in that it obliges us to consider dimensions other than those of the real or assumed inequality of these relations according to the level at which we are placed. We may well point out that social relations are unequal in a given context and that certain individuals are excluded because of this inequality. However, this exclusion is far from absolute.

It may prove to be true at one level while at another it may be totally absent. It is not a case of affirming that inequality is relative but rather of proposing an approach that makes it possible to refine the study of gender relations. As Tcherkézoff states: "Both inequality and equality establish a single level of practices: those with the required qualities are equal, the others are in a situation of inequality; the hierarchy therefore establishes several levels of practices". In other words, the notion of inequality (or of equality) makes only a very minor contribution to our understanding of the complexity of social relations. The notion of hierarchy, on the other hand, enables us to consider these social relations on several levels.

A certain convergence seems to emerge from this free interpretation of hierarchy according to Dumont and from French feminists, in particular. Of the few authors I have selected, Christine Delphy is probably the one who deals most directly with the notion of hierarchy. In an article published in 1991, she points out that most authors are interested in the (equal unequal) type of classification generated by the relationship between sex and gender. She proposes that we ask ourselves instead why sex should give rise to any classification at all. It is in the paradigm of hierarchy that she sees the driving force behind division. She considers hierarchy to be a component of gender.

Like Delphy, authors such as Anne-Marie Daune-Richard and Anne Marie Devreux are concerned by the fact that sex is a "socially constructed category" and not, as French sociology of the 1970s claimed, "a classification variable". Gender categories "are in fact constructed in and through the social relationship that both unites and opposes them: unites them because it refers to the same system of social division (based on sex); opposes them because the relationship is profoundly antagonistic". The study of the construction of social categories therefore necessarily implies that of the gender relation and the processes that determine its transformation "through its own specific dynamic". These authors go one step further, affirming that this relation crosses the whole of society according to a single logic that "assumes different forms in various arenas (of social life)".

Here, of course, they are referring to social reproduction as not simply a "duplication, but a continuous and complex process which produces the conditions necessary for the continued existence of a system". The process is therefore a dynamic one:

> The question of reproduction is therefore that of the conditions necessary for the preservation or evolution of the system which is constituted by the reciprocal relationship between genders. The object of analysis will therefore be to identify, characterize and qualify the elements that contribute

to its preservation and/or transformation: are there breaks, thresholds, shifts, and reinforcements/consolidation?

In light of these contributions, it appears that it is not the terms of the relationship that should most interest us, but rather the relationship itself, the dynamic interaction between categories. Along the same lines, Marie Claude Hurtig and Marie-France Pichevin write:

> When dealing with hierarchical social categories (White/Black, French/Immigrant, men/women), the categorization process, aside from its role in differentiating, in distinguishing similar from different, acquires a discriminatory function which is social, not just cognitive. What influences the way information is processed is the hierarchy between the categories which constitute the classification system, undoubtedly more than the specific characteristics of any given system (race, sex, etc.).

While this comment lies within the domain of perceptions, it undoubtedly is intended as an invitation to adopt a hierarchical approach to social categories rather than a contradictory and dual approach. In fact, it is not only the social categories themselves that are at issue here, but also the relationships between these categories. Monique Haicault, for example, reiterates the complexity of social relations, particularly gender relations, while maintaining that this complexity "is related to the availability of several forms of relations between their two terms".

This approach to the relationship between terms makes the study of social change possible. Obviously it is not the genders that are changing, but rather the relationship between them. Thus, "the gender relation changes, going from one state to another or from one degree to another, through its own specific dynamic". As presented and interpreted by these authors, the notion of hierarchy encourages us to focus on connections and relationships more than on the constituent elements of these relations. The notion of hierarchy invites us to move beyond static and unsophisticated approaches that simplistically oppose men and women, adults and children, and even social classes in a model of inequality based on exclusion.

The notion of hierarchy allows for the possibility of apprehending situations in which the relationship between the terms is neither entirely antagonistic nor entirely complementary. It is true that the system in which we live tends to lead us to perceive events and social relations in a binary and contradictory manner and, in reality that may often be the case. As Mary Douglas affirms:

> Individualistic thinking, like the political experience of hierarchy, is structured by analogy to the production and distribution process.... Women are at a disadvantage in such a system not only because they are likely to be treated as commodities ... but because they have no other way of thinking of themselves as women than in terms of commodities, of producers or purchasers in a system of marketing and trade.

Thus, without the possibility of thinking of the system differently from what it is in reality, any perspective of social change would be impossible. Eventually, reconsidering our environment according to a hierarchical system could favor "distinguishing differentiated categories of people and the awareness of their singularity".

The notion of hierarchy encourages us to consider social changes in a dynamic, nonlinear manner. The authors reviewed in this research conceive of social change as a modification of social relations. Although their focus is on gender relations, it does not exclude the possibility of simultaneously studying other relations. Daune-Richard and Devreux point out the importance of "combining, for analytical purposes, social class relations and gender relations, to which social relations between generations should undoubtedly be added". This is precisely the path I set out upon: taking into account a multiplicity of social relations that consider, in a non-deterministic fashion, that gender and generational relations cross the whole range of "social arenas."

The methodological choices regarding the approach to social change and social relations impose a treatment of the data that moves away from the dichotomy between the macro- and micro social levels. Class, gender, and generational relations within social arenas or spheres constitute the elements that structure the analysis. In the case of Colombia, the analysis is based on the fact that, as a country, it is tied to international development policies, including Canada's via CIDA's presence in the study region through income-generating projects for women. A study of the composition of these projects reveals that structural elements distinctive to Canadian society have direct and tangible repercussions on La Cocha women and on their interactions with men. In particular, gender relations in Canada and the ability of certain women to promote a specific conception of gender in development, whether or not one agrees with that conception; have been projected into a region of which most Canadian taxpayers have no knowledge.

Examining these social relations in the structural arena therefore constitutes a first level of analysis. This examination makes it possible to draw connections between contexts that, at first glance, are unrelated. The process, as a whole, sheds a particular light on the constraints to social change in a given environment. It is also important to show that while individuals or the social relations between them lie within the structural arena, the structure in turn can be detected in the arena of the individual and her-his daily life. In La Cocha, for example, social change in a development context has taken on completely different connotations depending on the hierarchical relations involving the various social categories; in other words, depending on whether one belongs to the poor or the rich peasantry, whether one is a woman or a man, a child, an adult, or whether one is a member of a community association.

Individuals and their daily lives therefore constitute a second level of analysis. Using life histories can prove to be extremely relevant for dealing with this aspect of research, in that one can focus on the gender relations that define women's and men's productive and reproductive activities. In the majority of studies on development as context for social change, when the subject of women is dealt with at all, it is handled as though women constituted a homogeneous social category whose members all share the same characteristics. Practice and experience, however, clearly show that such is not the case. Taking into account a factor such as age is sufficient to challenge this presumed homogeneity. Studies that focus on demonstrating the internal heterogeneity of social categories as defined by social scientists in general and by feminists in particular, when the social category is women, remain hard to come by.

To demonstrate that the effects of development, whether capitalist development in general or development programs and projects in particular- which at any rate work along the same lines- are felt differently by men and women, by youth and elders. It appears that women's development, especially in the case of women in the middle of their reproductive lives, implies not a lightening, but an intensification of their productive activities. Even when their participation in agricultural work increases, women are more and more confined to tasks that require patience, meticulousness, and dexterity that brings them no prestige. It is therefore to be expected that small income-generating projects for women will be abandoned or that they will be taken over by other social categories, most notably, men. This is precisely what has happened in La Cocha where male dominance and the weight of the patriarchal structures of the Colombian state have been confirmed.

Elucidating the connections between the social arena of the individual and that of the structure called for studying a third level that is neither exactly that of individuals nor exactly that of structures, but rather the social arena of associations and organizations. Studying the global structure of society and that of women's daily lives is unquestionably very important. However, without studying a "hinge" between them, such as associations, the connections between the first two social arenas would remain difficult to understand. In fact, change is likely to take on a more significant and more lasting social dimension only insofar as individuals are able to group together. The study of one of these associations, the Association for Peasant Development, has enabled us to take all hierarchical relations into consideration, particularly gender and generational hierarchies. The advantage of studying associations lies in the fact that their contours are quite clearly defined and that concrete signs of change are easily observable.

This third arena of study has shown that while it is true that income generating projects for women have not fundamentally changed their living conditions, the fact that some women and youth have wanted and sought out positions within the various committees of the peasant associations has shaken up people's view of gender and generational relations. Social change does not in fact necessarily take place exactly as planners have foreseen in the structural arena. Sometimes, people, through their own organizations, must impose their own views. Studying this kind of social change brings other social relations into play that was neither in the structural arena nor in that of individuals. In summary, the process I propose places the problem of social change in three different social arenas: global structure, daily life and individuals, and associations.

Because all of these arenas are interwoven it is difficult to assume that any one takes precedence over the others. In fact, knowledge of the historical, economic, and social structure is essential to understanding phenomena involving local populations and especially various categories of people within these populations. The weight of the structure can have more or less impact on individuals depending on how present the state and institutions (to give but an example) are in people's daily lives. However, if we assumed that individuals are completely at the mercy of transcendent factors, we could not speak of social change.

Therefore, in the structural arena, social change can be defined as the result of the combination of historical, political, and social factors favored by the shift in the relative weight of hierarchical relations and which has been reflected in the general configuration of society. Social change is not, however, only structural. In their more or less organized actions, individuals enter into a dynamic that constitutes both the outcome of and the basis for broader social change. Thus, social change can also be defined as the result of individual or group practices that modify the social relations in which they are involved. Thus defined, social change is therefore an ongoing process that cannot be measured in terms of the degree of success achieved by various categories of the population in their actions.

That is why it is important to examine their practices independently of the more general scope of their actions. In La Cocha, the striking thing is how the pace of change varies depending on the social relations that connect various social categories to the surrounding structures of society. The kind of hierarchies involved in these social relations, to a large extent, defines social change. In a word, social change must be approached in connection to social relations, keeping in mind that it is a process with multiple dimensions that varies depending on the social arena of the research.

DEVELOPMENTS IN HRM

The developments in the field of HRM are now well documented. Nevertheless, the debate on HRM issues continues even though its focus has changed over time. The main issue which occupied academics in the 1980s was the evolution of HRM. In this regard, the debate was mainly on the exploration of the salient aspects of the transformation of personnel management into HRM. Having done so, it moved on to issues pertaining to the incorporation of industrial relations into HRM; then the integration of HRM into business strategies, devolvement of HRM to line managers, and finally seeing HRM as a source of competitive advantage for organisations. Currently, there is an ongoing debate regarding the contribution of HRM to a firm's performance.

With these developments the nature of Human Resource (HR) function has changed from being reactive, prescriptive, and administrative to being proactive, descriptive and executive. While some seminal HRM research findings have been produced in recent years, research has often been based on a single country or the researchers look at issues in Western Europe or North America. Essentially, these studies have focused on HRM in advanced industrial societies in the West. As relatively very little work on comparative HRM research in developing countries has been done, some researchers have suggested the need for more comparative cross-national HRM studies.

This is all the more important because of the increasing levels of globalisation and internationalisation of business, the growth of new markets (such as in Africa, Eastern Europe, China, India, South-East Asia and Latin America), the growth of new international business blocs (such as NAFTA, the European Union, ASEAN) and an increased level of competition among firms at both national and international level. As the world develops into a 'global business village', there is a greater need to know how managers in various parts of the world cope with issues and problems related to management of human resources. Thus, we must highlight the major factors that impact on HRM policies and practices in different contexts as such an evaluation will contribute to the development of HRM theories and relevant policies and practices.

Although academics have responded positively to the challenges raised by the globalisation of business by investigating a number of issues and problems related to international business, again the comparative perspective has been put on the back burner. One possible way to investigate such questions is by identifying and examining the influence of the main factors and variables that impact on HRM in different cross-national settings. Several scholars note that national HR practices are determined by both 'culture-free' factors (such as age, size, and nature of organisation) and 'culture-bound' factors (such as national culture and institutions). It is now accepted that management practices including HRM are not universal but are 'socially constructed' in each society.

If the nature of HRM is known to be 'context-specific', then the degree and direction of influence of both culture-bound and culture-free factors on HRM vary from country to country and are responsible for the context-specific nature of HRM. For example, the strong impact of unions and other pressure groups on HRM in India presents the context-specific nature of such practices. On the other hand, the influence of competitive pressures marked by the downsizing of the workforce in the United Kingdom highlights the context specific nature of the UK HR function. Similarly, the response of unions to competitive pressures such as the introduction of new production technologies, large-scale restructuring and increasing work flexibility varies across countries. Union membership has declined significantly in countries such as the UK, France and the United States, whereas it has remained quite stable in Canada and Germany.

The above examples show that institutional configurations can mediate between environmental pressures and their effects on HR practices. Investigators have identified how important contingency variables such as the size, age, nature, life cycle stage of an organisation, level of technology used and presence of formal HR department can influence HR practices. However, other researchers in the field while acknowledging the role of contingency factors have noted that more complex culture-bound arguments must be applied to the field of HRM.

Research on the influence of the main factors on HRM in a cross-national context is therefore crucial for the growth and development of the field of HRM. This is particularly so in view of the major developments taking place in developing nations which have liberalised their economies and opened their doors to foreign investors. It is essential for practitioners to know the pattern of HRM systems prevalent in such developing countries. However, the achievement of such an objective does require more research. Focusing on developing nations would add a new impetus to HRM research and allow researchers to go beyond the current predominant emphasis on research in countries in the European Union and North America. Such an approach would also help researchers to examine the transferability of management systems and practices.

Until the 1970s, the view that management theories are universally applicable was quite pervasive. However, the influence of the 'convergence hypothesis' has now waned as sufficient evidence has been gathered against it. But the question still remains, to what extent does this contingency view apply to the relatively new field of cross-national HRM, given that most HRM models have been developed in the Anglo-Saxon world? McGaughey and De Cieri argue that organisations are becoming more similar in terms of macro-level variables (convergence), but are maintaining their culturally based dissimilarities in terms of micro-level variables (divergence).

This is a significant finding which perhaps can be applied to HRM in developing countries.

Although both contingent variables and national factors (mentioned above) are known to influence cross-national HRM, it is suggested that more meaningful cross-national HRM comparisons can be made by examining the influence of national factors on HRM. This thesis is based on the premise that national factors such as national culture and national institutions form the very basis of HR functions in any country. Therefore, in order to evaluate and highlight the context-specific nature of HRM in different national or regional settings, we need to delineate the major national factors that influence HR practices in such settings and the dilemma of factors to include under broad concepts of 'national culture' or 'institutions' needs to be resolved.

The term 'developing countries' is used in a broad generic sense and is used to represent all countries other than advanced industrialised societies which we refer to as developed countries. Some authors have used other terms such as 'less developed countries', 'newly industrialised countries', 'third world countries', 'emerging nations', 'emerging markets', and 'transitional economies' interchangeably for developing countries. For us, developing countries are the ones which are in their early growth stages of economic development and are in the process of industrialising or are still non-industrialised.

This is an ideal-type description as we know that all developing countries are at different stages of economic development. The existing literature shows that apart from a few journal articles dealing with single countries and the work of a few researchers, relatively very little has been written about HRM in developing nations. This was probably due to the limited number of researchable topics in mainly small economies with small companies and small wage employment sector. However, over the past two decades, foreign direct investment (FDI) has come to the developing parts of the world, bringing its share from 23 per cent in the mid-1980s to 37.2 per cent in 1997 (United Nations, 1998:9).

Though this amount decreased to 28 per cent in 1998 due to the financial crisis in Asia, FDI to Latin American countries has been rising continuously and is projected to rise in Asia. As a consequence, of 53,000 multinational corporations (MNCs) with 450,000 affiliates operating around the world, a total of 230,696 affiliates are now based in developing countries. As a result of such developments, there is now a sudden research interest in management in developing countries. The above facts highlight the great extent to which both developed and developing countries have now become interdependent on each other.

This is also evident from the creation of various economic international trading blocs and 'growth triangles'. However, it is important to recognise that the 'state-of-the-art' management practices and techniques which are dictated by unique configurations of different cultural and institutional factors, developed in the context of Western cultural values, cannot be uncritically adopted in developing countries. Therefore, there is now a need to research and highlight what kind of HR policies and practices are relevant for developing countries. Considering the above, what decision-makers in developing countries do, or fail to do, are of significant interest to both academics and practitioners in the rest of the world. Therefore, for the development of appropriate theory and practice, it has now become important for researchers to understand how HR is managed and what key factors determine HRM in developing countries.

In order to develop a conceptual framework to examine HRM in developing countries, it is important to define HRM in the broadest sense. There are several reasons for this. First, the existing literature suggests that the concept of HRM is relatively new and possibly non-existent in some regions of the developing world. Second, because several distinctive HR models can exist within firms in a particular country, each of which depends (along with a number of other factors, such as different institutions and national culture) on a number of distinct 'internal labour markets'. Within each labour market, HRM incorporates a range of sub-functions and practices which include systems for workforce governance, work organisation, staffing and development and reward systems.

HRM is therefore concerned with the management of all employment relationships in the firm, incorporating the management of managers as well as non-management labour. In line with these views, different scholars in the field of HRM have put forward a number of frameworks for conducting international HRM research. However, these frameworks are found to be normative in nature and many of them present a complex set of variables that cannot be tested empirically. On the contrary, Austin (1990) suggests an environmental analysis framework to enable managers in developing countries to practice effective management.

Based on a critical analysis of the existing frameworks in the field and over seven years of research in the HRM field, recently Budhwar and associates have proposed a framework for examining cross-national HRM. They have identified three levels of factors and variables which are known to influence HRM policies and practices and are worth considering for cross-national examinations. These are national factors involving national culture, national institutions, business sectors and dynamic business environment; contingent variables including age, size, nature, ownership, life cycle stage of organization, presence of trade unions and HR strategies and interests of different stakeholders; organisational strategies such as the ones proposed by Miles and Snow and Porter; and policies related to primary HR functions and internal labour markets.

However, considering that HRM in developing countries is in its infancy and the argument that HRM in a cross-national context can best be analysed by examining the influence of national factors, we propose to examine the impact of only four national factors on HRM in developing countries. These factors are: national culture, national institutions, dynamic business environment and industrial sector. These broad factors form the macro environment of organisations in a national context. Few would question the positioning of national culture, institutional arrangements and changing business dynamics in the external context as national factors. Perhaps it is the positioning of the industrial sector which requires justification. The study of national business systems, suggests that the industrial sector is best considered as a country level or national unit of analysis and is worth considering for national level evaluations and comparisons.

This inference is based on the premise that certain sectors (for example, the forest sector in Finland, which is an industrial complex of various businesses that has emerged over the past 130 years) are well connected to similar sectors in other competing countries and to markets all over the world. Examples of such critical sectors include the Finnish forest sector, the Danish milk products sector and the Japanese car sector. All can clearly be distinguished by the very nature of their social networks, ownership control relationships and vertical logistical links. However, all also clearly retain a 'national' character.

It is important to bear in mind that a sector is an accomplishment of many actors who work in different time periods and with diverse logics of action. There are always alternative interpretations and applications of the 'sectoral business recipe', based on simultaneous factions that emerge in the sectoral networks. It is, thus, logical to state that nation-states contain unique configurations of sectors, each trying to develop their own business recipe within the national business system. Recent research has therefore shown how HRM policies and practices are governed by a specific sector. Within the oil-dominating countries (such as Saudi Arabia and Iran), we expect some sector-specific HRM practices.

We have made a serious attempt to identify the main components of the four national factors. However, we are aware that this list is by no means exhaustive. Next, we present a brief discussion on the remaining national factors. A number of researchers including Easterby-Smith et al., Hofstede, Keesing Laurent, Schneider, Sparrow Sparrow and Hiltrop and Tayeb have highlighted and explained the influence of national culture on HRM policies and practices. The definition and scope of the concept of culture are, of course, debatable. It is therefore sensible to examine the impact of those aspects of national culture on HRM which have a sound theoretical base.

Moving to the third national factor, researchers in the field of cross-national HRM have considered in detail the impact of different national institutions on HRM policies and practices. There are a number of institutional systems whose influence on

HRM in a cross-national context must be interpreted. Finally, a number of the existing frameworks in the field do indicate the impact of a competitive business environment on HRM. However, like the factor of national culture, none of the existing frameworks in the field provide the main aspects of the competitive environment which can help to assess its impact on cross-national HRM. Although many of these dynamics are unique to each nation, a series of developments are pan-national and have been identified as major determinants of international HRM activity.

3

Multinationals and Industrial Development

It has been frequently noted that flows of foreign direct investment (FDI) have increased rapidly during the past decade. While much of the global stock of FDI exists within developed countries, recent evidence indicates that flows to developing countries have increased substantially: in 1997, developing countries received 37.2 per cent of the global flows of FDI. Furthermore, given the relatively small economic size of these economies, even a small amount of foreign investment can account for a large percentage of their total investment and therefore generate a significant impact. For example, in 1996, the total stock of inward FDI as a percentage of the gross domestic product in developing countries equaled 48.6 per cent.

Multiple market forces are behind the observed growth in FDI: reduction in costs of communication has eased the constraints on global rationalization of production and the information technology revolution has created markets for many new products and services. Increased world trade in services has further contributed to global FDI flows since services often require suppliers to have a physical presence in a market. However, changes in the market environment do not capture the whole story. Policy initiatives have also played a central role: many countries have gone further than simply removing barriers to inward FDI and have taken a more pro-active approach toward attracting FDI through the use of fiscal and financial incentives.

This new, more favorable, policy environment in many developing and formerly communist countries contrasts sharply with historical attitudes toward multinational firms in these countries. The spread of multinational firms was often viewed with suspicion and mistrust in such countries, particularly in those that pursued a strategy of import substitution. An important aim of import substitution policies was to encourage indigenous industrial development. Hostility toward multinationals was based on the perception that the entry of such firms was detrimental to domestic industrialization. The infant industry argument, or some derivation of it, often served as an intellectual justification for such policies.

However, a parallel tradition in development (at least among academic discussions) took a more optimistic view. In this tradition, multinationals were (and are) seen as agents that increase competition in the host economy, transfer modern technology, and help achieve a more efficient allocation of resources. The recent wave of liberalization of trade and FDI policies suggests that the optimistic view of FDI seems to be gaining the upper hand. One manifestation of this trend of liberalization is the proliferation of bilateral investment treaties across countries: there now exist 1,513 bilateral investment treaties among countries, compared with fewer than 400 at the beginning of 1990.

Of course, the failure of import substitution as a strategy for development is a crucial reason behind this remarkable turnaround in policies in many developing countries. Within the more optimistic view of FDI, a frequently cited benefit of inward FDI is that it pushes forward the process of industrial development by creating *linkages* with the rest of the economy. In this chapter, we explore the argument that FDI encourages industrial development through linkages.

First, we discuss the relevant economics literature that has attempted to formalize the concept of linkages. Second, we discuss the existing empirical evidence regarding linkages. In our first task, we begin by tracing the intellectual development of the idea of linkages by noting the debt owed to Hirschman who provided a concrete definition of the fundamental concepts. Next, we provide a discussion of some of the more recent theoretical analyses of the concept of linkages. Then, we discuss empirical evidence on linkages in light of the insights yielded by theory. Finally, we comment on the findings of both types of literature and note the policy implications of these findings.

FUNDAMENTAL CONCEPTS

In a classic work, Hirschman developed the concepts of backward and forward linkages and analyzed their importance for economic growth. In his own words:

> The setting up of an industry brings with it the availability of a new expanding market for its inputs whether or not these inputs are supplied initially from abroad.

This enhanced market exerts a backward pressure for establishing industries that supply the new entrants. He calls this process backward linkage effects:

> Every non-primary activity will induce attempts to supply through domestic production the inputs needed in that activity.

Similarly, forward linkage effects are created when one industry uses another industry's outputs as its inputs:

> Every activity that does not by its nature cater exclusively to final demands will induce attempts to utilize its outputs as inputs in some industries.

The sum of the backward linkage effect and the forward linkage effect gives the total linkage effect, which can be seen as the growth in new industries induced from establishing an industry. Hirschman was careful on the issue of backward linkages: he noted that linkages between parent and satellite industries are unlikely to be as important as those formed with larger industries that have a lower probability of forming. Another important point made by Hirschman was that multiple industries are likely to have a greater linkage effect when taken together, compared to simply adding up the individual effects. The presence of two or more industries may create enough demand to surpass the threshold required for establishing new industries, whereas the presence of only one of them would not.

Taking all of these industries together may provide enough incentive to create yet others. This cumulative effect may explain much of the acceleration of industrial growth seen early on in the development process. Regarding empirical implementation, Hirschman suggested that the importance of linkages in an economy could be approximated by the percentage of inputs purchased from other industries for backward linkages and the percentage of output sold to other industries for forward linkages. Industries with strong linkages in both directions (such as petroleum products and chemicals) can be distinguished from those with predominately forward linkages (such as metal mining and agriculture) and those with predominately backward linkages (such as grain mill products and leather products).

In this sense, Hirschman's scheme for development planning preceded and foresaw the recent debate regarding industrial targeting. Hirschman argued that part of the difficulty for underdeveloped economies is a lack of interdependence and linkages. Consequently, the development process must commence with industries that cater to final demand. This requirement leaves two possibilities: transformation of either primary goods or semi-manufactures into final products. Since the latter may provide stronger possibilities for linkages, Hirschman suggests that governments in such countries should assist industries involved in intermediate activities since these have strong potential for creating both backward and forward linkages.

Clearly, an accurate accounting of expected linkage effects is crucial for any plan to encourage investment in industries with the strongest linkages. Hirschman's suggested method for proceeding on this front was to use input-output data from more advanced countries with already existent industries to represent the linkages expected to form in some lesser-developed country. However, any extrapolation across countries runs the risk of error. For example, technologies adopted in lesser-developed countries might use a different mix of inputs, especially if other parameters (such as factor endowment ratios and trade policies) are not the same across countries.

Many of the failures of development prescriptions stem from failing to account for idiosyncrasies across countries. The entry of firms, especially large multinational firms in developing countries, may expand the total output of an industry through increased scale, enhanced competition, technology diffusion to local rivals, or general training of workers. This expansion in output of an industry may play a crucial role in bringing the scale of existing industries up to levels sufficient to generate backward and forward linkages needed for industrial development. As we shall see next, the theoretical economics literature on multinationals has indeed advanced this argument.

MULTINATIONALS AND LINKAGES: THEORY

The recent surge in the literature on industry linkages and international trade provides several concrete models of concepts originating in the development literature. In a recent paper, Rodríguez-Clare (1996a) takes up Hirschman's concept of linkages and develops a formal model to analyze the effects of multinationals on economic development. He relies on three premises to develop a model of the linkage concept. First, a greater variety of inputs leads to higher production efficiency, as captured by assuming a love of variety for inputs in the production of final goods (a weaker form of Hirschman's assumption that certain inputs were necessary for production).

Second, market size limits the available variety of specialized inputs due to inputs being produced with increasing returns to scale (related to Hirschman's specification of a minimum economic size). Third, proximity of supplier and user is required, since domestic firms must buy all of their inputs locally (to ensure that domestically produced inputs are essential to developing an industry in final goods). Under such circumstances, an economy will exhibit multiple equilibria: a good equilibrium with high wages (which coincides with the production of complex final goods and a wide variety of inputs) and a bad equilibrium with low wages (which coincides with the production of simple final goods and a small variety of inputs).

If the number of varieties of the intermediate good exceeds a threshold, then a country specializes in producing the more complex good. Since profits are zero due to the assumption of free entry, the higher wages in the good equilibrium imply that it Pareto dominates the bad equilibrium. To give multinationals a role in the process of industrial development, Rodríguez-Clare supposes that two economies exist with one in the bad equilibrium (a developing country) and the other in the good equilibrium (a developed country).

Under this scenario, firms in the high-wage economy may wish to take advantage of the cheap labor overseas by establishing a plant in the host country, while maintaining headquarters at home to enjoy access to the wide variety of specialized inputs available there. The crucial assumption is that specialized inputs cannot be exchanged internationally through arm's-length transactions and thus cannot be used by a firm unless it operates in the country where the inputs are produced. Consequently, only multinationals can combine the wide variety of specialized inputs from the developed country with the cheap labor from the developing country.

Rodríguez-Clare develops a statistic called the *linkage coefficient* to address the effect of multinationals on the host economy. The linkage coefficient measures the ratio of employment generated in upstream industries by a firm to the labor hired directly by that firm. A *positive linkage effect* arises if the multinational has a higher linkage coefficient than domestic firms. A positive linkage coefficient implies that an increase in the number of multinationals results in a greater variety of intermediate goods produced locally, which in turn increases the productivity of domestic firms and the domestic wage.

Positive linkages are most likely to result when the good that multinationals produce is more complex, the communication costs between the headquarters and the factory are higher and the source and host countries are more similar in terms of the variety of intermediates produced. The cost of communication is modeled as an iceberg-type transportation cost: a fraction of the composite input (produced from specialized source inputs) melts *en route* from the source headquarters to the host factory.

An increase in the cost of communication between the factory and headquarters causes a firm to purchase more goods locally, and hence raises its linkage coefficient. In addition, since the multinational is only able to purchase more inputs locally if they are produced, the linkage coefficient is increasing in the variety of intermediate goods produced in the host economy. Since firms using a greater variety of inputs tend to establish plants in countries with a smaller variety of intermediates, an implication of this analysis is that developing countries may not enjoy substantial linkages because multinational firms import their inputs from the source country.

This model operates under the principle of full employment, and the idea that foreign firms compete directly with domestic firms (hence creating a negative relationship between the number of firms in one country and another). In truth, underdeveloped countries do not possess full employment. A multinational may hire labor from the ranks of the unemployed, or from other industries that then replace their departed workers by drawing from the previously unemployed. In such a setting, not only the wage but the total wage bill (the wage times employment) should contribute to domestic welfare. A multinational's presence could generate large benefits by increasing employment, even if wages increase only slightly.

Furthermore, the existence of multiple final goods industries would further complicate the scenario, since one would have to know from which industry the labor is being displaced. Consider three industries, A, B, C, which have linkage coefficients in descending magnitude. If a multinational enters in industry B, then it may have a negative impact on the host economy if it draws labor from industry A. However, the converse will hold if the addition of this firm draws labor from industry C. Which scenario is more likely? What happens if we allow multinationals to pay a higher wage than local firms do? This query is not merely of theoretical concern: multinationals are indeed often observed paying higher wages than local firms, especially in developing countries. Can the added labor income be enough to offset a mild negative linkage effect? While such questions are beyond the scope of Rodríguez-Clare's model, their importance can hardly be overstated.

In another interesting paper, Markusen and Venables construct a model with linkages to address the potential for cumulative causation in industrial development - the ability of the formation of an upstream industry to generate the later formation of a downstream industry. The entry of multinationals affects the host economy in two potentially opposing directions. On one hand, multinationals replace domestic firms through a *competition effect*: the entry of multinationals lowers the price index for the final good, which causes the exit of domestic producers of final goods to restore equilibrium. On the other hand, multinationals may create conditions beneficial to local industries through a *linkage effect*: the entry of multinationals may raise the demand for intermediates, which causes the domestic production of intermediate goods to expand.

An important variable for assessing the linkage effect is the *input-output coefficient*, which measures the ratio of the intermediate required relative to the per unit total input requirement of the downstream industry. Whether this ratio for the multinational firms exceeds the ratio for the domestic firms influences whether the linkage effect is positive. The two ratios may differ due to differences in technology (the multinational firms may use more intermediates relative to primary factors than do domestic firms) or differences in sourcing (multinationals may source from abroad). If this ratio is greater for multinational firms than for domestic firms, then the multinational uses local intermediate goods more intensively than the domestic industry. Thus, this ratio is the analogue to Rodríguez-Clare's employment-based measurement.

The Markusen-Venables model also exhibits multiple equilibria. Starting from the good equilibrium where the domestic economy already supports its own upstream and downstream producers, multinational activity can generate various consequences depending on the relative strengths of the competition and linkage effects. In general, the competition effect decreases the number of domestic firms (both upstream and downstream), while the linkage effect may increase both if multinationals use intermediates more intensively than domestic firms do. The various consequences are most easily understood by considering a few special cases. These cases are chosen to illustrate how the characteristics of the multinational investment project and of the domestic industry influence the magnitude and direction of the effects.

First, suppose multinationals source no intermediates locally. Then, the linkage effect must reduce the number of domestic firms (both upstream and downstream), which reinforces the competition effect. Second, alternatively assume that multinational production merely displaces foreign firms serving the domestic market through exports. Such a scenario arises if foreign firms decide to switch to being multinationals, a common occurrence (and hence not merely a theoretical exercise). Then, the competition effect is zero, and provided the multinationals source some intermediates locally; the linkage effect increases the number of domestic firms (both upstream and downstream).

Third, instead of assuming intermediate goods are near perfect substitutes so that the forward linkages, whereby additional upstream firms (through enhanced variety) induce entry of downstream firms, are shut down. Then, multinational firms purely displace domestic downstream firms, so the number of domestic downstream firms falls although the number of domestic upstream firms may rise. This last case illustrates the role of the love of variety for intermediates in inducing forward linkages and hence cumulative causation in industrial development.

Even starting with no initial domestic production (the bad equilibrium), backward linkages generated by multinational firms may be strong enough to induce the development of a domestic upstream industry. The domestic economy would be observed having its own upstream industry but not yet its own downstream industry (only multinational production). Forward linkages may then induce the development of a domestic downstream industry. Ultimately, the multinational presence serves as a catalyst to the development of the entire domestic industry. The expansion of domestic production may be so strong that it eventually drives the multinational out of the host country, as occurred in the bicycle and personal computer industries in Taiwan.

Matouschek and Venables take a deeper look at the interaction between competition effects and backward linkages created by the entry of a multinational firm into the local market. They analyze the effects of investments in the downstream and then the upstream industry. They break the overall effect of multinational entry into two parts: an initial production effect and a feedback effect. The initial production effect is the immediate change in local production: the multinational production alters the output levels of domestic firms (through crowding out) in that industry as well as in upstream production. The number of downstream firms adjusts to restore zero profits, but the number of upstream firms is held constant in determining this piece of the overall effect.

Next, the *feedback effect* occurs once changes in the upstream industry impact the downstream sector through changes in the price of upstream varieties (which are felt as cost changes to those downstream). Here, entry and exit of upstream firms affect both the variety of intermediates available as well as the intensity of competition. The initial production effect in the downstream industry depends on two important parameters: relative local supply and the measure of local substitutes. The *relative local supply* is the ratio of the additional local supply generated by the foreign investment project relative to the local supply generated by a local firm. It depends on the export orientation (of the project and the local firms) and the extent that the project is import replacing. Relative local supply is decreasing in the export orientation of the multinational relative to local firms. If the project sells less of its output locally than do local firms (and the project is not import replacing), then the relative local supply is less than unity because the project is more export oriented than local firms.

Relative local supply is also decreasing in the extent that multinational output merely replaces imports of the downstream good from foreign countries. If the multinational has the same export orientation as local firms, then relative local supply is unity if the multinational's output does not displace any imports from abroad but zero if it fully displaces them (sells the same amount locally through FDI as it did before through trade). The initial production effect can be negative; as if the project sells all its output locally while local firms export some of their output and the project displaces no imports.

The local substitute's index states the number of units of local sales by local firms that are displaced by one unit of local sales by the foreign investment project. A value of zero means that local firms compete in completely different markets; while a value of one means local firms compete in the same market segment. Intermediate values between zero and one indicate the degree of competition. Consider different possible values for these two parameters to illustrate their impact. When local substitutes take a value of one (compete in same market) and relative local supply is zero (multinational sales merely displace imports, or no multinational production is sold locally, for example), then the initial production effect is simply the foreign investment project's own production: no crowding out of local firms occurs in the downstream market.

On the other hand, if relative local supply is one (such as if the project sells the same amount locally as one local firm but does not displace any imports), then no initial production effect results: multinational production fully crowds out local production so local production in the downstream market is unchanged. Hence, the initial production effect is decreasing in the relative local supply. Similarly, the initial production effect is also decreasing in the local substitute's index. The initial production effect in the upstream industry depends on the level of relative local sourcing, which is the project's usage of local inputs per unit of output relative to the usage by local firms.

A value of one means the project uses local inputs to the same degree as local firms, while a value of zero means the project buys all of its inputs from abroad (or uses none). The initial production effect in the upstream industry is increasing in relative local sourcing but decreasing in relative local supply.

Putting the initial production effects in the upstream and downstream industries together, the initial production effect of the project is larger, the larger the export orientation or import replacement of the project, the lesser the degree that the project competes directly with local firms, and the larger the usage of local intermediate goods by the project.

In the next round, the feedback effect captures inter-industry effects generated by the project. Positive feedback effects are possible because increases in the demand for upstream goods induce the entry of upstream firms (which in turn causes entry of downstream firms due to reduced costs). Characteristics of each industry also affect the magnitude of the feedback effect. The feedback is greater if the upstream industry has a greater degree of imperfect competition. Backward linkages result in forward linkages, like the cumulative causation described in Markusen and Venables and initially seen in Rodríguez-Clare.

If the initial production effect is zero and relative local sourcing is unity, the project generates no feedback effect. Feedback effects strengthen welfare gains: the reduced input costs lead to a reduced price for the final good and hence welfare benefits through consumer surplus. A relatively export-oriented project generates even greater welfare gains, which may help explain the export performance requirements that multinationals often face in developing countries. A welfare reduction will occur if the project has a relative local sourcing coefficient less than one and is export oriented. The more the output expansion and welfare gain, the higher the elasticity of demand, the greater the potential for expansion of sales at the expense of imports, and the greater the potential for expanding exports in the downstream industry.

Next, consider investing in a project in the upstream industry. Such an investment will lower the price of inputs for the downstream industry, increasing the demand for upstream production. There is also a substitution effect, where the lower price for one intermediate may reduce demand for others. However, more downstream firms enter due to higher profits (the feedback effect), which may offset the substitution effect. Additionally, if local industry supply is perfectly elastic, then there is no net result. Forward linkages require an initial production effect upstream in order to affect the downstream industry. Furthermore, forward linkages are decreasing in both local substitution and export orientation. If the former equals one, or if all output is exported, then there are no forward linkages. Finally, larger welfare gains result if the downstream industry is more open to international trade and competition or if the upstream industry is more imperfectly competitive.

So far, three different models have proposed three different linkage measurements. To recapitulate, Rodríguez-Clare's statistic depends on the relative local job creating capabilities of multinational and domestic firms. Markusen and Venables use the competition effect to determine whether multinationals crowd out local firms and the input-output coefficient to compare the use of locally produced intermediate goods across multinational and local firms. Finally, Matschusek and Venables use two similar measures, relative local supply and relative local sourcing, to capture the crowding out of local production or imports and the demand resulting for locally produced intermediate goods. Rodríguez-Clare examines linkages in a general equilibrium setting where the emphasis is on wage effects, while the other two conduct their analyses in partial equilibrium where the emphasis is on price effects.

The last approach is somewhat more appealing as it provides a more complete view of how linkages affect the local economy. For empirical purposes, the relative local sourcing and Markusen-Venables indices are the easiest to quantify. The others involve job or demand creation, which can be analyzed theoretically using a *ceteris paribus* assumption, but would be difficult to implement empirically. The competition or crowding out effects may be apparent *ex post* (for assessing existing projects), but would be hard to determine *ex ante* (for assessing planned projects, such as for host country approval).

Other theoretical papers consider the role linkages play in trade liberalization. None of these models contains FDI: instead of foreign firms becoming multinational, these models have concurrent exit of foreign firms and entry of domestic firms to shift production into the domestic economy. In Krugman and Venables, if transportation costs are sufficiently low, the presence of backwards and forwards linkages leads to agglomeration and a core-periphery dichotomy with its resultant wage gap. As costs fall to zero, the two economies again see production in both sectors and a convergence of wages. The other papers build off these results. Puga and Venables show that when cost linkages outweigh demand linkages, the upstream industries will be the first to flee the domestic economy, and the industries with weaker linkages will lead the exodus. Extending these models to allow for FDI would seem to be productive avenues for future research.

EMPIRICAL EVIDENCE ON LINKAGES

Schive (1990) provides some empirical work on linkages from FDI in Taiwan. Since his work precedes the theoretical models discussed above, he does not use the above-mentioned measures. Nevertheless, his study shows that FDI in Taiwan tended to concentrate in industries with strong backward linkages. Initially, enterprises controlled by non-Chinese investors tended to import more and form enclaves, with little interaction with the rest of the economy. Over time, however, these firms tended to increase the percentage of inputs that they bought domestically. He postulates that perhaps these firms need time to determine which local suppliers could provide for their needs and points to evidence showing that those firms which set up shop later tended to import a lesser percentage from the start.

Perhaps this shift occurred because later entrants had time to observe and learn from the behavior of earlier entrants. However, this learning effect may tell only part of the story. It is also likely that foreign firms begin to buy more local inputs due to a domestic learning effect: domestic suppliers may also need time to determine the needs of foreign firms and to learn to supply those needs at competitive prices. Thus, the later entrants enjoyed a better selection of locally produced inputs from which to choose.

Furthermore, Schive's observation those foreign-based non-Chinese firms tended to import a higher percentage of their inputs than domestic firms may not capture the full picture. Foreign firms could also use a higher level of inputs per unit of output, so that the resulting linkages effect may be stronger than the corresponding effect for Chinese foreign firms. Borrowing from Rodríguez-Clare's linkage coefficient concept, foreign firms might also create more jobs depending on the types of inputs they buy, despite their higher tendency to import. For example, if inputs demanded by multinationals require more labor per unit of output than those demanded by local firms, then the multinational's demand may actually create more jobs upstream than local firms.

Three other case studies precede the recent theoretical papers on linkages and FDI. Stewart studies linkages in a random sample of manufacturing firms located in the Limerick Mid-West Region of the Republic of Ireland. Stewart measures linkages in several different ways: backwards national linkages (BNL) are defined as the sum across firms of total inputs minus imports plus wages paid to employees at the plant (pre-tax). Similarly, backward regional linkages (BRL) are defined as the sum of inputs bought in the region plus the local wage. Finally, the difference between sales and exports is called forward national linkages (FNL) while forward regional linkages (FRL) equal regional sales across firms. The author notes that there are indeed several flaws with these measurements.

First, the effect of wages in BRL may be overstated due to taxes. Second, redistribution of resources (labor and capital) results when a foreign firm replaces a domestic one and in this case, since there was high unemployment in this region during the survey period, this redistribution may not prove a significant issue in terms of labor. Furthermore, these measures also ignore secondary effects, which are captured by the cumulative causation analysis developed in Markusen and Venables and advanced by Matouschek and Venables. The new theory and the linkage measurements developed take some of these effects into account, showing immediately how older empirical studies may benefit from the new theory. His analysis concludes that foreign firms fail to develop either backwards or forward linkages.

Irish firms generate larger linkages as a percentage of output compared to foreign firms, but fewer of them are regional. He proposes that fiscal incentives and the region's characteristics attract firms that are less likely to develop linkages. In 1964, regional linkages as a percentage of output were as follows: 39.3 per cent for US firms, 22.1 per cent for British firms, and 27.4 per cent for Irish firms. In 1970, the figure for US firms had fallen to 28.7 per cent, comparable to the 29.5 per cent for Irish firms, both of which were paltry, compared to the 44.9 per cent witnessed with British firms. British firms provide an excellent example of the general trend that multinationals tend to buy more locally as time goes on, while the behavior of US firms runs counter to it.

The British firms also illustrate the benefits of proximity to the host country, despite the claim by Rodríguez-Clare that proximity lowers communication costs and hence decreases the level of local purchasing. This counter result may well be due to some of the dynamics referred to in the Taiwanese example. Irish suppliers, by having a closer connection with the British than the US firms, both in terms of geography and the cultural spillover that results, may find it easier to determine the needs of British suppliers as opposed to US firms. British firms may likewise find it easier than US firms to purchase from Irish suppliers due to proximity. In addition, US firms may have a better selection of intermediates to choose from in their own domestic market owing to the larger size of the US market.

The Irish experience has also been studied by Barry and Bradley who find that foreign factories are much more likely to import their inputs than are local factories. This result again casts doubt on the proposition that multinationals generate significant local linkages. However, Barry and Bradley also find that foreign firms have a higher productivity than domestic plants. Furthermore, those industries with high levels of FDI tend to have higher wages. Lim and Fong examine Singapore, starting in the early 1960s when there were few linkages because US tariffs (placed only on the value added) created the incentive for intra-firm trade. They conducted three case studies of long-established, export-oriented, multinational firms in Singapore's electronics industry.

Their conclusion was that, with limited government interference (as in Singapore), export-oriented multinationals can indeed create linkages. In a recent book, Moran provides anecdotal evidence strongly suggestive of extensive backward linkages from FDI in the Mexican auto industry. Within five years of the initial investment, there were 300 domestic producers of parts and accessories, of which 110 had annual sales of more than one million dollars. These case studies present some evidence that FDI results in linkages, especially backward linkages, since multinationals often locate simple manufacturing operations in developing countries to take advantage of low local wages. However, none of these studies provides a rigorous econometric study to help determine whether any of these trends or results is statistically significant. Certainly much more rigorous work, taking advantage of the new measurements developed in recent research, would add significant value to the empirical literature analyzing linkages and multinationals.

In this, we have provided a selective survey of the theoretical and empirical literature on linkages from FDI. At present, there does not exist a strong connection between theory and empirical evidence. Part of the problem may simply be that it is difficult to empirically implement the theoretical models. However, much of the advances in the theoretical modeling of linkages are relatively recent, so most empirical work pre-dates the formal theory. In general, there is strong theoretical support for the idea that FDI can play a crucial role in industrial development by generating backward and forward linkages in the host economy. On the empirical side, the evidence is mixed. While some studies support the linkage effects of FDI, others fail to find such effects.

However, much of the existing empirical evidence does not correspond directly to the theory and therefore should not be viewed as a direct test of existing theories. A fresh attack on the problem of measurement of linkages needs to be undertaken using the issues identified by modern theory. Finally, linkages are but only one of the potential channels through which FDI impacts a host economy. Any policy formulation based primarily on the notion of linkages would be misguided.

Increased competition, technology transfer, increased access to world markets due to spillovers to local firms, and worker training are some of the other channels through which FDI can benefit the host economy, and such benefits can be realized despite the absence of linkages. Hence, policy formulation should be based on a more holistic view of FDI.

4

Foreign Manufacturing
An Analysis of Discriminating Characteristics

Studies evaluating the impact of foreign direct investment (FDI) on host developing countries have usually addressed themselves to quantifying gross or net generation of incomes, savings, foreign exchange, and employment by individual or total FDI projects. This evaluation approach ignores the domestic alternative that may be possible in most cases (with or without foreign technology and loans). The direct balance of payment (BOP) effect in the case of an import substitution project is very likely to be negative and could be so even in the case of a local firm. From the point of view of evaluating the impact of FCEs on various parameters of development, therefore, examination of aspects that distinguish them from their local counterparts is more important.

Furthermore, it has been argued, for instance by Cohen (1975), and Newfarmer and Marsh (1981), that the impact of FDI on development would be 'minimal' if the foreign controlled and local firms behaved in a similar way. The current state of knowledge on conduct and performance differences between foreign and local firms in developing countries is deficient in many respects. Besides having a limited choice of parameters compared and sample size, the existing studies have seldom controlled for extraneous influences and interaction among the variables, since most of them have been conducted in univariate context.

This chapter compares some important aspects of conduct and performance of foreign controlled and local firms (FCEs and LCEs respectively) in forty-nine Indian manufacturing industries in a more comprehensive framework. The analysis covers different elements of market structure and performance, choice of technology, employee compensation behaviour, linkages with the domestic economy, export performance, and financial policy and management. The significance of the differences between the two groups of firms across forty-nine industries is first evaluated in terms of a univariate statistical criterion.

The variables identified by the univariate test as important in differentiating the two groups are then simultaneously included in a multivariate test to control for possible mutual interaction. The final discriminating variables are, thus, selected through step-wise discriminant analysis from among those identified by the univariate analysis. This chapter begins by examining the characteristics of MNEs which may lead to differences in the behaviour of FCEs and LCEs. In the light of these characteristics and the existing empirical evidence, it then formulates a set of hypotheses on the expected nature of differences pertaining to different parameters. The findings of the empirical analysis in the univariate and multivariate frameworks, respectively, are presented, and the chapter concludes with a summary of the major findings and the limitations of the analysis.

FCES AND LCES-HYPOTHESES

FCEs share the ownership of certain unique intangible assets with parent MNEs such as brand goodwill, knowledge, organizational skills, access to marketing and information networks, etc. Because of the ownership advantages, the asset bundles of FCEs are different from those of their local counterparts. This fact may lead to differences in the mode of rivalry of the two groups of firms. The FCEs' rivalry may be dominated by non-rice competition based on product differentiation to maximize the revenue productivity of advantages such as the brand goodwill that they hold. The mode of rivalry might reflect on their scale of operations, advertising behaviour, and profit margins.

The access to information on world markets and opportunities coupled with the MNEs' objective of global profit maximization may result in rationalization of production on the basis of international division of labour, which may lead to the higher dependence of FCEs on international trade. FCEs' perception of risks may also be different because of their access to better information. The centralization of strategic decision-making responding to global opportunities in MNEs may lead to a different investment and financing behaviour, propensity to undertake R&D, raw material sourcing, export behaviour, profit repatriation behaviour, etc., of FCEs.

The decisions to enter, diversify, and undertake R&D of MNE affiliates in Canada have been found to be less determined by the local conditions than in case of their local counterparts. The factor proportions and the employee compensation behaviour may show differences because of grooming of MNEs in an environment of capital abundance or labour scarcity. The experienced and more professional organizational skills of MNEs may lead to more optimal financial and inventory management.

Taking leads from these general characteristics of MNEs, and drawing upon the existing empirical knowledge, we can now proceed to formulate the hypotheses concerning the nature of differences between FCEs and their counterparts in terms of different parameters of behaviour. These parameters have been classified into seven broad headings: market structure, conduct, and performance; choice of technique; employee compensation behaviour; vertical inter-firm linkage generation in the local economy; export performance; financial policy and tax planning; and financial management. The variables proxying each of these parameters and their definitions are also indicated.

The impact of penetration of MNEs on host country market structures directly and indirectly (through their competitive behaviour) has received considerable attention in the recent literature. Market structure and performance can be influenced by FCEs through the relative scale of their operation, and other aspects of competitive behaviour. In some countries, particularly in Latin America, there is evidence that MNEs have influenced the local market structures through their acquisition and merger behaviour. These, however, are not important in the Indian case because of government regulations.

SCALE OF OPERATIONS

The scale of operation of firms is an important determinant of the market structure of the industry. There are no clear-cut *a priori* reasons for expecting differences in the relative scales of operations of FCEs and their local counterparts. However, as has been observed earlier, FCEs are expected to prefer non-price competition and sell more differentiated products. Such form of rivalry is often accompanied by extensive advertising and marketing campaigns to disseminate the differentiating features of the product among potential customers. The advertising activity is known to enjoy significant economies of scale and is most cost effective if carried out at the national scale rather than at regional or local levels. It can therefore be expected that FCEs will prefer to set up operations that intend to serve national markets.

Hence the relative scale of their operations is likely to be larger than that of a firm not following a similar strategy. This expectation perhaps explains the conclusion of Lall, which was reached on the basis of a survey that the 'larger and more industrially advanced a host economy, the more will TNC affiliates tend to exceed their local competitors in size'. Available empirical evidence also indicates that FCEs are on average larger than their local counterparts, and is provided, for example, by Kidron in the case of India; Newfarmer and Mueller in Mexico and Brazil; and Lall and Streeten in India, Colombia and Malaysia.

A number of studies have observed a significant correlation between the degree of presence of MNEs and seller concentration. Examples are: Rosenbluth in the case of Canada; Radhu in Pakistan; Willmore (1976) in Guatemala; Newfarmer and Mueller and Connor in Mexico and Brazil; and Parry in Australia. These correlations, however, can be misleading, as the sources of entry barriers that give rise to concentration and the sources of FDI overlap substantially. Evans for Brazil, Lall for Malaysia, and Blomstrom (1986) for Mexico find the positive influence of foreign ownership on industry concentration even after controlling for the entry barriers. In view of the above theoretical reasons, and in the light of the empirical evidence, the scale of operations of FCEs will be hypothesized to be larger than that of their local counterparts in Indian manufacturing.

The scale of operation will be proxied through the average volume of net sales per firm (SIZEi). Firms manipulate the external constraints placed on their expansion through their advertising, R&D, product diversification, collusion, merger and takeover behaviour (Hay and Morris 1979:30). In view of the limitations of data on products diversification and collusion behaviour, and the government regulations on merger and takeovers, we shall consider here only the advertising and R&D.

Advertising activity is the source of brand goodwill and an important aspect of non-price rivalry. However, there is a general lack of evidence on the comparative advertising behaviour of FCEs and local firms. Caves has argued that the skills of MNEs in differentiating their products prompt them to prefer non-price competitive rivalry, such as through advertising campaigns. The presence of MNEs may dispose an industry towards non-price competition and hence may increase the general level of advertising expenditure of the industry. Caves et al., and Gupta (1983), found the foreign share in industry sales to have a significant positive influence in explaining the proportion of advertising expenditure in Canadian manufacturing industries.

This could be due to two reasons: one, the foreign subsidiaries spend relatively higher proportion to their income on advertising so that the industry average of advertising expenditure rises in proportion to their presence; and two, the foreign subsidiaries induce the industry to pursue non-price rivalry, and both foreign and local firms spend a higher proportion of income on advertising. Which of the two effects is dominant, however, is not clear from the two studies. Willmore found FCEs to spend a higher proportion of sales revenue on advertising than their local counterparts in Brazil even after controlling for firm size and industry. We shall, therefore, examine the hypothesis that FCEs spend a higher proportion of their income on advertising (ADSi) than their local counterparts.

R&D activity is the main source of the technological edge that MNEs enjoy. It is logical, therefore, to expect MNEs to concentrate their R&D activity near their headquarters (Vernon 1974). The US Tariff Commission confirmed that US MNEs do concentrate most of their R&D in the United States. Creamer, on the basis of a survey of over 900 US MNEs having overseas R&D, found that the bulk of their R&D activity was undertaken in the United States only. Similar figures were reported by Mansfield et al. in a more recent survey. Furthermore, the overseas R&D was carried out primarily in the industrialized countries (two-thirds of the total overseas R&D activity done by US MNEs being in three countries, namely Canada, the United Kingdom, and West Germany).

Only a 'negligible share' of the overseas R&D found its way to the developing countries. The implications of this finding are that affiliates of MNEs, particularly in the developing countries, are likely to undertake little R&D. On the other hand, there may be several compelling reasons for a local firm to undertake R&D. For instance, local firms do not enjoy the continuous access to laboratories of the parent firm abroad as FCEs do. The local firms that obtain technology from abroad on a licensing basis may be forced to undertake R&D to absorb, adapt, and modernize the technology. The fixed life span (usually 5-7 years) of foreign technical collaborations and restrictions placed by the Indian government on their renewals may make the licencees anxious to absorb the technology during the life of the collaboration agreement.

Most of the studies that analysed R&D intensity found the locally controlled firms to be more R&D intensive than their foreign controlled counterparts. Examples are: Subrahmanian for the Indian chemical industry; UNCTAD for the Indian capital goods industry; Evans, and Gordon and Fowler for the pharmaceutical industries in Brazil and Canada, respectively; and Ragachand in the case of Canada. On the basis of a detailed examination of different aspects of innovative activity of foreign and local firms in Latin American countries, controlling for age and scale of operation, Fairchild and Sosin reached the conclusion that domestic firms had a higher level of internal innovative activity, whereas foreign firms relied more heavily on sources external to the subsidiary. Lall found a positive relationship between foreign ownership and R&D in the Indian engineering industry but a negative one in the chemical industry thus affording no generalization. We shall verify the hypothesis that in India, FCEs spend a lower proportion of their income on R&D (RDSi) than their local counterparts.

PERFORMANCE

The performance of FCEs and LCEs has been compared in terms of profitability and factor productivities. A number of studies have found higher labour productivity in the case of FCEs, for example, Fairchild and Sosin in various Latin American countries and Willmore in Brazil. But a large part of the difference could be on account of their observed higher capital intensity. Tyler in Brazil, Vendrell-Alda in Argentina, and Agarwal in India, have attempted to compare total factor productivities of FCEs and LCEs. The differences appeared to be significant in the case of India. The lack of data on physical labour inputs, inflation adjusted book value of capital stock, physical quantity of output, and rates of capital utilization in our data base does not permit us to make any meaningful comparison of performance in terms of factor productivities. We shall, therefore, confine ourselves to comparisons of profitability and growth rate.

FCEs can be expected to enjoy higher profitability than their local counterparts because of their monopolistic ownership of intangible assets. It has been observed earlier that this fact may induce them to pursue a non-price mode of rivalry. A part of prices charged by them may be monopoly rents for goodwill and other intangible assets held. Evidence from the literature gives the impression that FCEs fare better than local firms in terms of profitability. However, when extraneous factors were controlled for, the observed differences did not remain statistically significant.

Examples are from Lall in the case of Colombia and India; Gershenberg and Ryan in Uganda; Fairchild and Sosin in Latin American countries. Subrahmanian, Fairchild, and Newfarmer and Marsh also did not find any significant differences between profitability of FCEs and their local counterparts in Indian, Mexican, and Brazilian case studies, respectively. The reported profits, however, need not necessarily reflect the true profits, since they are subject to possible manipulations such as transfer prices. We shall, none the less, examine whether FCEs have higher profitability. Following current practice, profit margins on sales (PCMi) rather than the rate of return will be used to represent profitability.

Growth is also an important aspect of performance of firms. The managerial theories of the firm have considered maximization of growth to be the basic objective of the managerial firm (subject to a certain minimum profit constraint). The sources of growth may include expansion of the existing product line, vertical integration, conglomerate diversification, and acquisition. FCEs may be considered to be better equipped to undertake expansion, integration, or diversification for the reasons that facilitate their initial entry, namely ownership advantages. However, the decision pertaining to the expansion of FCEs may not only be taken in view of the local opportunities but may also be influenced by the parent enterprise's global strategy.

Furthermore, in India firms need to procure an industrial licence from the government (and an additional clearance under the FERA or MRTP Acts for firms coming under their purview) before effecting any plans of substantial expansion of existing product line, integration, diversification, or acquisition. Though the industrial policy statements of the government have repeatedly assured a non-discriminatory treatment in industrial licensing to all FCEs with foreign equity up to 40 per cent, it is possible that the purely local firms could be enjoying a preference over FCEs in actual implementation of the policy.

Thus, while FCEs may enjoy an edge over their local counterparts in terms of resources for growth, they may be constrained by the global strategy of the parent enterprise and Indian government policy. In the absence of information on possible weights of these contradictory factors we are unable to reach a definite prediction on relative rates of growth of FCEs and their counterparts. Empirical studies have usually confined themselves to comparisons of growth rates between developed country firms that stayed at home and those which undertook foreign investments and became multinational. Therefore, growth rates (GROWi) of FCEs and local firms will be compared without *a priori* prediction.

CHOICE OF TECHNOLOGY

Choice of technology by the foreign firms has perhaps been the most controversial issue till date. The *a priori* reasoning has been that technologies of FCEs are appropriate to the factor endowments of their home countries, which are typically capital abundant. Reuber *et al.* found that in over 70 per cent of the cases MNEs transferred the process technology to developing countries without any adaptations. Courtney and Leipziger, and Leipziger, however, found that MNE subsidiaries in developing countries employed different techniques, in most cases more labour-intensive than their counterparts in industrialized countries. Among the several factors that might discourage adaptations of the imported technology to make it more appropriate to the factor proportions of the developing countries is the possibility of technological rigidity.

Marsh *et al.*, find a close association between capital intensity and technological rigidity. They find that MNEs usually concentrate in capital intensive sectors which often suffer from a technological rigidity that limits the scope for influencing the technological choice. Morley and Smith reached similar conclusions.

Most of the studies that compared factor proportions have noted a higher capital intensity of operations of foreign firms compared to that of local firms. Examples are: Forsyth and Solomon in the case of Ghana; Gershenberg and Ryan in Uganda; Newfarmer and Marsh in the Brazilian electrical equipment industry; Biersteker in Nigeria; Radhu in Pakistan; Wells in Indonesia; Agarwal in India; Jo in South Korea; Chen in Indonesia and Thailand; Balasubramanyam in Indonesia; Meller and Mizala in six Latin American countries; and Willmore in Brazil. On the other hand, Cohen in the case of Taiwan, South Korea and Singapore; Reidel also in Taiwan, and

Jo in South Korea found that the export-oriented foreign subsidiaries did not employ a significantly different technology from that of the local export-oriented firms.

Chung and Lee in the case of Korea; Mason in the case of Mexico and Philippines; and Chen in the case of Hong Kong, Malaysia, and Taiwan also could not find any significant difference in capital intensities, possibly due to the export-oriented nature of these economies. Kirim also did not find any significant difference in capital intensity on the basis of nationality in the Turkish pharmaceutical industry (controlling for size and degree of vertical integration factors). ILO (1984), on the basis of studies in a number of developing countries noted that MNE affiliates tended to be more capital intensive but that their capital intensity was explained in terms of other characteristics such as size rather than by multinationality. The evidence, therefore, generally confirms the view that MNEs employ technology that is relatively more capital intensive compared to that used by local firms when producing mainly for local markets. In the case of manufacture for exports, however, FCEs employ technology not significantly different from that employed by their local counterparts.

Since the firms studied here are predominantly local market oriented we shall verify the higher capital intensity or, alternatively, lower labour intensity - of FCEs as compared with their local counterparts. There are problems in measuring capital intensity due to the unavailability of data on the physical quantity of employed labour in the company annual reports, our ultimate source of data. Measurement of capital also suffers from problems relating to different vintages of capital and rates of capital exhaustion (utilization), differing accounting rules, and price changes over time. In the absence of any better index, we are led to use a wages: fixed assets ratio as an admittedly crude indicator of labour:capital ratio (LKRi).

Because of their grooming in an environment of labour scarcity and high wages, MNE affiliates are expected to pay higher wages and salaries than their local counterparts in developing countries. A number of studies seem to support this expectation, for instance, Markensten for Swedish MNEs in India; Gershenberg and Ryan in Uganda; Mason in the Philippines and Mexico; Possas in Brazil; and ILO. Chee reported that, while there was a significant difference between wage payments by foreign and local firms to managerial and skilled workers, no significant difference was observed in the case of unskilled workers. Cohen did not find any clear pattern on the relative employee compensation behaviour of foreign firms in the case of export-oriented firms in South Korea, Singapore, and Taiwan.

Lim, while examining the determinants of average hourly wages in West Malaysian manufacturing industries, inferred that higher wages paid by foreign firms were largely due to greater capital intensity and productivity of their production processes. Similar conclusions were reached by Dunning and Morgan in a six-country study where they observed that, normalizing for industry and country differences, MNEs do in general pay higher wages than indigenous firms but that the margin of difference is not as great as is sometimes alleged. Thus the existing evidence 'does not affirm any pervasive differences due strictly to their transnational statuses.

Furthermore, a part of the higher wages paid by FCEs may be on account of possible differences in skills not controlled for in any of these studies. Balasubramanyam in the case of Indonesia, and Willmore in the case of Brazil find average wages paid by FCEs to be significantly higher than their local counterparts, but they attribute them to the quality of human capital differences. We shall, none the less, attempt to compare an index of employee compensation behaviour between foreign and local firms; we can expect it to be higher for the former.

Measurement of relative rates of wages and salaries, however, is not without problems. Companies in India, in general, do not report total number of their employees in their annual statements of accounts. Therefore, even though the total wage bill is presented, it is not possible to compute average levels of wages. However, the number and the gross emoluments of all employees in receipt of Rs 3,000 per month or more are given. Siddharthan and Dasgupta (1983), and Lall and Mohammad have used, the proportion of earnings of high income employees in the total wage bill as a proxy of managerial and/or skill intensity (SKIL2).

The proportion of high income employees may differ between industries due to their differing requirements of skills. However, one often finds wide variation in the proportion of such employees across different firms in the same industry. There could be two possible explanations for such intra-industry variation: (a) inter-firm variations in employee compensation behaviour or pay policies, or (b) inter-firm qualitative differences in skills (such as higher qualifications and experience or motivation). Hence, differences in the proportion of high income employees (HIE) between FCEs and LCEs may be due to variations in either pay policies or the quality of the personnel employed, or both. In both cases, FCEs are likely to have a higher HIE.

The vertical inter-firm linkages created by an enterprise have valuable implications for the development of the host economy. The volume of vertical backward linkages generated is determined by two decisions concerning the sourcing of raw materials and intermediate products of the firm: 'import or procure locally' and 'make or buy'. Performance of FCEs and LCEs will be compared in terms of both these aspects.

IMPORTATION VS. DOMESTIC PROCUREMENT

A number of studies have compared the dependence of foreign and local firms on imported raw materials in order to get an idea of the extent of linkages generated in the domestic economy. FCEs can be expected to import a higher proportion of their raw materials and other inputs than local firms, because of their familiarity with foreign suppliers and the alleged inadequacies of local producers, and sometimes to provide a market for products of their associates elsewhere. Cohen in the case of South Korea, Taiwan, and Singapore, and Reidel also in Taiwan, has found that the export-oriented foreign firms import a greater proportion of their inputs than their local counterparts.

Even foreign firms producing predominantly for domestic markets have been found to depend more on imports than their local counterparts, in studies by Kelkar and Subrahmanian and Pillai in India; McAleese and McDonald in

Ireland; Jo in South Korea; and Newfarmer and Marsh in the Brazilian electrical industry. Lall and Streeten, in a study of six countries including India, however, did not find any significant difference between the import dependence of foreign and local firms. Here we shall verify the hypothesized higher dependence of FCEs on imported raw materials (IMPi) for our sample of Indian manufacturing industries.

The 'make or buy' decision essentially relates to the degree of vertical integration. The latter is inversely related to subcontracting parts of the production run to unassociated vendors. In countries like India, which have evolved a strict trade and exchange control regime that restricts the freedom of firms to import, subcontracting may be a more important aspect of a firm's decision-making concerning the sourcing of intermediates and raw materials. A number of market failures may tempt the firm to internalize the manufacture of intermediate inputs such as the certainty of delivery schedules and quality standards.

Certain monopoly rent may also be associated with vertical integration. On the other hand, the firms can internalize part of scale economies in the manufacture of intermediates and can escape problems of industrial relations by sub-contracting their production to other firms. In India's case, promotion of subcontracting is also one of the objectives of the government's industrial policy (the promotion of ancillary industries). The degree of vertical integration will, therefore, be determined by the relative weights of these factors which may vary from industry to industry and from firm to firm. There are no clues as to whether FCEs may tend to subcontract a greater or lower proportion of their requirements of intermediates.

Among the empirical studies, Cohen in the case of export-oriented firms in Taiwan, South Korea and Singapore found local firms to be having a greater degree of vertical integration. Newfarmer and Marsh, and Willmore, found a reverse pattern in the case of Brazil. UNCTC could not find any significant difference between the extent of sub-contracting of a foreign subsidiary and a local company in India which both produced trucks. Therefore, no definite pattern emerges from the existing work. We shall compare the degree of vertical integration (VASi) of foreign and local firms in our sample of Indian manufacturing without making a prediction.

EXPORT PERFORMANCE

As part of the multinational enterprises, FCEs enjoy several advantages over their local counterparts in export markets: captive access to market information networks, marketing outlets, brand loyalty, etc. Hence, other things being the same, FCEs are better equipped to tap export markets than their local counterparts. MNEs have evidently played an important role in the rapid expansion of manufactured exports of some South-east Asian countries during the 1970s. The decision to export from the host country, however, is an important aspect of the global strategy of the enterprise. Hence, the relative export performance of FCEs may be determined more by their global corporate strategy than by export advantages.

In India's case there are additional reasons for expecting better export performance of FCEs than that of their local counterparts. In addition to general export incentives, FCEs are encouraged by the government to export through both direct and indirect means. Under the provisions of FERA, 1973, foreign firms are permitted to retain a higher level (51 or 74 per cent) of foreign equity than the general ceiling of 40 per cent if they manufacture predominantly for the export market. Expansion into industrial activities, otherwise not open to FCE with over 40 per cent foreign equity (such as non-core sectors or those reserved for the small-scale sector), is permitted if production is meant for export.

Further, the government of India sometimes imposes export obligations on foreign collaboration approvals or on industrial licences to foreign controlled firms for expansion/diversification. It is evident that roughly 20 per cent of foreign collaborations approved between 1974 and 1978 had certain export obligations. The findings of empirical studies comparing export performance of FCEs and local firms in different countries have been mixed. Based on a study of the export-oriented firms in South Korea, Taiwan, and Singapore, Cohen concluded that local firms were somewhat more likely to export than foreign firms, while Reidel found no significant difference in the export performance of the two groups of firms in Taiwan (except in the case of electronics).

Some studies compared the proportion of exports in sales of firms predominantly producing for domestic markets, and found that foreign controlled firms performed relatively poorly. Examples are: Lall and Streeten, and Subrahmanian and Pillai, for India; Jenkins for Mexico; Kirim for the Turkish pharmaceutical industry; and Solomon and Ingham for the British mechanical industry. Studies by Morgenstern and Muller for ten Latin American countries; Newfarmer and Marsh for the Brazilian electric equipment industry; and Fairchild and Sosin also for Latin American countries, could not find any significant difference. Lall and Mohammad found a positive, though weak, influence of degree of foreign ownership on industry's export performance in India.

But that does not necessarily imply a superior export performance of FCEs compared to their local counterparts. Furthermore, in their study the influence of foreign ownership appeared to be significant only in the absence of another independent variable with which it was collinear. Here we shall examine whether FCEs export a significantly higher proportion of their turnover (EXPi) than their local counterparts in Indian manufacturing industries.

The proportion of retained earnings in disposable profit (retention ratio), and ratio of borrowings to shareholders funds (leverage ratio), are considered to be the two central financial policy decisions of firms. These two together determine the valuation ratio and cost of obtaining funds for the firm. The (corporate income) tax planning is also an important aspect of financial strategy because it influences the volume of cash flow and the effective cost of investments. The behaviour of FCEs and LCEs will be compared in terms of each of the three components of the financial strategy.

Apart from influencing the market valuation of a firm's stock, the retention vs. pay out behaviour of the corporate sector is an important parameter of the saving/investment situation in the country. Since the retention ratio determines the valuation of a firm's capital, it is subject to a stock market constraint. A high retention ratio and consequently low pay out ratio may lead to a decline in the market valuation of the firm. A too low stock price may not only affect the flow of external funds to it but may also activate bulls to mount a take-over raid. FCEs may be less susceptible to this constraint as big chunks of share capital held by the foreign share holders are not traded locally.

Given the stock market constraint, the retention vs. pay out decision of FCEs may be influenced by among other things, the relative attractiveness of investment in the host country, the investment opportunities, proportion and pattern of distribution of local share holdings, and the parent's perception of the role of affiliates in their global strategy. These factors vary from firm to firm. No *a priori* reasoning for expecting a difference in the retention ratios of FCEs and local firms in any particular manner is possible. Jo found FCEs to retain a significantly lower proportion of profits than their local counterparts. In this exercise, however, the extraneous factors had not been controlled for. The retention behaviour (REPi) of two groups of firms will be compared here without making any prediction.

The proportion of borrowed funds in the financing of capital requirements determines the cost of funds for the firm. FCEs have an additional incentive to depend more on the locally raised loans because they reduce their exposure to exchange risk. Their better credit-worthiness and strong financial position ensure a flow of the desired volume of funds to them. On the other hand, higher cash flow on account of their hypothesized higher profitability may reduce their borrowing requirements. The findings of empirical studies are mixed. Subrahmanian found FCEs to depend less on borrowed funds than their local counterparts in nine of the twelve pairs of firms studied in India. While Lall in the case of India, and Gershenberg and Ryan in the case of Uganda, could not find any significant difference in the borrowing requirements of FCEs. Here again, the leverage ratio (LEVi) of FCEs and their local counterparts will be compared without any firm prediction.

Rates of corporate income tax in India in general are high. However, to encourage investments a number of concessions are permitted, such as tax holiday for new investment, accelerated depreciation, and allowances like investment allowance and weighted deductions. Therefore, the effective rate of tax applicable to a company becomes a function of tax planning which can even reduce the tax liability of an otherwise profitable company to an insignificant sum. Another factor which might influence the effective rates of tax is profitability.

Though the prescribed rates of tax are flat (a slightly higher rate for closely-held companies and a lower rate for widely-held companies), an element of progression has been brought in by imposing a surtax for companies earning supernormal profits. One might expect that FCEs may be at a disadvantage compared to the local firms in their ability to reduce tax liability, their being alien to the land. Second, supposedly high profitability of their operations might attract surtax. Both factors will lead the effective tax rate for FCEs to be higher. Therefore, the effective rate of tax (ERT) for FCEs can be expected to be higher than their local counterparts.

Two aspects of financial management - inventory and cash management - are considered here for the purposes of comparison.

A certain amount of inventory is necessary for running production processes in manufacturing activity. However, large accumulation of inventory adds to the cost of capital. Inventory management, therefore, is an important indicator of the efficiency of marketing and procurement networks. Since possession of efficient management and organizational skills is considered to be one of the intangible assets held by MNEs, one can expect FCEs to be able to manage with a smaller volume of inventory per unit of sales compared to their local counterparts. Performance of FCEs has not yet been compared with that of their local counterparts in terms of this aspect of managerial efficiency. In the absence of any empirical evidence we shall prefer to go by the expectation that FCEs' inventory requirements per unit of sales (INSi) are lower.

In addition to holding the necessary volume of inventory a manufacturing firm needs liquidity to cover the lag between input procurement and recovery of sales proceeds. This requirement of liquid assets is referred to as working capital. Having a bearing on the total capital employed, and hence cost, working capital management is an important aspect of financial management. Furthermore, a firm with a comfortable liquidity position may obtain a competitive advantage over its rivals by offering liberal suppliers' credits.

Liquidity requirements of a firm may also depend upon the efficiency of procurement and distribution channels. Reasons for the difference between the liquidity positions of FCEs and local firms are not quite clear, nor are there any empirical studies on this aspect. Therefore, the relative liquidity position of FCEs and local firms will be compared without any *a priori* prediction. Liquidity is defined as the difference between current assets and current liabilities. Hence, it is measured by the current ratio (CUR).

The empirical analysis includes comparisons of FCEs and LCEs in terms of the fifteen parameters identified above. A look at the means reveals that for variables, SIZE, ADS, RDS, PCM, HIE, IMP, and ERT the mean differences are in accordance with the predictions. In the case of three variables, LKR, EXP, and INS, the differences are contrary to the expectations, in particular a higher LKR for FCEs. But the difference may not be statistically significant because the standard deviation of LKR is high for FCEs. On average, FCEs export a lower proportion of their sales and have a higher inventory per unit of sales, compared to the local firms. Among the variables for which we did not have a definite prediction, the mean for FCEs is higher in the case of VAS and CUR indicating their greater degree of vertical integration and richer liquidity position on average. FCEs have a lower mean in the case of GROW, LEV, and REP.

Examination of the statistical significance of these mean differences is conducted in two stages. In the first stage the univariate tests of significance of the differences are performed. The findings of the univariate tests may sometimes be misleading because they do not take into account the interaction among the discriminating variables. In the second stage, therefore, the variables found to be important discriminators in the univariate test are considered simultaneously in a multivariate framework.

The univariate test applied here is non-parametric. Non-parametric tests have the advantage of not assuming any specific distribution of the population under analysis. Hence they are uniquely suited to behavioural science data. Among the various non-parametric tests, the Wilcoxon Matched-Pairs Signed-Ranks Test is one of the more powerful ones, as it utilizes information on both the direction and the magnitude of the differences within pairs. It gives more weight to a pair that shows a large difference than to a pair that shows a smaller difference. It has been used for similar purposes by Mason, Willmore, Agarwal, and Chung and Lee. For more than twenty-five observations, T (the test statistics) is normally distributed with

$$\text{mean} = \frac{n'(n'+1)}{4} \qquad \text{variance} = \frac{n'(n'+1)(2n'+1)}{24}$$

where n2 is number of non-zero differences. Hence standard normal variate Z can be calculated by dividing the difference between T and its mean by its standard deviation.

Since six of the forty-nine industries in our data base have no representation of FCEs, we shall confine our analysis to forty-three matched pairs of industries. The test can be, as usual, either one- or two-tailed. Of the five variables representing different aspects of market structure and performance, four (SIZE, RDS, PCM, and GROW) were significant. The direction of differences suggests that FCEs have significantly larger scales of operation and enjoy higher profit margins than their local counterparts. This result is in line with the general impression and the hypotheses formulated above. These findings also indicate that FCEs spend a relatively smaller proportion of their income on R&D and seem to be growing at a slower rate than their local counterparts. However, one needs to control for the possible interaction among the variables before reaching a final conclusion.

The analysis, however, fails to bring out any significant differences in the intensity of advertisement expenditures of the

FCEs and LCEs. It is possible that FCEs spend significantly more on advertising in advertising intensive industries. Thus giving equal weight to all industries may not be appropriate. To correct for this the advertising intensity of FCEs and LCEs was weighted for the industry's share in total advertising expenditure by the sample firms. Though the weighting improved the Z statistics from 0.84 to 1.37, it continued to remain insignificant. In view of MNE's predisposition towards product differentiation, advertising intensity of FCEs was expected to be more than that of LCEs. This result, however, does not rule out any impact of FCEs on this aspect of market structure. As indicated above, it is possible that penetration of MNEs in an industry induces the firms to adopt a non-price mode of rivalry, which increases the general level of advertising activity in the industry.

The only way of checking this is to examine the dynamic pattern of advertising behaviour of industry firms *vis-à-vis* the entry of FCEs. Moreover, FCEs enjoy a dowry of intangible assets and hence are able to internalize the benefits of a part of the advertising done by their parent and associate firms in the rest of the world. Hence the current advertising expenditure of FCEs may yield proportionately higher returns than that of LCEs. Another reason why FCEs may be getting more mileage out of the same proportion of income spent on advertising could be due to economies of scale. FCEs have been found to have significantly larger scales of operation. Hence, the scale of their advertising is larger than that of LCEs.

The factor proportions of FCEs are also not significantly different than those of LCEs. However, caution needs to be applied while interpreting results pertaining to this variable because of the limitations of measurement. The difference in terms of proportion of high income employees (HIE) is significant at the one per cent level. This finding, however, is subject to confirmation in multivariate tests. Of the two sources of vertical local inter-firm linkages compared, FCEs' behaviour is not significantly different in terms of import dependence. The difference continues to remain insignificant even if the import dependence of FCEs and LCEs is weighted for the industry's share in total imports by the sample firms.

Most of the studies done for other countries found FCEs to have a tendency to import a higher proportion of raw materials and intermediate goods than the local firms. In India's case this result may be an outcome of the strict exchange and import regulations, and the high priority attached to import substitution. In addition to quantitative restrictions on imports and high tariffs, the government's tendency to canalize most of the bulk imports may have contributed to this result. Behaviour of FCEs regarding the 'make or buy' decision is significantly different, as revealed by the higher degree of vertical integration (VAS).

The export orientation of FCEs does not seem to be significantly different from their local counterparts. Again, weighting of export performance by industry's share in total exports of the sample firms makes no difference to the result. It indicates that FCEs in India are largely local market oriented. The aspects of an enterprise's financial policy considered here, namely retention and leverage ratios, are significant in discriminating between FCEs and LCEs. This suggests a lower propensity on the part of FCEs to retain profits and to depend on external sources of financing. The tax planning variable is also significant and has the hypothesized sign.

Of the two aspects of financial management, liquidity and inventory management, only the former is significant in differentiating the two groups of firms. FCEs appear to have greater liquidity than their local counterparts. FCEs do not reveal any significantly different inventory behaviour compared to their local counterparts. Inventory requirements are also dependent upon the degree of vertical integration. The fact that FCEs do not require a significantly larger volume of inventory than the LCEs, in spite of the greater degree of vertical integration of their operations, might indicate their efficiency of inventory management.

The univariate analysis of statistical significance of differences has identified ten of the fifteen variables used as possible discriminants. These are: SIZE, PCM, RDS, GROW, HIE, VAS, REP, LEV, ERT, and CUR. In order to take care of the possible interaction among them the significance of mean differences will now be examined in the multivariate framework with the help of the step-wise discriminant analysis. The discriminant analysis involves the fitting of linear discriminant score functions on the basis of observed data on a number of discriminating variables of individuals whose group membership is known.

These functions (sometimes known as classification functions) can classify further cases into the groups on the basis of values of discriminating variables. In our case discriminant analysis can be used to examine whether FCEs differ from their local counterparts, and if so, in terms of which characteristics. Riedel, Solomon and Forsyth, and Solomon and Ingham, have made use of discriminant analysis for similar purposes. An individual observation is classified into the group for which the discriminant score on the basis of its observed values is higher. The goodness of fit is judged in terms of significance of mean difference between groups which can be expressed as F-ratio, and the ability of the fitted discriminant functions in correctly classifying the individual cases.

The discriminant analysis has three assumptions. First, no variable may be a linear combination of other discriminating variable. Second, the population co-variance matrices are similar for each group. Third, each group is drawn from a population which has a multivariate normal distribution. It has been shown; however, that discriminant analysis is a rather robust technique and can tolerate some deviation from these assumptions. In our case, since data are drawn from the same set of industries (forty-three for FCEs and forty-nine for LCEs) for both groups the covariance matrices are expected to be identical.

Since all the ten variables may not prove to be good discriminators, a step-wise procedure was used to select the significant ones. The procedure begins by selecting the individual variable which provides the greatest univariate discrimination (in terms of groups mean difference or partial F-ratio or F to enter). It then pairs the first variable with each of the remaining variables to locate the combination which produces the greatest discrimination. The variable which contributed to the best pair is selected. In the third step, the procedure goes on to combine the first two with each of the remaining variables to form triplets.

The best triplet determines the third variable to be entered, and so on. The step-wise procedure produces an optimal - not necessarily the best-set of discriminating variables.

Each correlation coefficient in this matrix is an estimate of the degree of relationship between the corresponding pair of variables *within the groups,* usually different from the total correlation, which is influenced by the differences. No two variables are found to be highly correlated so as to violate the assumption of the analysis. The procedure selects only five of the ten variables to be significant (at 5 per cent or higher level in terms of partial F-ratio) discriminants, namely SIZE, PCM, HIE, VAS, and CUR.

The other five RDS, GROW, LEV, REP, and ERT, are not significant in the multivariate context. These variables might be good discriminators on their own, but they do not add to the discriminating information contributed by the significant variables. Hence their unique contributions to the analysis are inadequate. They were, therefore, excluded from the subsequent analysis. The total F-value at the fifth step indicates that the two groups indeed differ significantly (at the one per cent level). The discriminant functions are able to classify nearly 85 per cent of observations correctly. Hence, they appear to be good fits.

The findings of the discriminant analysis suggest that of the five parameters of market structure, conduct and performance, only SIZE and PCM are able to distinguish FCEs and LCEs significantly. Both of these findings are in tune with our hypotheses and corroborate with the findings of a number of previous empirical studies. FCEs enjoy higher profit margins independently of their larger scales of operation (SIZE). The theoretical and empirical explanation of this difference in profitability performance needs to be examined in a greater detail.

The R&D intensity and growth rates which were found to be significantly different in the case of the univariate test are no longer able to distinguish the FCEs from their local counterparts in the multivariate case. The growth rates were perhaps influenced by scale of operation and not by the foreign ownership. Therefore, when scale of operation was controlled for, the significance of growth rate variation vanished. R&D intensity's interaction is, however, not so clear. The proportion of high income employees (HIE) continues to be a significant discriminant. In fact, this variable explains the maximum variation between the two groups. HIE could be higher in the case of FCEs due either to their tendency to employ more talented personnel or to their general tendency to pay their employees better. Which of the two tendencies is dominant, however, is not clear.

Of the seven possible explanatory variables included in the equation, only skill intensity and foreign share turn out to be significant determinants of HIE with positive signs in the single equation framework. But the relationship between HIE and FS is subject to simultaneity bias as the former has been found to be a significant determinant of the latter. When this simultaneity of their relationship was sought to be controlled for through two-stage least squares, the significance of even FS vanished and only SKIL1 remained a significant explanatory variable.

The high proportion of high income employees in the case of FCEs thus appears to be on account of their tendency to employ qualitatively superior personnel than their local counterparts, as observed by Balasubramanyam in the case of Indonesia, and Willmore in Brazil. However, more detailed micro-level research is needed on this aspect before a definitive statement can be made. FCE's tendency to employ qualitatively superior personnel may be an aspect of the non-price rivalry and may lend them a formidable competitive advantage in skill intensive industries, and can be a source of contrived entry barrier.

The degree of vertical integration (VAS) of FCEs is significantly greater than that of their local counterparts. This suggests that operations of FCEs generate fewer vertical inter-firm domestic linkages than those of LCEs. The government of India's policy of encouraging subcontracting to generate inter-firm linkages, therefore, seems to have found lesser favour with FCEs. The generation of linkages constitutes a boost to the development of the local industries. The performance of FCEs in this respect, therefore, appears to be inferior to that of LCEs.

Aspects of a firm's financial strategy, namely retention and leverage behaviour (REP and LEV), and the tax planning behaviour (ERT), were also not significant discriminators in the multivariate context. It appears that these variables are influenced more by the scale of operation and profit margin than by the nationality of ownership of the firm. CUR is significant even in the multivariate context, which suggests that FCEs enjoy richer long-term sources of financing their current assets. The comfortable liquidity position which FCEs enjoy is independent of their larger scales of operations and their higher profit margins. They might be using their strong working capital position as a source of competitive advantage.

The above analysis suggests that, compared to local firms, FCEs in Indian manufacturing have significantly larger scales of operations, enjoy higher profit margins, and are more vertically integrated and cash rich firms with better paid personnel. This, however, is a general picture. Some industry variation in the relative characteristics of foreign and local firms does exist as indicated by misclassification of some cases by the discriminant functions. FCEs in eight industries and LCEs in six industries do not wear the respective group's characteristics as specified by the discriminant functions on the basis of the whole sample.

Five of the eight cases where FCEs have been misclassified are those where FCEs are of only a marginal significance with their combined shares in industry sales under 10 per cent, namely breweries and distilleries, steel forgings, foundries and engineering workshops, cement, and paper and board products. In these industries, a few FCEs that continue to exist are there for historical reasons. They seem to enjoy no competitive edge and hence their characteristics do not reflect the distance that FCEs maintain from their local counterparts in other industries.

In fact, market power in these sectors is enjoyed by certain local companies affiliated with local large industrial conglomerates such as United Breweries, and Mohan Meakins in breweries and distilleries; Bihar Alloy Steel (Birla) in forgings: Mukand Iron, FACOR, Tata Yodogawa in foundries; ACC in cement; Central Pulp Mills in paper and board products. In the other three industries, metal products, paints and varnishes, and industrial and medical gases, although FCEs still enjoy substantial market shares their behaviour does not appear to be very different from their local counterparts.

All the six cases where LCEs have been misclassified, perhaps with the exception of industrial and medical gases, have one thing in common: LCEs in these industries are relatively larger firms affiliated with local large industrial conglomerates and with technology imported under licensing. With the goodwill backup of the parent (local) business house and technology from western MNEs they have almost matched the asset bundle of FCEs and hence have closely resembled them in terms of the discriminating characteristics. The instances are Tata Engineering and Locomotive, Hindustan Motors, Bajaj Auto in motor vehicles; Mysore Kirloskar in machine tools; J.K. Synthetics, Baroda Rayon, Indian Organic Chemicals, Nirlon Synthetic Fibres in man-made fibres; Hydrabad Asbestos in asbestos and asbestos cement; and Modi Continental Tyres in automotive tyres and tubes.

This chapter has examined the firm characteristics that distinguish FCEs from their local counterparts. The analysis of discriminating characteristics is important for evaluating the indirect effects of operation of FCEs which may sometimes be considerable in the host developing countries. The current state of knowledge on this aspect was found to be deficient in many respects. The distinguishing characteristics considered here included fifteen diverse aspects of firms' conduct and performance.

The statistical significance of the variables in actually discriminating the two groups of firms was examined for the sample of forty-nine three-digit Indian manufacturing industries in both univariate and multivariate frameworks. The findings of multivariate analysis indicate that a number of characteristics are able to discriminate FCEs and LCEs only on account of extraneous factors. Hence, findings of studies made in a univariate context need a fresh look. Among the different aspects of market structure, behaviour, and performance only larger scale of operations and higher profit margins (on sales) distinguished FCEs from their local counterparts.

Their advertising intensity was found to be not significantly different from that of local firms. They might, however, still enjoy an edge over their counterparts in this respect, on account of internalization of a part of the goodwill generated by advertising done by their associate companies and of economies of scale in advertising. The R&D intensity and growth rate of FCEs were both found to be lower only in the univariate test. The factor proportions also did not appear to be any different. A significantly higher proportion of employees of FCEs are in a high income category. This appears to be on account of the tendency of FCEs to employ qualitatively superior personnel than their local counterparts. This tendency could be an aspect of non-price rivalry, particularly in skill-intensive industries, and a source of contrived entry barrier.

Among the two sources of vertical local inter-firm linkages, FCEs' behaviour with regard to 'import or procure-locally' does not significantly differ from that of their local counterparts. This finding could possibly be an outcome of the strict foreign trade and exchange regulations exercised by the government. In terms of the other important source of linkages, 'make or buy', however, FCEs differ significantly from their local counterparts. FCEs have a higher degree of vertical integration and hence their operations generate fewer inter-firm linkages. Despite their advantage in export markets, and various fiscal incentives and government policy regulations to induce them to export, the proportion of their output that the FCEs export is not significantly different from that of their local counterparts.

Behaviour of FCEs in terms of retention ratio, dependence on external funds (leverage), or tax planning appeared to be different only on account of extraneous factors rather than because of foreign ownership. FCEs enjoy a more comfortable liquidity position due to their better long-term sources of funding working capital. This position can be used to secure a competitive advantage through their ability to extend liberal (suppliers) credits. In terms of inventory management, however, their performance was not very different.

The above analysis, therefore, brings out five major differences between foreign and local counterparts: the scale of operation, the profit margins, the proportion of employees in high income categories, the degree of vertical integration, and liquidity ratio. In a few industries, however, local firms affiliated with large local conglomerates with technology obtained on licensing from abroad closely resembled their foreign counterparts in all the dimensions covered here.

Further, as this exercise was conducted in a comparative static framework it does not bring out the dynamic influences of the entry of FCEs into an industry on different aspects of the conduct of local firms. Since firms in an industry mutually interact, the behaviour of local firms could be altered, through competitive and demonstration effects, by the very presence of foreign rivals. For instance, the presence of FCEs could have raised the general standards of advertising and other modes of non-price rivalry in an industry. This aspect of the effects of FCEs can be captured through dynamic analysis.

5

The Differential Effects of Patriarchy on Women in Cameroon

In light of recent attempts by the World Bank, International Monetary Fund (IMF), and bilateral donors to institute reforms aimed at promoting market liberalization in sub-Saharan Africa, women in development (WID) scholars have presented compelling evidence that women farmers, as the primary food producers in Africa, have been adversely affected (Gladwin 1991a). The structural adjustment policies (SAPs) called for by these donors - currency devaluation, increases in food prices and interest rates, decreases in wages and hiring rates, trade liberalization, removal of input subsidies, and decreases in budget deficits - were designed to stimulate long-term development in economically depressed developing countries.

The assumption that SAPs were gender-neutral, when in fact they were gender-blind, led to their failure to improve agricultural production in many cases, despite incentives to agricultural producers. For example, fertilizer subsidy removal programs called for under SAPs had a deleterious effect on many women farmers in Malawi and Cameroon because rising food prices and lack of access to credit in some regions left women unable to purchase fertilizer, resulting in low crop yields and food deficits. Most studies have focused on the adverse effects of SAPs. The question in the debate over market liberalization is whether it actually benefits women farmers: do women with access to productive markets for cash crops also gain access to productive resources like land and capital via input markets?

Women's access to the market depends on the particular interaction of capitalism and patriarchy in society. Patriarchy has been defined as "a system of social structures and practices in which men dominate, oppress, and exploit women". In areas where women are denied access to land and other productive resources such as fertilizer, credit, and training, patriarchy impedes women's entry into the market, and agricultural production suffers. By contrast, women's access to these resources and their participation in the market improves their household provisioning capacity and achieves greater equality.

Many of the feminist theoretical frameworks address gender inequality through capitalism and patriarchy. In this chapter, we discuss these different theoretical approaches and analyze their usefulness in explaining differences in women's market access in two provinces in Cameroon, the Francophone West Province and the Anglophone Northwest Province. Data used for this comparison are drawn from both secondary sources and primary sources. After describing and comparing the different feminist frameworks, we employ common themes from them to examine the effects of the interaction between capitalism and patriarchy on market access in Cameroon. Dual systems theory posits that gender relations are determined by the particular articulation of capitalism and patriarchy present in society.

The gender relations framework considers all aspects of social inequality in a holistic framework. We conclude that both frameworks are useful in explaining women's differential access to markets, land, and other means of production in Cameroon. We postulate that the often conflictual nature of capitalism and patriarchy can create an opportunity to promote gender equality. Cameroon provides a provocative setting for this discussion because recent agricultural developments there illuminate many of the effects of women's differential access to the market and implications for agricultural productivity.

Once proudly self-sufficient in food production, Cameroon has recently experienced a decline in production and exports.

Land conflicts have erupted as the population expands. Landholdings have become increasingly concentrated, often in the hands of urban elites. Women farmers in some areas have always had to "beg" for land. Currently they witness their tenuous usufruct rights being challenged by rural development schemes that give land title to elite urban males. In other regions, women are able to inherit and purchase farmland for the first time. The recent land tenure conflicts and declining agricultural production provide an opportunity to analyze the differential effects of capitalism and patriarchy on women farmers' access to the market in the two regions.

GENDER FRAMEWORKS

There are several theoretical frameworks for addressing gender inequality. The primary perspectives are liberal feminism, radical feminism, Marxist-socialist feminism, gender relations theory, and dual systems theory. Radical feminism and Marxist-socialist feminism differ from liberal feminism in that they analyze gender equality vis-à-vis underlying social structures: patriarchy and capitalism, respectively (Gordon 1996). Both gender relations and dual systems theory explore gender inequality through a synthesis of Marxist and radical feminist theory.

Liberal feminism originated among primarily white, middle-class, Western women. Its emphasis on "individualism, freedom of choice, and equality of rights and opportunities for women and men" was viewed as "moderate and consistent with the liberal ideology of capitalist democracy" and led to its popularity within the development field. The problem, according to WID enthusiasts, was not that modernization was undesirable, but that women had not benefited from it. Liberal feminists believe that women suffer "numerous small-scale deprivations," such as prejudice and sexism that result in unequal access to employment and educational opportunities.

The solution was to integrate women more fully into the development process by improving women's access to the market through education, training, technology, and land rights. Policymakers and planners needed to recognize women's productive roles and incorporate their needs into development strategies. Liberal feminism provided the theoretical inspiration for the feminist initiatives within development that became popular in the 1970s. These efforts came about from the realization that "market forces had not led to gender-neutral outcomes". However, more than a decade of WID efforts failed to alter gender inequalities in development significantly. This failure to address the underlying social structures (i.e., patriarchy and the gender division of labor) that cause gender inequality has contributed to its limited success. In other words, structural inequality, not poor planning, is the problem.

Radical feminism also analyzes women's subordination in terms of a system of male domination called patriarchy, defined by Sylvia Walby above. Male domination asserts itself in myriad public and private ways, including work, sexuality, violence, and even conversation and housework. Some examples include women being excluded from higher paying jobs, the double standard involving sexual relations, men's domination over women in conversation (length of speaking time and "taking the floor"), and housework being deemed a "woman's job" so that men can be "off-duty" from and not responsible for such work. Many scholars, however, debate whether or not women can be viewed as a homogeneous group, with essential differences between them and men, rather than also disaggregating by class and ethnicity.

Marxist feminism can take many forms but generally posits that women's subordination is a direct result of capitalism. Gender inequalities are caused by the economic exploitation of one class by another. Although many Marxist feminists address patriarchy, capitalism is considered the primary cause of gender inequality. Naila Kabeer identifies three different Marxist-influenced frameworks of gender analysis in development: dependency, global capitalist patriarchy, and gender relations.

The dependency critique is based on the notion that capitalism relies on a relationship of dependency between the "Third World" and the "First World." As Maria Mies (1993:56) explains, "The poverty of the underdeveloped nations is not a result of 'natural' lagging behind but the direct consequence of the overdevelopment of the rich industrial countries who exploit the so-called periphery in Africa, South America, and Asia." A similar system of exploitation exists between men and women, and gender inequality can only be understood within the larger system of dependency and inequality created by capitalism. Feminists who subscribe to the notions of dependency analyze gender inequalities in relation to capitalism's exploitation of labor, and class differences are believed to be more important than gender differences.

Proponents of the "global capitalist patriarchy" school, another group of Marxist-influenced scholars, argue that class is not more important than gender and that patriarchy cannot be viewed separately from capitalism. The beliefs of this framework are exemplified by Mies, who suggests that men exploit women not as members of the ruling class but as men exploiting a difference in power; consequently, women cannot achieve equality within a capitalist system. Mies argues that capitalism and patriarchy function as one system ("capitalist patriarchy") because capitalism is "necessarily patriarchal". One example is that women's work as housewives and unpaid laborers contributes to the reproduction of the labor force and subsidizes men's low-paid work, which is part of "underdeveloped capitalism".

GENDER RELATIONS THEORY

Kabeer's gender relations theory offers another framework. Whereas the liberal individualism of the WID perspective portrays women as "making individual choices in the face of prejudice and constraint" and the dependency and capitalist patriarchy frameworks "present women as having no choices at all in the face of overarching structures of power", the gender relations framework examines the effects of social relations between men and women on power and equality.

The focus shifts from an analysis of women as isolated individuals at the mercy of a patriarchal system to the power relations between men and women. No single system of domination such as capitalism or patriarchy is given primacy. This approach emphasizes the specific ways in which broad systems of domination are manifested at the individual level. Because of the holistic nature of the approach, all forms of social inequality (i.e., class and race) in men's and women's lives are considered inseparable from gender.

DUAL SYSTEMS THEORY

The dual systems theory of Walby addresses how both patriarchy and capitalism play a causal role and must be analyzed to understand contemporary gender inequality because they can interact differently and produce different outcomes depending on the context. Even if capitalism and patriarchy are usually interrelated and symbiotic systems, capitalism can erode patriarchy in some situations, but in other situations, patriarchy can hinder capitalism. A dual systems approach can reveal opportunities to promote gender equality within existing capitalist and patriarchal systems by enhancing policymakers' understanding of the constraints faced by women.

The dual systems approach has much in common with Kabeer's gender relations framework. Both extol the value of recognizing capitalism and patriarchy as separate, distinct systems and both are interested in examining the relationship among women, men, and social structures. The two approaches emphasize the diversity of experience of men and women and reject sweeping generalizations.

The importance of other causal factors in inequality such as race, class, ethnicity, and poverty is cited. Perhaps most significantly, both authors also agree that the contradictory natures of capitalism and patriarchy create an opportunity for feminist reform. The differences between these two frameworks are subtle. Gender relations theory seems more concerned with situating analysis at the macro level, "exploring how the relations of class and gender mediate social realities, translating broader processes of change into concrete gains and losses for different groups of women and men". The dual systems framework places more emphasis on capitalism and patriarchy as causal factors in gender inequality.

There are several common themes between the dual systems and gender relations theories: (1) capitalism and patriarchy are dynamic and variable systems; (2) capitalism and patriarchy are separate and often conflicting systems; and (3) the conflict of interest between capitalism and patriarchy can promote gender equality. Each of these themes is discussed below and revisited in the Conclusion. Because capitalism and patriarchy are dynamic and variable systems, they can function well together at one point but conflict later. For example, African patriarchy allowed for some colonial expansion in the past, whereas colonial and neocolonial capitalism likewise sustained and strengthened patriarchy.

Continued capitalist expansion, however, is now undermined in many areas by African patriarchal systems that inhibit women's participation in the market. Since women produce most of the food crops in Africa, women require access to the market if agricultural commercialization in these commodities is to flourish. Patriarchy and capitalism can also exhibit various manifestations depending on the situation. Kabeer describes the variable nature of patriarchy: "while male dominance may be a near-universal phenomenon, it generally operates in more concealed and variable ways than that allowed by the global patriarchal model. " Patriarchy can be expressed in such obvious ways as male violence against women or unequal opportunities for men and women.

Like patriarchy, capitalism can be expressed in various forms. April Gordon distinguishes between capitalism and underdeveloped capitalism. Underdeveloped capitalism is caused by the "failure of capitalism to fully transform the pre-capitalist mode of production," resulting in a "distorted quasi capitalism". Underdeveloped capitalism relies on the unpaid subsistence labor of women to subsidize men's participation in the workforce and provide for the reproduction of labor, resulting in low wages for men. Thus, underdeveloped capitalism exploits both women and men. It perpetuates the reliance called the "economy of affection," which Goran Hyden defines as "a network of support, communications and interaction among structurally defined groups connected by blood, kin, community or other affinities, for example, religion". African farmers "stand with one foot in the economy of affection and the other in the wider national economy".

On the positive side, the economy of affection serves as a safety net for people in need and acts to channel resources to those with limited access to the formal sector. On the negative side, the social obligations it imposes on people can limit their ability to operate effectively outside their community and in the market economy. The idea that capitalism and patriarchy are separate and often conflicting systems is fairly new. Radical and Marxist feminists assume that a harmony of interests binds patriarchy and capitalism into a system of capitalist patriarchy, whereas proponents of dual systems and gender-relations theory believe that patriarchy and capitalism are distinct systems.

Gordon states that "capitalism seeks to exploit labor, [while] patriarchy seeks to exploit women". Both Gordon and Walby reject Mies's thesis that capitalism is inherently patriarchal and offer compelling evidence to the contrary. Gordon argues that capitalism cannot be inherently patriarchal because there is often a conflict of interests between capitalism and patriarchy that creates a dysfunctional relationship. For example, patriarchy can thwart capitalism's efforts to mobilize labor and produce a surplus, such as when women are denied access to education, productive resources, or employment opportunities. However, capitalism can undermine patriarchy as women enter the workforce, become wage earners, and gain autonomy and status as decision makers.

Kabeer concurs, arguing that the gender relations framework views capitalism and patriarchy as interdependent but distinct systems and endeavors to analyze the "variable, sometimes contradictory, outcomes of the interaction of specific forms of gender subordination and different processes of production". In this chapter, we argue that the conflict of interest between capitalism and patriarchy can promote gender equality. Because the relationship between capitalism and patriarchy is so often conflictual and dysfunctional, efforts to improve the situation can result in more equitable gender relations.

At the policy level, increasing awareness of the debilitating effects of patriarchy on capitalism has created demand for more equitable reforms. Capitalism has also unintentionally decreased gender disparity in some areas by offering opportunities (i.e., wages, education, and training) to women that result in increased independence. Even the negative effects of capitalism can undermine patriarchy, as when women enter the workforce to augment family income and subsequently gain more autonomy and status within the household and as African women find or create opportunities for greater equality within currently "hegemonic global capitalism".

At present, Africa is a lamentable mix of precapitalist and capitalist systems that are exploitative, inequitable, and unsustainable and that tie Africans into a "disadvantageous dependency relationship with the global capitalist economy". It is not capitalism per se but underdeveloped capitalism that is the problem. To ameliorate this problem two approaches are possible. One disengages Africa from capitalistic development, advocated by those who regard capitalism as inherently onerous, exploitative, and expressive. The other argues that Africa needs an improved form of capitalism that permits all people to have access to the market.

Many Marxist-influenced scholars advocate disengagement, called "delinking," from formal top-down development programs. Others argue that Africa needs reforms so that it can be more capitalist, allowing people to produce for the market and thereby benefit. Capitalist market reforms can "promote the entrepreneurial and productive forces in society that have been stymied by the familial mode of production and underdeveloped capitalism".

With its dependence on market forces, capitalism has the potential to undermine patriarchy and the familial mode of production. As such, peasants need to be tied more strongly to the market to counteract their obligations to their "economy of affection." This may assist women farmers as "further market penetration may open up new opportunities for women that were not there before.... Market penetration is an asset to women as much as it is a constraint". However, capitalist market reforms must address the issue of institutional sexism in order to benefit women.

Access to the market can improve women's lives in several ways. Cash crops provide women with an important strategy to improve household provisioning capacity and food security. A food-secure household is one with multiple livelihood strategies that include both subsistence and income-producing activities. When women have a cash crop, they are better able to procure the necessary assets to produce or buy food for the household, as well as other commodities and services. Improved nutrition is an additional potential benefit of women's cash cropping as long as subsistence production is maintained.

Studies have shown that the mother's income has a greater effect on child nutrition than the overall household income because African women tend to spend their income differently from men, retaining less for personal use and spending more on food for the family. Also writing on Cameroon, Judith Krieger reports an increase in children's nutritional status from agricultural commercialization because as women produce or sell cash crops; they have more and diverse foodstuffs, as well as greater income. Other benefits of women's market participation are more subtle and include increased autonomy, status, self-esteem, and decision-making power in the household.

What are some of the factors that affect market access? Access to land is one of the biggest determinants of the success of agricultural commercialization. Changes in African land tenure systems are having an effect on market access. African customary land tenure systems are based on the belief that all households in a community have a right to land for cultivation. However, the control of land in a community is affected by gender, class, and age.

Throughout much of Africa, men own land, and women have use of the land through their spouses and male relatives. The influence of colonialism, political changes, and, more recently, international donors has aided the shift away from customary land tenure systems toward Western styled privatization in an attempt to facilitate the commercialization process. Those who advocate change assume that greater tenure security provides an incentive for long-term agricultural investment, which in turn will stimulate agricultural production.

However, land title and land registration programs implemented by governments have had mixed results.

Miriam Goheen reports that Cameroonian land policies typically benefit well-placed individuals who are educated and wealthy. Privatization schemes sometimes have the effect of taking land out of production and away from smallholders who produce both for household and national consumption because many of the people who purchase land are elites who are motivated by a desire to have collateral for credit and loans and never have any intention of planting crops. The shift toward land privatization has often adversely affected certain groups, notably women, pastoralists, and poor households. Land privatization schemes are not gender neutral. Women are at a disadvantage in acquiring land because they often have no property, little or no cash income, and minimal political power. Moreover, they must contend with a strong male bias against women owning land.

A crucial issue surrounding agricultural commercialization is whether cash crop production takes land away from subsistence production. If land is scarce, then cash cropping may replace some of the area previously devoted to subsistence crops. In other cases, the area allocated for subsistence production is similar for both cash-cropping and noncash-cropping farmers. If women are excluded from cash-crop production, competition over planting cash crops versus subsistence crops may result. Men are most often the winners in this situation, and women lose food-crop land to commercial production.

However, commercial production does not automatically lead to a decline in subsistence production, particularly if women farmers are involved. Farmers can simultaneously increase subsistence and cash-crop production by increasing the productivity per area by using inputs such as fertilizer acquired through cash-crop production. In fact, although access to yield-increasing inputs such as fertilizer is important if women are to succeed in cash cropping, the rate of adoption and application of fertilizer is low among women farmers because they lack sufficient access to credit or cash to purchase it. In some places in Africa, the removal of fertilizer subsidies, as mandated by

SAPs, has caused a decline in fertilizer use since the higher prices mean it is no longer cost efficient for many crops.

Until 1990, Cameroon was often touted as a "success story" in sub-Saharan Africa because of the relative political stability and economic growth it had experienced since independence. Agriculture, employing over 80 percent of the labor force, was arguably the driving force behind the country's economic development. Agricultural production grew by 4.2 percent annually between 1965 and 1980, easily surpassing the sub-Saharan average of 1.9 percent. Until recently, the country remained virtually self-sufficient in food production. In 1984, only 2.6 percent of the food consumed in-country came from net imports, mostly of wheat and rice.

Recently, the country experienced a decline in agricultural production while having a population growth rate of 3.2 percent. The decline in the agricultural sector was caused by a number of factors, including at the farmer level inadequate access to labor, inputs, infrastructure, technology, and resources. In 1986, the economy suffered a drop in the price of oil, a major export that precipitated an economic crisis continuing to the present. Cameroon is divided into ten provinces, eight Francophone and two, the Northwest and Southwest Provinces, Anglophone. Cameroon has diverse agro ecological zones that support a variety of subsistence and cash crops.

Millet, peanut, and sorghum are the staple crops in the north; maize, beans, yams, banana, and plantain are found in the west and central regions; and cassava is important in the east and south. Of the export crops, cotton is important in the north; Arabica coffee in the West and Northwest provinces; tea in the Southern Province; and Robusta coffee and cocoa in the Central, East, and Southern Provinces. The overwhelming majority of coffee growers belong to a coffee cooperative that provides access to credit, fertilizer, and other inputs. The introduction between 1940 and 1960 of coffee as a permanent tree crop has had an impact on land tenure claims. Traditionally, when farmers died, the chief might repossess some of his subjects' land; now the permanent presence of coffee trees gives farmers' heirs a stronger claim to the land.

As the primary unit of production, the household organizes labor, production, consumption, and distribution. More than 90 percent of the food consumed in the household is homegrown, primarily by women. Since the 1950s, women farmers in the northwestern area known as the Grassfields have been considered the backbone of the country's agriculture. Women are responsible for subsistence production and may or may not cultivate a cash crop. Women provide labor for men's coffee fields, intercropping their food crops with the trees in some regions, including the West Province. Men primarily produce cash crops for market sale. Husbands and wives do not necessarily pool their resources or their labor but instead often keep separate budgets and assume separate, but complementary, roles.

Women farmers in Cameroon, in their multiple roles as primary food producers, child bearers, and household managers, have suffered the most from the economic crisis. Although women's high level of participation in agricultural production has traditionally contributed to their relatively high social status, this status has recently been undermined in some regions by the effects of the worsening economy. Whereas in the past, women were valued as food producers and household provisioners, decreased access to the market in some areas has resulted in increased social stratification and a "feminization of poverty".

A gender analysis of the Northwest and West provinces of Cameroon reveals differences in agricultural production attributable to differential access to resources - primarily land, cash crops, and fertilizer. Research conducted by Christina Gladwin in 1989 served as the primary source of data for this analysis. She interviewed a total of thirty-six male and female smallholder farmers: fifteen women and ten men in Kom, Northwest Province, and seven women and four men in the West Province near Dschang. In addition, this chapter relies on research conducted by Steven Staal at approximately the same location as Gladwin's research. Goheen's book on gender and agriculture in the Grassfields region supplements the data from the Northwest Province.

The analysis focuses on access to land, cash crops, and fertilizer. In both regions, the interviews were generally conducted with a single respondent who would report information for the entire household. For example, if a man was interviewed, he would report maize data, including land size, fertilizer use, and yield, even though the maize was grown by his wife. Similarly, women would report household coffee data, which in the Northwest Province is predominantly grown by men. Of the thirty-six households interviewed in both regions, 27 percent in the Northwest Province and 43 percent in the West Province were female-headed.

The Northwest Province in the Bamenda Grassfields is the principal maize producing region in the country. The area comprises numerous independent, hierarchic chiefdoms centered on a chief authority called the fon. Gladwin's research was conducted among the Tikars in the Kom chiefdom. Population density in the province is relatively low, with about fifty-three persons per square kilometer, and the average fallow period for maize fields is three years. Maize, beans, yams, and coffee are the primary crops. Poor market infrastructure in the region has hampered commercial production. During the rainy season, many roads become impassable, and transportation costs rise dramatically.

The availability of arable land has declined due to increasing population density, resource degradation, and ill-conceived government land reform policies designed to promote privatization. National and traditional land tenure policies have evolved in response to increasing population pressure on the land in an attempt to regulate access to this most precious of resources. In 1974, the government sought to arrest the trend toward decreased production and increased food imports by implementing new land ordinances that were intended to provide secure title to land and thereby increase investment. However, these policies have provided benefits mostly to elite farmers, whereas smallholder farmers, the majority of whom are women, are increasingly marginalized.

Much of the newly acquired land, purchased by rural elites (modern "Big Men") intent on amassing personal fortunes, has not been put under production but serves as collateral for other business ventures, causing food production in the area to decline. In response to land pressures, women farmers in many regions have been pushed to marginal fields. The gender ideology of the Nso' region in the Northwest Province dictates that "men own the fields, women own the crops", so women are forced to beg their male relatives for permission to use land. The patriarchal bias inherent in the Northwest Province undermines women's access to land, and increasing gender inequality has caused more conflicts. Because of declining soil fertility, women in the Nso' region cultivate twice as much land as they did in the 1950s, and the distance to fields has increased. Such constraints have had a negative effect on subsistence production, household food security, and gender equality.

Cases such as this one have fueled the debate that commercialization harms women farmers. In addition, land conflicts have increased in the region. Many traditional leaders and villagers do not recognize the national policies, which they view as anathema to traditional tenure customs. The increasing rural stratification between the elite and smallholders has exacerbated the grim situation of poor farmers with little access to credit, education, employment opportunities, or land. In some areas, women have lost their farms to coffee growers. Under the present system in the Northwest, the "intensification of market relations ... has created a greater power differential between men and women" as men's access to productive resources increases at the expense of women's access.

Only 4 percent of the women owned coffee land, compared to 100 percent of the men. None of the respondents - male or female - had ever purchased farmland. The distinction between buying and owning land is purely monetary: people own plots that were given to them, usually by a relative and no money changes hands. Most of the land women used to grow food crops was "begged" from male relatives. The land situation in Kom is similar to the situation described for Nso' in the Northwest Province: women are "essentially excluded from ownership, inheritance, and real control of land both by the current structure of customary tenure and by national land and development policies".

In the Northwest Province, maize and coffee are the primary crops. Women typically have maize fields separate from their husbands' coffee plots, but there is also some intercropping. Women are responsible for maize production, and men grow the cash crop of coffee. Only 4 percent of the women in the Kom sample grew coffee, but 8 percent grew other cash crops (sweet potatoes and green beans). The average and median sizes of the maize plots were 2.3 hectares and 2 hectares, respectively, and 1.3 hectares and 1 hectare for coffee plots. Fertilizer use in the Northwest Province was suboptimal in terms of the number of farmers applying it, as well as the quantities applied. Acquisition of fertilizer in Kom was primarily a man's responsibility, since men had better access to credit and cash. Of the female-headed households, only 25 percent applied chemical fertilizer, indicating women's reliance on men for this resource.

Of the households applying fertilizer, 46 percent purchased fertilizer on credit (in most cases from a men's coffee cooperative); 15 percent used money from a njangi (a savings cooperative); and 38 percent paid cash. Women who did not have a cash crop or other source of income were dependent on their male relatives to buy their fertilizer for them because the men had better access to credit institutions. Fertilizer use on maize was so low in the region because men usually only bought fertilizer for the women if they had money left over from their own cash crop. However, of the men who grew coffee in the Kom sample, 16 percent gave their fertilizer to their wives to use on maize instead of applying it to the coffee.

This sharing of fertilizer reflects a national trend. Suboptimal fertilizer rates for both maize and coffee are probably related to decreased yields and declining coffee prices. The overwhelming majority of households in the Northwest Province experienced food insecurity. The average and median maize yields for the households surveyed were 3.5 and 3.3 bags per hectare, respectively. Maize lasted an average of 8.2 months, which meant that 80 percent of the households were low on maize for the year and had to purchase it. A small percentage (12 percent) of the households was able to sell surplus maize.

The Francophone West Province is the smallest and most densely populated region in the country, with an average of about 250 persons per square kilometer in 1986. It is important agriculturally; in 1984, it produced 41 percent of the country's maize, 40 percent of the yams, 52 percent of the potatoes, and the majority of the coffee. The staple crops of the region include maize, plantain, beans, cocoyams/taro, yams, groundnuts, and cassava. The temperate climate, access to the urban markets of Yaoundé and Douala, and high returns per unit of land have recently encouraged the production of market garden crops such as cabbage, lettuce, Irish potatoes, leeks, tomatoes, and carrots.

As the population increased and land became increasingly scarce, land tenure conflicts erupted. Unlike in the less populated Northwest Province, traditional tenure systems in the West Province evolved to cope with the effects of population pressure and government policies. Recent changes in the traditional tenure system have allowed women to inherit directly and even to purchase land: "female ownership of land is now accepted where it was unthinkable a generation ago". Fearful that prospective sons-in-law may not be able to acquire sufficient land to feed their household, many Bamiléké fathers now give daughters land to ensure those daughters' and their future offspring's well-being. Many women in the West Province not only own and control their own coffee plots but also intercrop food crops in their husbands' and sons' coffee fields.

Women in Dschang, West Province, have much greater access to land than women in Kom. In the sample, 43 percent of the women and 50 percent of the men had bought their own farmland. The average time of purchase was eleven years prior to the interview for women and twenty-four years for men. The type of farmland was not consistently reported. In some cases, it was for growing coffee, but in other cases, the crop grown was not specified. However, of the women who purchased farmland in the Dschang sample, 67 percent reported that it was coffee land. All of the women who grew coffee (73 percent) owned their own coffee land.

The women who had not purchased their own land had been given coffee plots by their husbands or male relatives. One woman reported that it was normal for a husband to give his wife a coffee plot at marriage if he had enough land. Staal reported that among the farmers he surveyed, 58 percent of female coffee land had been inherited, 18 percent purchased, and 24 percent had been "begged." However, in the Highlands region of his sample, the amount of coffee land that had been purchased by women was much higher. The data for women's access to food-crop land revealed a different story: only 5 percent was inherited, 9 percent was purchased, and 86 percent had been "begged." As for the men, the overwhelming majority relied on inherited land for their coffee and food-crop land (97 and 96 percent, respectively); only approximately 3 percent was purchased.

Maize and coffee are typically intercropped. In Dschang, 73 percent of the households practiced intercropping, whereas 23 percent reported separate maize and coffee plots. Like Kom, women grow all the maize, and men grow coffee. However, in sharp contrast to Kom, the majority of women in the Dschang sample also grow cash crops: 73 percent of the women had income from their own coffee plots and 18 percent had additional cash crops of vegetables or a maize/beans mixture. Some of the younger men in the region also grew market garden crops. For the households that practiced intercropping, average and median plot sizes were 3.4 hectares and 3 hectares, respectively. When crops were grown separately, both maize and coffee plots averaged 1.3 hectares. Median plot sizes were 1.3 and 0.8 hectares for maize and coffee, respectively.

Chemical fertilizer use among respondents in the Dschang sample was high: 100 percent for men and 91 percent for women. Staal (1990) reported that fertilizer use in the West Province as a whole was high: 75 percent of farms used chemical fertilizer, compared to the national average of 33 percent. This is partly due to declining fallow periods and the subsequent need to improve soil fertility; it may also be related to the greater availability of subsidized fertilizer in the West Province. Fertilizer use in the Dschang sample was higher than the Kom sample for both food crops and coffee.

Fertilizer use in Gladwin's Dschang sample was reported separately for each cropping pattern. For intercropped systems of maize and coffee, average and median fertilizer rates were 96.3 kilograms per hectare and 75 kilograms per hectare, respectively. The fertilizer rate for crops grown separately averaged 70 kilograms per hectare for maize and 245 kilograms per hectare for coffee. In the West Province, 30 percent of the respondents applying fertilizer did not indicate how they acquired it, but all of them belonged to the coffee cooperative. Of the other 70 percent, 30 percent received fertilizer on credit from the coffee cooperative, 20 percent used njangi money, and 20 percent paid cash. Of the female-headed households in the sample, all were able to purchase fertilizer.

The food security data from the West Province reveal a stark contrast to conditions in the Northwest Province. Only 18 percent of the households surveyed in Dschang experienced a maize deficit and had to purchase maize, and 64 percent of the women reported selling maize. Maize lasted an average of 11.2 months. The average and median maize yields were 6.5 and 4 bags per hectare, respectively. Cash-crop preferences have shifted. World prices for coffee hit a record low between 1986 and 1990, and prices received by farmers also dropped because producer prices set by the national marketing board had been substantially lower than world market prices. In response to this disincentive, farmers in the West Province began diverting fertilizer and labor from coffee plots to food crops.

Farmers maintained coffee plots in spite of diminishing returns because of continued access to credit and fertilizer, as well as the more secure claim on the land that trees provide. However, under these government pricing policies, the future for tree crops looked bleak. Some enterprising farmers turned to food crop production as an attractive option because their markets were less regulated by the government, allowing farmers to increase their profits. Staal suggested that women in the West Province have generally benefited from these changes in agricultural production. Because they controlled the increasingly lucrative food crop production sector and contributed significantly to coffee and market garden production, women were potentially in a position to increase their income as urban markets swelled and demand increased. In contrast, Goheen found no benefits for women in Nso' because they did not generally sell their food crops in the market.

The trend toward market garden crop production in the West Province can provide further opportunities for women farmers who have access to the market. This province affords easier market access because of its relatively good roads and closer proximity to the urban centers of Yaoundé and Douala. This lends support to Abe Goldman's premise that marketing opportunities rather than population pressure can play a primary role in inducing agricultural intensification. Staal states that "the barriers to women's entry into the agricultural marketplace are being rapidly breached," and food and beverage crops have great potential as cash crops, but women still need more secure access to land.

The data from these two regions demonstrate the different outcomes produced from varying degrees of market access. Food security was higher in the West Province, where women were more integrated into the market. In the Northwest Province, 80 percent of the households surveyed experienced a maize deficiency, as compared to only 18 percent of households in the West. The farmers in the West Province experienced more food security than producers in the Northwest because of their increased fertilizer use and access to land and cash crops. In the West Province, 91 percent of the women applied fertilizer, compared to 52 percent in the Northwest. Men also applied more fertilizer in the West: 100 percent used it, whereas only 67 percent applied it in the Northwest.

The regional differences in women's access to land and cash crops are startling. Due to the evolving traditional land tenure system, women farmers in the West Province now have access to land that they did not have in the past. In the West Province, 73 percent of the women had at least one cash crop (usually coffee), whereas only 4 percent of the women in the Northwest Province had their own coffee plots. Considering that women spend their income provisioning the family, the benefits of women's access to cash crops are considerable.

This income has even allowed many women to purchase land, and 43 percent of the women in the West Province have done so. Income from the sale of coffee also allowed women to procure their own fertilizer, which benefited both coffee and maize production. Women farmers in the West Province probably resort to buying land more readily than their male counterparts because they have the cash and do not receive as much through inheritance. However, it should be noted that when women in the West Province do inherit land, it is predominantly coffee land and not food-crop land, perhaps because of the more permanent nature of coffee land.

Women farmers in the West Province are not being displaced by agricultural intensification as predicted by Boserup because they are integrated into the market, have access to such agricultural resources as land and fertilizer, and are able to grow cash crops. Nor did cash cropping in the West Province displace subsistence production; rather, there was an increase in fertilizer use in households in which women grew cash crops; maize production increased, and women were able to sell their surplus maize. By contrast, women farmers in the Northwest Province are being displaced and pushed toward marginal land with minimal access to cash crops and agricultural resources.

What accounts for the differences in the two regions? The dual systems and gender relations frameworks (with their three themes centered on capitalism and patriarchy) help elucidate the differential effects of capitalism and patriarchy on women's access to the market.

The situation in the Northwest Province is best described as one of underdeveloped capitalism, whereas capitalism in the West Province is more developed. The two patriarchal systems of these regions are also characterized by sharp differences. Women are poorly integrated into the market in the Northwest because inflexible gender ideologies restrict their access to land and other resources. In describing the situation in the Nso' chiefdom in the Northwest Province, Goheen writes that "the ways in which capitalist relations are locally incorporated are significantly shaped by indigenous cultural systems".

The indigenous patriarchal system of the Nso' in the Northwest Province has been "maintained and reinforced within the post-colonial state by the coalition between regional and national male elites". The increasingly broad influence of the local fons has not had positive repercussions for women in the area. In contrast, the patriarchal ideology in the West Province changed to allow women to inherit and even purchase land, resulting in both women's and men's high level of integration into the market. With agricultural commercialization, access to land in the Northwest Province decreased, but in the West Province it increased. This disparity is due to the particular way that capitalism interacted with patriarchy.

The social system in the West Province has adapted to changing conditions caused by increasing population growth and expanding markets, but the social system of the Nso' in the Northwest Province has remained "recalcitrant in the face of changes brought by colonialism, the marketplace, and national independence". The "economy of affection" aptly describes the fon-centered social organization throughout the Northwest Province. Women are identified with farming and food, whereas men concentrate their energies on investing in kin networks and improving their influence with the fon to gain access to more land, labor, and, consequently, power. Traditional land tenure policies dictate that "men own the fields, women own the crops," and women have generally been denied access to cash crops such as coffee that the men use to strengthen their position within the community, thus elevating their status.

In the Northwest Province, the rigid patriarchal system did not allow capitalism to evolve and produced negative results, demonstrating that capitalism and patriarchy are two separate and conflicting systems. The patriarchal social system limited women's access to agricultural resources and undermined their efforts to increase agricultural productivity. The outcome was poor land use, poor yields, and poor market integration. Women were not able to contribute to coffee production other than as laborers on their husbands' plots because they were denied plots of their own. In addition to gender, class was also an important factor in determining access to land. Smallholder farmers, male and female alike, were disadvantaged in their attempts to register for land titles.

Similarly, agricultural production suffered. Agricultural commercialization is failing in the Northwest Province not because of capitalism and the market but because of patriarchal biases and male control over crucial productive resources. In the West Province, capitalism and patriarchy did not conflict. The Bamiléké patriarchal system was more flexible and evolved to give women access to land and cash crops. This allowed women to cultivate their own coffee and vegetable plots, purchase fertilizer and other inputs, and sell the surplus food crops. The superior market infrastructure of the West Province - an example of what Gordon terms "real capitalism" - encouraged and support increased agricultural productivity in the region.

The conflict of interest between capitalism and patriarchy is evident in the lower food security in the Northwest Province, where women do not have income from a cash crop to buy fertilizer to put on food crops. The patriarchal gender ideology prevalent in the region restricts women's access to land and other resources and severely limits women's ability to produce cash crops for the market. Gender equality increased in the West Province due to the initial conflict of interest between capitalism and patriarchy (i.e., women traditionally could not buy or inherit land) that has since lessened. Capitalist forces in the West Province have begun to overcome the patriarchal system of the Bamiléké, and women are taking the first steps toward achieving gender equality by growing cash crops and buying land. Women who have their own sources of income are less dependent on their husbands' income for household provisioning and can experience an elevation in their status and power as decision makers within the household.

Gender reforms resulting from the conflictual relationship between capitalism and patriarchy occur as a defiant response to the negative effects of underdeveloped capitalism. Modest changes permit some women to participate more successfully as entrepreneurs. Some elite urban women have been able to acquire urban land because their knowledge of national procedures has improved through education and participation in women's development projects. Many women in Nso' are electing to remain single and raise children on their own because they see no advantage in marriage, providing evidence of capitalism-induced family transformation. Capitalism serves to weaken ties among family members, ethnic groups, and lineages while promoting class formation, nuclear families, and individualism.

In conclusion, the evidence both supports and can be analyzed in terms of the three themes concerning the interaction of capitalism and patriarchy. The dual systems theory complements the gender relations framework and provides a useful framework for analyzing women's differential market access within Cameroon. When capitalism and patriarchy are viewed as separate and conflicting systems, the opportunities to promote gender equality are revealed. Agricultural commercialization in particular and capitalist development in general presents a threat to African patriarchal systems but offer opportunities to improve women's lives.

In order to have a positive impact on smallholder farmers, market liberalization reforms must address the underlying structural causes of gender inequality. As more egalitarian policies are implemented, patriarchal systems will be undermined and women will benefit. Do agricultural commercialization and market liberalization benefit women farmers?

The answer is yes, if women have access to resources such as land, credit, and fertilizer that allow them to grow and sell cash crops and thus participate in both input and product markets. In Cameroon's Northwest Province, women's limited access to both kinds of markets increases gender inequality, marginalizes and impoverishes women, and threatens regional and national food security. However, in the West Province, women's increased access to these markets promotes gender equality, empowers women, and increases household food security. The differences in women's access to markets in the two Cameroonian provinces shows that market liberalization can and does benefit women farmers.

6

Gender Ideology in Northern Luzon, the Philippines

The Igorot say, "Women are good with money." From bank managers to moneylenders, from small vendors to regional vegetable dealers, from tiny shops to national and international enterprises, women dominate the Cordillera economy, and gender ideology justifies this dominance. This situation runs counter to the frequent assumption that women lose out in the process of capitalist or market development. Starting with the work of Henry Lewis Morgan and Friedrich Engels and reinterpreted in the highly influential work of Boserup, there has been a dominant thread of research that argues that the introduction of capitalism and of capitalist agriculture has a detrimental effect on the status of women and gender relations.

This assumption of a universal impact has grown out of the experience of implementing development programs. From a modernization perspective, the assumption was made that women would benefit equally from any economic and social transformations from traditional to modern society. However, this perspective has often led to adoption of "formulas," "development blueprints", and "add women and stir" interventions, rather than to good, locally grounded projects.

The Marxist dependency critique of the modernization approach was based on similar assumptions that women would share equally in any benefits from the transformation of class and dependency relations. The depressing experience of women in communist countries and in newly liberated states such as Mozambique showed that equality for women would only come from action targeted at transforming gender relations; understanding preexisting gender relations was critical to developing effective interventions. From a Marxist feminist and a socialist-feminist perspective, gender and class are intertwined dual systems dependent on each other that needed to be transformed to improve the equity and equality of gender relations.

Much of this debate has seen capitalism and gender as systems of stratification. Both modernization and neoconservative models are based on the same premise, that the class that accumulates is the engine of growth rather than the exploiter. Judith Lorber, for instance, argues that "as a social institution, gender is a process of creating distinguishable social statuses for the assignments of rights and responsibilities. As part of a stratification system that ranks these statuses unequally, gender is a major building block in the social structures built on these unequal statuses". These models of the impact of development on social and gender relations have been questioned in relation to understanding the role of local processes.

As early as 1985, Fiona Wilson argued that many studies on the impact of agricultural commercialization on gender relations were "apolitical, ahistoric interpretations that are insensitive to the complexity of existing social inequalities located in relations of class, gender or ethnicity". When looking at more general outcomes, a review article on cash cropping contends that most of the negative effects of cash crops are not a result of the nature of the undertaking but of the social, political, and economic context in which they are produced. A reexamination of works by early authors such as Anne Whitehead and Susan Rogers showed that under the aegis of various development and state projects, cash cropping had serious negative implications for women and household viability and that gender ideology plays a critical role in this.

It is essential to consider the trail of failed projects, gender relations, and ideology when formulating interventions or when analyzing the impact of economic processes such as agricultural commercialization. New trends in feminist theory questioned the role of universal theories as the locus of action to address inequities and inequality. The early 1990s saw the fluorescence of a new critique in feminism that had been growing throughout the 1980s. Non-Western feminists began to question the Western model of exploitative gender relations as universal, the assumption of a universal solution, the right of white Western feminists to speak on behalf of all women, and the assumption that women in developed countries are at the apex of an evolutionary continuum.

They pointed out that this perspective discounts the local actions of women and ignores the particular and unique nature of specific local gender relations. Discussing Igbo women, Ifi Amadiume argues that Third World women are frequently active in resisting and transforming gender inequities and have often done so longer and more effectively than Western women. These critiques emphasize the importance of delineating the nature of local gender ideology and gender relations from the outset and of seeing the impact of various policies and interventions in the context of local actions and local processes.

The movement against monolithic theory also calls for understanding gender as "process, constantly being created and recreated". Pernille Sørensen demonstrates the value of both understanding the role of local action in socioeconomic change and in understanding gender as a process in her work on the impact of gender ideology on agricultural commercialization among the Busoga of Uganda. In this study, she argues that although "men have appeared to have gained total control over food production ... closer examination reveals an increased significance in marital bargaining and a movement from established gender roles to more negotiable relationships".

In this chapter, the idea that gender relations are systems of stratification in all contexts. In the case of the Sagada Igorots of Northern Luzon, gender ideology does not represent a strong system of stratification. Sagadan society has been characterized by a high degree of gender equality, and cash cropping has not had a negative impact on the status or roles of women. Instead, cash cropping has had a negative impact by exacerbating class differentiation and affecting how various categories of women have experienced the growth of cash cropping and the increase in agricultural commercialization. I argue that these changes have not taken place along arbitrary lines but along preexisting inequities and arenas of struggles for power and resources.

In analyzing who won and who lost of the historical events that have shaped the present-day integration into capitalist markets and into the Philippine state, outline the nature of stratification and gender relations found in Sagada at the turn of the century, and then consider the specific form agricultural commercialization has taken and its implications for class relations and gender ideology.

Located in the Cordillera Central, Sagada is about 150 kilometers northwest of Baguio City and 19 kilometers off the national highway. It is composed of eighteen barrios with a total population of about 10,000 in an area of roughly 100 square kilometers. The population has been steadily shrinking because of out-migration since the 1960s. The landscape is dominated by rice terraces, sweet potato fields, vegetable gardens, banana plants, grasslands, and pine forests. The average farm size is about 1.5 hectares. Each barrio is a small cluster of twenty-five to 175 houses nestled between fields, grasslands, and forests.

The Sagada economy is based on agriculture (subsistence, cash cropping, and livestock production), artisanal cloth production, carpentry, medium-scale weaving industries, small and large shops (some specializing in dry goods and canned foods and others in agricultural tools and inputs), and a thriving tourist trade (with its guest houses, restaurants, and guides). Remittances from out-migrants and overseas workers play a large role in the prosperity of Sagada. Most families have been involved to some degree in the regional, national, and international market economy as artisans, laborers, professionals, and entrepreneurs. Most families have members who are overseas migrants or workers.

Sagadans have a strong pride in their traditions and history; but they have adopted "modern comforts" and become successful in a global economy, to a surprising degree on their own terms. This success builds from a long history of pre-colonial trade that continued from the Spanish period to the present day. Women were important traders in the local and regional system.

The Sagada Igorots have been characterized by a high degree of gender equality that extends to most spheres of society. Albert Bacdayan found a "high degree of inter changeability" in tasks between men and women. Shared tasks accounted for 93 percent of domestic tasks, 87 percent of subsistence production, and 50 percent of religious functions. There is no specific ranking of these tasks as less or more prestigious on the basis of the person who does them. No strong domestic division of labor exists. Both men and women routinely carry babies, bathe children, and tend to sick family members, do dishes, cook meals, and clean houses. Even tasks that are considered "women's work," such as laundry, are often done by men when women are pregnant and lactating.

Inheritance patterns show a similar lack of gender bias but manifest an age bias. In inheritance, which takes place at the time of marriage, the oldest child, male or female, inherits the largest share of land or the best land. The youngest, male or female, inherits the house, the care of aging parents, and the fields the parents reserved for their own use. Recent trends in inheritance have shown a bias toward women in this latter form of inheritance because it is believed that a girl will take this responsibility more seriously than a boy. This is a bilateral inheritance system; both the father and the mother endow each child with land and goods at marriage. Access to various resources through personal inheritance, clan affiliation, and various forms of communal property is not limited by gender, and each spouse makes a significant contribution to the household.

Traditional political and some religious structures seem to exclude women. However, except for the actual meetings in the men's houses, which women attend but in which they do not participate, women have strong rights and important roles in political and ritual life. This apparent lack of political involvement is not as significant as it seems because women are present and active in the actual process in which decisions are reached. All problems and important topics are discussed, by both men and women, in public meetings at people's homes, and dap-ay (councils) ratify the decisions reached through these discussions.

Women are important religious actors both in agricultural and domestic traditional religious rituals, have significant roles in public traditional religious rituals, and are often the "keepers" of important religious and ritual knowledge that appears to be performed only by men in the dap-ay. When considering the gender ideology of Sagada and the division of labor in Sagadan society, Bacdayan argued that men and women are equal human beings and that "a girl is also a boy and a boy is also a girl".

These gender relations have not remained untested. The American bias toward men was clear in their educational policies and in their systems of credit and employment. Boys were privileged over girls during the American period on the islands, but this period started in Sagada in 1904 with the arrival of the Episcopal missionaries, as the initial graduation figures in the local Episcopal high school show. The roll of graduates from the local high schools documents a dramatic change in the gender split in education over a generation. The first generation of educated Igorots showed a distinct gender bias in education, with ten men educated for each woman in the early American period.

The next generation shows an equal number of women and men educated. When asked why this was so, it was most commonly explained that once education was seen to bring prosperity and came to be considered a form of inheritance, all members of the family were seen to have a right to obtain as much as they could manage and the family could afford. However, in recent years, there has been a stated bias toward educating girls over boys. Girls are seen as a better investment, both in terms of remittances from educated children and because they are considered to be more likely to complete their education. Moreover, the survey also showed a tendency for professional men to marry professional women and a tendency for less educated men to marry women who have a higher education than they do.

In economic life, the Episcopal bias also benefited men, who were given preferential credit and employment, but within a generation women became more important economic actors, owning and operating many of the businesses in the community. This change is usually attributed to the greater business acumen and discipline with money that women are seen to have compared to men. Almost universally, women manage the household accounts, and decisions about expenditures are made with men. Lorelei Cristologo Mendoza concludes in her study of household decision-making in three Cordillera villages that "the wife not only participates in the management of matters concerning household and family, but also of farming and livelihood [and] executive management of the budget is the wife's domain."

However, under certain circumstances, men share in the decision-making process. "The larger the relative share of the husband's cash earnings compared to that of his wife, the more joint decision making there is rather than the wife deciding by herself. Wives who have finished a secondary education are more likely to share decision-making power concerning important expenditures with their husbands". CristologoMendoza notes that Sagadan couples were more likely to make joint decisions than members of the other two villages (who represent different Igorot ethnic groups). Sagadan people consider men to be less responsible with money than women, and to be subject to pressures that encourage them to waste money, such as drinking, treating male friends, and gambling.

While gender relations have remained relatively equitable even with the development of the cash economy, class relations have changed substantially. There has been a growing disparity between rich and poor in access to wealth, power, and labor, which has far outstripped the obligations of redistribution, mutual help, and the egalitarian tendencies of the precapitalist economy that previously controlled accumulation.

At the turn of the century, Sagadan society had a social structure that was based on the dialectical relationship between highly egalitarian values and political institutions and a socially and ritually reinforced status hierarchy. All men were equal members of the local men's houses (dap-ay). In the dap-ay, all decisions were reached by unanimous consent. However, all men and women also inherited one of two statuses, kadangian (high status) or kodo (commoner status), which determined marriage, social position, and social and ritual obligations. This uneasy mix of egalitarian and hierarchical structures was the source of considerable social tension.

At the time of the first American contacts, two factors determined rank: ritual activity and inherited goods and lands. Rank was determined as much as by what a family gave away as by what a family inherited. A person was born to a specific rank, but this status needed to be validated through redistributive rituals that gave a person access to forms of festive labor, which enabled expansion of irrigated lands and access to power and authority within the dap-ay. This hierarchy also allowed for social mobility. If a wealthy commoner could do the right rituals and accrue the necessary rice lands and artifacts, his or her children could then become kadangian.

Articulate and wise commoners could also gain considerable power in the community and translate this skill into the capacity to accumulate wealth and influence. Being kadangian gave individuals certain rights and privileges, but these were mitigated by various egalitarian communal institutions and customs. One such system was that of community and clan ownership of resources and the rights that came with community membership. Every member, male or female, had the right to use wood from the clan lands, open fields, and use vacant lands; each had the right to live in an empty house or have some free help in building his or her own house.

Private landownership was also limited by custom. None of the land could be owned by outsiders, and families could not own more land than they could farm by themselves. This put a natural cap on the extent to which any community member could accumulate land and wealth. All members had access to labor through a system of various forms of cooperative and mutual help institutions (ob-obbo). These usually took the form of one-on-one reciprocal relationships and included the obligation to give goods or forms of help in a crisis or in a life cycle event and to exchange labor on a day-for-a-day basis with friends, kin, and neighbors.

The limits on landownership, the pressure for elites to validate rank through redistributive feasting and the need for elites to work through egalitarian political institutions effectively limited class differentiation. But the capacity to accumulate wealth and change statuses within the local system was not static and functioned because of fierce local pressure on elites to conform to social norms. New or expanded economic opportunities have seriously changed this uneasy system of checks and balances. Despite the fact that cash cropping is only the most recent Sagadan economic activity, along with tourism and economic migration, it has had a profound influence on Sagadan day-to-day life. Because of gender ideology, the effects for women have either been neutral or positive when compared to men in the equivalent class or status positions.

Vegetable production began in Sagada in the 1950s, but it was largely confined to the barrio of Balugang (also known as Bugang) and to a few families in other barrios, such as Demang, until the early 1980s. In Central Sagada (which comprises the barrios of Dagdag, Demang, Patay, and Ambasing, the focus of this study), fewer than ten families earned an income from gardening in the late 1970s. By 1991, approximately 100 vegetable producers worked on different scales and had access to different resources and opportunities. The majority of these gardeners and a large number of their spouses were interviewed for this study.

The gender division of labor in agriculture differs from subsistence agriculture to cash cropping. In subsistence cultivation of rice and camote (sweet potato), women provide most of the day-to-day labor. They are also the main bearers and transmitters of the specialized knowledge about techniques, diseases, varieties, and characteristics. Research done in 1979 with Susan Russell, Tom Killip, and Joachim Voss in the Buguias region of the Cordillera Central found that the gender division of labor had changed with vegetable farming. Men did most of the day-to-day labor, and women came in to work during peak periods.

This is also the case in Sagada. However, unlike in other areas of the Cordillera Central such as Buguias, the development of vegetable farming has not meant a complete shift away from subsistence agriculture in Sagada. Instead, the pattern is closer to that for Kabayan, where some rice fields have been taken out of production for vegetable farming, but most of the families engaged in vegetable production have access to rice fields that they own, borrow, or sharecrop. Either spouse, through his or her property or personal networks, may provide the land on which vegetables are produced for the market. In Sagada, the typical pattern of soil conservation involves fallowing and the rotation of vegetable crops with subsistence crops.

Vegetable growing is a male occupation in Sagada, and men provide the majority of labor in the fields. Although women do not provide labor, they participate in production decisions. Moreover, they are instrumental in other economic activities, such as out-migration, petty marketing, or wage work that complements or underwrites the cash-crop production. This strategy is critical because of the uncertain nature of the market for vegetables. One Sagadan vegetable gardener called the seasonal glut of vegetables in the market in Baguio "the green tide." Another gardener explained that he earns a profit once in every four harvests; occasionally he takes a loss, but more often he breaks even. Unlike in Sagada, this pattern has caused farmers in other areas of the Cordillera Central to sink into massive indebtedness and virtual tenancy.

CASE STUDIES

The following six case studies illustrate the range of commercial producers in terms of entry into commercial enterprises, household strategies to allocate capital and labor, and scale of operation. In each case, women are critical participants, active in money management and farm/business decisions. First, I discuss a small-scale gardener household, for whom commercial production generates cash; the next two households considered are medium-scale producers, but the latter has greater resources (labor and capital) and therefore is more secure in its production.

Elite community members have even greater access to resources, as the fourth and fifth case studies show, although the traditional elite is involved in traditional redistributive actions and reciprocal exchanges, which the municipal/regional elite disdain or bypass. The final example shows how rich relatives benefit from hiring poor relatives to perform the labor, whereas the poor get some privilege but not income from the connection.

Until 1985, Richard and Jane had been working for other gardeners as laborers but were encouraged to start gardening for them. From 1985 to 1989, they began gardening, using their savings to buy seeds, tools, and inputs and borrowing land from an uncle. But they ran out of cash, and from 1989 to 1991, they worked as casual laborers for others. From saved money, they started gardening again in 1991. All the gardening labor is provided either by the couple, by their family, or through reciprocal labor.

Inputs are purchased locally because the biggest input dealer is a woman from a powerful local family who gives them credit. Occasionally, they borrow inputs from other gardeners, repaying them in kind during the same season. Usually they sell to one of two Sagadan women who are local vegetable dealers. If these dealers' prices are low, they pool their vegetables with other small gardeners in a rented fierra (a type of small truck), and sell to the highest bidder they can find in Baguio. They also grow cheap, low-input crops such as Chinese greens, which Jane sells door-to-door or in the Saturday market. Crop and marketing decisions are made jointly; they also grow some rice, beans, corn, squash, and sweet potatoes for home consumption using family labor.

About 15 percent of the gardeners follow this strategy. They use inherited or borrowed land, family labor, and their savings gained through working as casual laborers for others. They try to get access to capital using family ties. Sometimes they are successful, but their extended families are also often cash-poor. Various family members usually help with child care, subsistence farming, and emergency needs. These gardeners usually enter into an agreement with a local input supplier who sells goods at a high price but will wait until the end of the growing season to be paid.

They have a limit on the amount they can borrow, and if they do not pay promptly, they must pay interest rates of 5 to 10 percent per month. Even if a harvest is poor, these debts are paid first. They depend on community support during crises and cannot be seen to default on loans. In the barrio, one's word and reputation are a major form of "capital." With debts paid, they can get cooperative labor and have access to clan and communal resources. These gardeners grow a variety of crops, retail low-value ones rather than selling them to a wholesaler, and live on their subsistence production. Gardening tends to be a source of cash rather than a major form of livelihood.

The majority of the gardeners (approximately 55 percent) have mediumsize operations. Edward worked for others as a laborer until 1983, when his father helped him get started in farming by giving advice and lending tools. Edward's capital came from his savings as a laborer and from Teresita's earnings as a weaver. He and Teresita grow cabbage for the wholesale market and some Chinese greens, green beans, corn, and onions for the retail market. They started by using only Edward's fields and growing more retail than wholesale crops. Over the years, the ratio of retail to wholesale has changed; now their major production is wholesale.

They rented centrally located land with an assured water supply to grow cabbage. Seedlings and retail crops are grown on their own land, which is distant and has a seasonal water supply. Edward works the fields on a daily basis. Teresita and their older children work at peak labor times, and they use reciprocal labor for harvesting and packing. Edward and Teresita send their produce with other gardeners in a rented fierra to sell to the highest bidder, which entails meeting the agents of various dealers en route and bargaining over the price. These prices are written down, and the sellers then go to Baguio City with these various "bids" and cash in the best. They grow cabbage rather than peppers because cabbage can be harvested over time and can be left in the field for a few weeks if prices are poor.

Teresita does weaving on a piecework basis for a local businesswoman, and both she and Edward do casual labor if available. Teresita sells the retail crops in the Saturday market, and their children sell retail crops door-to-door in the barrio. They also grow rice, sweet potatoes, beans, corn, and squash for their own consumption. Like Jane, Teresita manages the money, but the couple makes the production and marketing decisions together. Inputs are obtained on credit from the largest local input seller; they pay their bills after the harvest to avoid interest. Teresita's money from piecework is used to buy inputs in Baguio. They also borrow inputs from other gardeners and return these in kind. Edward argues that "gardening is like gambling. It's not much of a profit but we have something to feed the pigs and share with the children."

Edward and Teresita have been more successful than Richard and Jane. Their farming activities have expanded due to sporadic market success and changed with the family's developmental cycle. As their children have grown older, they have had access to more labor and found ways to diversify cash income. Children's labor is used to produce subsistence crops, which frees Teresita to look for alternative work. However, they do not produce sufficient surplus or have available labor to expand their activities like the larger producers. The kinds of vegetables these medium scale producers grow do not produce the larger windfalls but allow some flexibility and a chance to "play the market" by staggering their planting and harvesting. Although Teresita does not work on a day-to-day basis in the vegetable business, her income is critical to the family enterprise; she handles the accounts and is an equal partner in the production and marketing decisions.

Andrew and Rachel were both twenty-one when they began gardening at the time of their marriage in 1981. Rachel's father established a series of gardens on the land that she inherited. He planted the initial crops, and Andrew's parents paid for the seeds, fertilizers, and pesticides for the first season. Andrew's elder brother, a skilled gardener, gave him advice, and the whole family provided labor. They have continued to grow vegetables using the proceeds of previous harvests supplemented with capital provided by their parents at no interest. Like the previous two families, they use a system of reciprocal exchange with fellow gardeners, which enable them to borrow inputs in emergencies. These they return in kind and without interest during the growing season.

Their children are young, so they use a combination of reciprocal labor, family labor (siblings and parents), and hired labor at peak labor times. They buy fertilizers and pesticides and sell their produce to a cousin. At various times of the year, Rachel takes a load of vegetables to the town of Isabela in Quezon Province. This trip can be lucrative, but it requires selling small amounts to a variety of wholesalers and retail vendors, as well as spending an extended time in Isabela. To go to Baguio or Isabela, they rent Andrew's brother's fierra at a reduced rate and pay a driver. They bring back rice and rice bran to pay for the return trip.

While Andrew engages in full-time gardening, Rachel weaves blankets or textiles, engages in casual labor in others' fields, works with her husband, and works in their rice and camote fields with her mother, and oversees her small piggery. They have been able to build a house on their earnings. They grow a variety of capital-intensive crops for the Baguio market and low-input, low-value crops for the local market.

Andrew and Rachel have a more secure footing as gardeners. They follow much the same subsistence/market and mixed-income strategy as Edward and Teresita but have far more intrahousehold resources on which to call. Their families can provide free labor, cheap transportation, and easy access to cheaper inputs, cheap or interest-free capital, and preferential prices. They can defer payment to their input supplier because of the close family relationship they enjoy with her. These sorts of family ties enable a group of producers to have a relatively secure income with the capacity to hire labor, rent land, and expand production. Family ties have provided them a debt-free start; cheap capital; and favorable prices for inputs, products, and transportation. All of the previous three cases differ from the next example of elite gardeners, who form less than 10 percent of the total.

Both Roman and Patricia come from affluent families among the traditional elites (kadangian). They inherited larger properties and many rice fields. Their high-status wedding provided them with a large lump sum of cash. Roman began gardening after the marriage in 1970, using the land he inherited. His father built them a house, bought their tools, and provided the initial capital. They grow cabbage and peppers for the wholesale market on a wide rice field near a constant water supply using children's, hired, and reciprocal labor. They also grow fruit and coffee for the local market.

The household does not have problems with capital because both Roman and Patricia are moneylenders, loaning substantial sums of money (as much as U. S. $1,000 at a time) at high interest rates (5 to 10 percent per month). They work their own rice and camote fields with hired, reciprocal and children's labor and raise pigs for sale in the local market. Roman and Patricia follow a mixed strategy for marketing produce. They stagger crops, hoping to market some early and some at the end of the season. They buy other gardeners' produce and are thus able to send two to three fierra loads to both Isabela and Baguio.

Roman normally goes with these loads and brings back inputs, rice, and pig food for sale to local consumers and for his own use. Occasionally, they sell some produce early in the season to a dealer who harvests the crop, or they sell a portion to another gardener who is gambling on the market. Roman sells to the highest bidder and does not have a permanent relationship with any one dealer. Patricia manages the household money and makes all the production and expenditure decisions with Roman. They hold their money jointly and make joint decisions on lending money. They are also seen as individual moneylenders because borrowers approach them individually, depending on the ties they can draw on for preferential rates and repayment schedules.

There are few producers in the barrio who are as affluent as Roman and Patricia, although some "secure producers," such as Andrew and Rachel, have the potential of becoming this affluent. This barrio elite couple has good lands, secure sources of cash, and enough surplus to pursue activities such as money lending to get high returns. For them, increasing their wealth involves diversifying investments rather than seeking alternative labor opportunities. Their high standing in the community grows out of their kadangian status and is reinforced through appropriate redistributive rituals and careful adherence to norms of reciprocal exchange and appropriate behavior.

Graal, a nurse in the provincial center 19 kilometers away, and Peter, an accountant and the son of one of Sagada's wealthy businesswomen, began their vegetable operation in 1985, but neither does the day-to-day work. Rather, they have hired a couple of workers on a monthly basis. Peter and Graal's brothers help harvest during peak labor periods. They grow cucumbers, potatoes, and peppers, crops that require substantial capital. Cucumbers are risky but bring a high return because they rarely glut the market. Peter and Graal know only the basics of gardening and rely on the expertise of the hired laborers. They buy all their inputs in Baguio and borrow capital from the local credit union at an interest level well below the local moneylenders' rate (1.5 percent per month).

Graal works in the provincial capital and has extensive business concerns, such as a sizable commercial piggery run with hired help. Their children study at the local private high school and in the university. Hence, they do not grow any crops for home consumption. Peter may even go to Saudi Arabia to work as an accountant to provide the resources to expand their business interests. Producers like Peter and Graal are few and powerful and have flexibility in meeting market changes. They see themselves as rational modern farmers. Their social standing provides access to cheap credit, cheap labor, and regional resources, but they are not bound by local social pressures.

Some people in this category have been known to cheat their employees and default on loans. Their "credit" comes from their standing as members of the regional elite, as professionals, and in particular from their regional political clout. Unlike the barrio elite, their word is notoriously not their bond. Gardening may be only a short-term proposition, and if market prices fall, they move their capital into another sector. They have few kin and community ties, illustrated by their casual attitude toward repayment or meeting their obligations. Few elites can afford to disregard such ties completely. Instead, many use kin ties for access to cheap labor but have an obligation to help kin if the harvest fails. These producers engage in a form of sharecropping with poorer relatives or friends, as the following case illustrates.

Irving has an agronomy degree and worked for the government for a few years after graduation. In 1986, he quit, married Soledad, bought a fierra from Soledad's brother, and began to garden in Sagada. Irwin and Soledad do not actually work the fields but have a sharecropping arrangement with Irwin's brother Edwin and his cousin Fred. Soledad runs a medium-size dry goods shop. The couple provides Irwin's relatives with some land, capital, and inputs; at the end of the season, the workers pay back the expenses and the interest on the loan and then split the profit with Soledad and Irwin. They borrow money from the bank (at 1.7 percent per month) to provide the inputs, run a passenger route to the provincial capital and buy inputs there, and market the produce (onions, potatoes, celery, cabbage, and peppers) to the highest bidder in Tabuk and Baguio, using their own fierra for transport. In addition, they grow a number of home consumption crops, grow fruit for sale, and run a commercial piggery. They are not sure if they will plant this season (or if vegetable farming is lucrative) because their other activities are becoming more profitable and Edwin will soon go to the university.

There are four producers in Central Sagada in a position to use relatives in this way. With alternative forms of income and ownership of fierra s, they make use of the fierras to buy cheap inputs and fund a few sharecroppers. The relatives work for the cost of the inputs and split whatever profit remains on a fifty-fifty basis. Because they are closely tied to the wealthy relative, they are obliged to take the price he or she has negotiated. Often the relationship is not discussed in kin terms, and the rich relatives call these men "hired" laborers. Other poor producers use strategies such as working for rich relatives as domestic helpers and low-paid laborers to earn the right to have these cousins act as their patrons. The rich families benefit from cheap, loyal, and reliable labor. The poorer relations gain privileges but little access to wealth.

The people who have truly benefited from the vegetable boom are the moneylenders, the input dealers, and the vegetable dealers. Moneylenders are most commonly middle-class and elite women who operate other commercial enterprises, although they can also be men. They lend at usurious rates, and repayment is expected over a season or over a period of months. Input dealers are most commonly women. Unlike money lending, which continues to show some gender parity, input dealing has changed over time.

Men initially controlled these businesses but have tended to turn them over to their daughters at marriage and retire to manage their other enterprises. Input dealers are de facto moneylenders because almost all the gardeners buy on credit and pay a high interest rate. Kin ties can be used to gain access to cheap credit in return for a period of working as cheap labor. Dealers and moneylenders have to provide lavish redistributive feasts to operate in the community. Local structures give them access to wealth and labor only as long as they conform to local expectations. One woman, who tried to build a business on this form of usury, was stripped of her stock when she refused to make a feast on the death of her kadangian father. Eventually, she was forced sell her businesses and lands and to leave the community.

All the vegetable dealers in Sagada are women, as are most dealers throughout the region. This is a lucrative trade, and many act as de facto moneylenders and input dealers, using their return trips to transport inputs bought at large economic centers. The two women who work in Sagada as dealers enjoy their access to local gardeners as ka-ilian (town mates). Outsiders are not welcome to do business within the community, so these women have special access. Women also dominate the stalls in Baguio City, and their (mostly male) agents bargain with the gardeners along the route to Baguio. In these transactions, village origin is not critical, but most prefer to do business with Igorots over lowlanders or Chinese merchants.

The women who control the circuits of capital, inputs, and distribution within the community of Sagada are wealthy and stand to gain a great deal from their exclusive access. Sagadans jealously control who does business in the community; it is a local joke that one has to marry into the community to do business there. In part, this is true because the community is able to exercise some degree of social control over its own population. In return, community members accept a considerable level of exploitation by the elites, who validate their status through locally sanctioned mechanisms.

In the case of Sagada, local action and processes have a clear impact on the nature of social transformations brought about by commercialization and the development of capitalist markets. A gender ideology that posits women as equal to men and considers women to be more effective economic actors than men has not been affected by cash cropping and the development of capitalist markets in Sagada. Nor did coming into contact with a gender ideology that was marked by extreme stratification (i.e., American gender ideology of the colonial period) have a negative effect on women, gender relations, or local gender ideology. Given the contradiction in Sagadan society between egalitarianism and hierarchy, the introduction of the market has allowed certain members of the community to become wealthy, predominantly at the expense of the poorer members of the same community. The beneficiaries are women as often as men, and given the gender bias in business and education, it may be that women benefit the most.

The struggle for power is situated in the control over resources by various status groups and not the control over resources along gender lines. When new resources become available, then social relations shift along traditional lines. The Sagada case effectively illustrates that the shift is mediated by local institutions. The same tension between egalitarianism and hierarchy has limited the ways in which local elites can act, has made this affluence conditional on meeting social norms, and has allowed the poorer members of the community more food security and power than they would enjoy in an equivalent lowland Philippine community. Sagadans are proud of the fact that the poorest man or woman can and does interact with the richest man or woman in the community and is treated as an equal.

Women in Sagada have been able to make use of new resources to expand their roles within the community, but this mobility has been constrained by differences in wealth and status, so that some women benefit more than others, and some benefit at the expense of others. In the case of vegetable farming, the women who control the circuits of capital, inputs, and distribution exploit the labor of the poor men and women who make up the majority of the gardeners.

7

Gendered and Racialized Labor in the Post-colonial Philippines

The epigraphs that introduce this chapter are part of the gendered and racialized discourses that construct and manage low-skilled Filipina labor in the Philippines today. The first is an excerpt from a guidebook that characterizes the Philippines as a series of golf destinations for the (mostly Asian) golf tourist. Its author, a local Filipino writer and golfer, places Filipina service in the familiar tradition of accommodating colonial servant who happens to be the recipient of the trickle-down benevolence of golf development. The umbrella girl, holding an umbrella over the vacationing golfer while he walks up and down the fairways, epitomizes the gendered relations of labor that the transnational leisure class has come to depend on for its exotic "royalty trip."

The second epigraph is a quotation from former Secretary of Tourism Tony Gonzales describing the available exploitable labor force at the Clark Special Economic Zone (CSEZ or Clark hereafter), earlier the site of the United States' Clark Air Force Base. At Clark, one of Gonzales's pet projects involved the conversion of part of the military grounds into a privately run "leisure estate," complete with a twenty-seven-hole golf course and the cheap, "trainable" labor to make such an enterprise profitable and attractive to investors. Plentiful numbers of malleable, willing, and desperate workers are the present-day boon for global capital. For both men, the overabundance of labor is not a problem that has larger socioeconomic causes and consequences but rather a unique opportunity for corporate investors and tourists.

The sentiments in the epigraphs construct a moment in which recourse to the potentials and joys of economic neoliberalization requires the suspension of a critique of the neocolonial Philippine economy. Here, the racialized and gendered labor of the Filipina body (as surplus, as trainable) not only justifies and enables the discourses of uplift so necessary to the project of Philippine economic development and modernization, it also ensures and distinguishes the privileged positions these men occupy in Philippine society.

The body of the Filipina- as a trope of manageable, cheap, and available "service" in state and private development discourses and as a material laboring presence in the modern Filipino diaspora- operates as a crucial bridge between the colonial period and the present day in the Philippines. Specifically, I examine the ways in which Filipina bodies are crucial to the narratives and projects of progress and modernity operating within the transforming space of a former American military base in the Philippines. What are the critical continuities of colonial discourses and structures of racialized and gendered labor in an ostensibly post-military, post-occupation space?

In tandem with this analysis, it is also important to examine the ways in which the Filipina body enables critical linkages between empire and modernity for scholars and activists invested in issues of feminism and post-coloniality in the changing and uneven terrains of globalization. What also occurs in the epigraphs above is the elision of the protracted colonial history of the Philippines through the innocuous narratives of leisure and service, as if such a history was already safely over and the pleasures of hospitality can again be enjoyed without colonial guilt. Indeed, in the epigraphs, the provision of much-needed jobs to the "people there" is rendered philanthropic- the effect of neoliberal economic policies the Philippine state has embraced in the past twenty-five years, through which the state cedes even basic welfare concerns to corporate and private interests.

Yet, I argue, we must challenge this formulation of neoliberal benevolence to account for the kind of ideological labor that goes into maintaining these discourses as absent of and separated from colonial histories. As exemplars of the bodies of well-trained "service" evoked in these less-than-innocent innocent epigraphs, Filipinas are evidence that U.S. colonial rule is a continuing legacy in the Philippines and not a historical aberration or concluded event. That is, Filipina laborers embody a particular gendered material history of empire that troubles the disappearance of past and contemporary dominations. The colonial and post-colonial are intimately foundational to the modern global age, and most critically through the body of Filipina labor. Thus this project is also a counter-narrative to both governmental and corporate claims that sweep the colonial under the rug of the global.

Through ethnography of the Clark Special Economic Zone, I highlight the continuing and crucial links between the structures and discourses of a "historical" empire and the structures and discourses of globalization. This ethnography explores the spatial, discursive, and cultural practices at work in what Raymond Williams might call the "structures of feeling" of globalization: those aspects of the social that rationalize the neoliberal economic policies endemic in these spaces. As Wendy Brown argues, such neoliberal political rationality emerges as "governmentality- a mode of governance encompassing but not limited to the state, and one which produces subjects, forms of citizenship and behavior, and a new organization of the social."

Williams and Brown's insistence on the multivalent institutional and social aspects of domination is significant for this ethnography. Neo-liberalism as I use it here refers not only to the economic policies epitomized by the market fundamentalism of the Washington Consensus but also to the cultural technologies that extend market values to other aspects of social life. At Clark, the culture fostered by the primacy of neoliberal economic rule is a crucial part of the mode of governance that structures the lived reality in this space. In my ethnography, I examine the centrality of gendered and racialized labor in the colonial narratives of uplift and the neoliberal discourses that accompany projects of development, modernization, and "progress" in Clark. By foregrounding the work of cultural institutions in this economically over determined space, I also extend the existing scholarship on export processing zones through cultural analysis.

Following Catherine Lutz's call for more ethnographies of empire to track the "topography of U.S. power," my analysis of present-day Clark is a moment where metanarratives of modernity can be broken down and concretely connected to an ongoing American imperial project. An examination of the culture of domination that remains and flourishes at Clark illustrates the ways in which the supposed historical distance of imperialism continues to inform the present and future lived realities of its inhabitants.

If we consider how ideological formations of domination are worked through and entrenched in culture, particularly through gendered hierarchies, then facile periodizations and spatializations of imperialism based on military occupations are at once problematic and specious. In U.S. postcolonial studies in particular, the interrogation of contemporary cultures of domination plays a large part in implicating the United States as an imperialist presence. The sentiments embedded in the epigraphs evoke the still-structuring presence of imperial discourses of exceptionalism and innocence in the contemporary incarnation of a former military base.

The last part of this chapter looks at those patriarchies of globalization, local and otherwise, that overlap to constrain the life choices of the primarily female workforce that comprises most of the service sector at Clark and, in particular, the Mimosa Leisure Estate's golf and country club. Elaborating on the discourses about "trainable" labor for the "royalty trip" of tourist-consumers illustrated in the epigraphs, I look at the ways different kinds of narratives produced by management and other elites elucidate how Filipina bodies are framed within the modernizing borders of Clark. However, as a contrast to the over determined casting of Filipina as passive, I conclude with other kinds of narratives about gendered and racialized labor on the golf course- the narratives of the women workers themselves.

Contemporary scholarship on globalization analyzes capital and labor flows in the era of transnationalism. Arguing for an alternative geography of globalization that pays attention to the ways global processes become congealed and are lived out in places such as cities and export processing zones, Saskia Sassen urges us to pay attention to immobilities and boundedness as well as fluidity. Following Sassen's attention to these "countergeographics" of globalization, in this project I turn to the space of American empire at "home" in the Philippines. Here, I hope to map the colonial structures of feeling, gendered and racialized nostalgia, and the different kinds of discursive and material labor that underpin the project of Western-style modernity in a former American military base.

Taking into account M. Jacqui Alexander and Chandra Mohanty's work on the transnational flows of gendered and racialized labor, in this chapter I consider the ways that continuities and discontinuities between "colonial legacies" and "state and capital formations" map a process of recolonization. As Alexander, Mohanty, and other feminist scholars point out, the networks of desire and labor so central to today's world-system are steeped in familiar vocabularies and transactions that are carried out through the currency of gendered and racialized bodies. That is, the contemporary mobilities of some are bought at the expense of the constrained movement of others.

As Cynthia Enloe has noted, "Paying serious attention to women can expose how much power it takes to maintain the international political system in its present form." In my analysis of those who have "stayed home," I use a "multinational and multilocational approach to questions of gender" to examine contemporary formations of feminized labor in a historically militarized zone. Sassen notes that the gendering of labor in these sites is paramount to the spread of economic globalization. Filipino/American and feminist scholarship on migrant labor flows and the political economy of "love" and care giving probe the crucial role that U.S. structures and cultures of imperialism play in the contemporary world order.

This critical body of work links contemporary patterns of Filipina labor migration to racialized and gendered structures and ideologies set up during the American colonial era and exploited in its aftermath. I seek to supplement existing scholarship on the gendered nature of Filipino Diasporas, which looks particularly at domestics, nannies, nurses, and entertainers, by focusing on those who "stay behind" and labor "at home." Such gendering of labor draws heavily from imperial structures, dynamics, and discourses, which continue to flourish and shape these spaces and processes long after the last gunship has officially departed.

The social structures of free trade and tourism at Clark is not just about the economics of transnational capital, but also just as importantly about evoking a social feeling or "setting a mood" for and of domination. An integral part of the affective structure of modernity produced by Clark rests on the familiar positioning of Filipinas as the bodies of service in a transnational age and on the continued use of the space by a different set of postcolonial elites. Centering gender in this examination of discourses and cultures of modernity in the post-colony, I draw on a deliberately eclectic range of objects, practices, spaces and narratives to interrupt monolithic and masculinized theories of modernity.

This project's objects of analysis- the military base, the Clark Museum and golf clubhouse situated within it, guidebook narratives, and the stories of the people who work within the special economic zone- are evidence that the artifactuality of empire and war, as Oscar V. Campomanes has argued, remains. To examine the artifacts of empire returns us to the discourses and material structures that continue to shape the gendered and racialized violence of historical amnesia and neocolonial capital that inform and support the apparatus of nation-states.

For instance, how do the relations of labor and leisure at the renovated golf clubhouse at Clark hold on to and further elaborate the gendered and racialized discourses of its former incarnation as a military institution? How might they work against and alongside the narratives of guidebooks and the stories of the laborers who work in these sites? What do these relations have to do with the larger issue of the Philippine state's continuing struggles for economic and political stability and legitimacy?

However, interviews with the caddies, umbrella girls, and groundskeepers were in-depth and yielded consistent similarities in responses and findings. The interviews were conducted one-on-one at the subject's workplace or where the most privacy was available. The exceptions to this were those instances where the golf course staff member invited a companion or two to accompany her on the interview. Although not official primary informants, these companions overwhelmingly confirmed the interview subject's opinions and added examples and anecdotes of their own, adding to the richness of my interviews. While everyone who was interviewed signed formal releases, I have chosen to keep my informants, particularly the golf course staff, anonymous.

Most of the questions centered on the conditions, routines, and regulations enforced at their workplace. What kinds of interactions and transactions occurred between the various types of people who populated the space? How did they view their own participation in their jobs? What hierarchies structured the transition of the military base to a "leisure" and commercial zone geared toward elite consumption? During this time, toured the base grounds on different days, observing various facilities such as the clubhouse, the golf course, and the base museum. The ethnography focuses on conversations with the staff and observations of the Clark Special Economic Zone and is supplemented by my readings of the narratives of occupation, "progress," and modernity in the historical exhibit of Clark Air Base in the Clark Museum and the contemporary culture of leisure in the Mimosa Leisure Estate's golf and country club.

In tying together these various artifacts to map out a countergeographics of globalization that links the historical occupation of Clark to the present-day framing of the former base as a bastion of modernization link the eclectic "evidence" of museum displays, the text of a contemporary guidebook, the culture of a golf country club, and the experience of its workers to illustrate the work it takes to recast a former military base as a space where neo-liberalism works its benevolent magic.

In mainstream histories, the War of 1898, more popularly known as the Spanish-American War, was a war between a declining Old World empire and a "young" New World imperial power. Waged against the declining and over-stretched Spanish empire, the decisive battles took place in the colonial territories of Puerto Rico, Cuba, and the Philippines. Many of these histories not only downplay the deliberate and premeditated acquisition of former Spanish territories by the United States, but ignore the long-standing native revolutions against the Spanish as a crucial element in the United States' easy success.

Indeed, native-led anti-colonial movements continued against American intervention and occupation after the Treaty of Paris that ceded these former Spanish territories to the United States. In the Philippines, the Philippine-American War between the native "insurgent" government and the colonial government of the United States lasted long after its official end in 1902. Bringing "civilization" to America's "little brown brother" was a violent and protracted affair. The infrastructures of large military bases that remain in the central and northern Philippines are the legacies of sustained and violent American occupation. Clark Air Base was one of the larger military reservations that the United States established at the beginning of its colonial rule in the Philippines to aid in the "pacification" of the populace.

Its predecessor at the site near Angeles, Fort Stotsenburg, was a post for the U.S. cavalry and a training ground for the Philippine Scouts, native collaborators recruited by the U.S. Army for their knowledge of the diverse languages and terrains of Luzon, the northern portion of the Philippines. During American occupation (1898-1946, excepting the period that it was occupied by the Japanese army during World War II), it was a stronghold not only for quashing native rebellion, but also for protecting growing American interests in the region.

After Philippine independence in 1946, American troops stayed on to "secure" the region through the Cold War, occupying large amounts of Philippine territory that had been ceded to U.S. military jurisdiction under the 1947 Military Bases Agreement and Military Assistance Pact. The American military did not officially return the leased lands until 1991, when the Mount Pinatubo disaster accelerated the process. By that time, the Philippine and American governments had established a working relationship that allowed for the U.S. to provide aid, training, and intelligence to the Philippine military in exchange for the bases. These continuing neocolonial "special relations" abetted the Philippine state's anti-poor and anti-Communist state campaigns, which peaked during the Cold War.

Today, Clark, like other former American military reservations in the Philippines, is a special economic zone, holding on to the kinds of autonomy it had during American occupation. When the American military bases reverted to Philippine control, a great deal of speculation arose over the fate of these highly developed properties. After much congressional and public debate, the federal government decided that they would be overseen by state-run development companies, which, in partnership with private corporations, would convert the former military infrastructures into commercial, manufacturing, and leisure zones. In April 1999, the Clark Development Corporation became the "implementing arm of the bases' conversion and developing authority for CSEZ."

The driving vision behind this public-private investment and development partnership was an understanding of the military properties as bastions of Western modernity in the hands of a country that remains largely agricultural and largely in debt. Steven C. McKay points out that despite the Philippines' relatively high labor costs (compared with China and Central America), its export processing zone program ranks in the top five worldwide because of the ways these zones have been renovated and taken over by private developers. Clark's economic importance as a special economic zone is evidence of the Philippines' continued dependence on foreign investment and exchange.

In fact, the ways that the CSEZ operates today are reminiscent of the base's independent status during the years it was under U.S. jurisdiction: the development company has the final say in cases where an action might conflict with local governance. The Philippine government, concerned with the impending massive unemployment from the vacating military lessees, assigned Clark as a protected investment and manufacturing zone, offering tax incentives to potential investors. Subsequently, drawn by the lack of bureaucratic red tape, the abundance of workers, the minimal regulations, and the site's easy-to-reach location, many foreign and domestic corporations have transferred their operations here.

The vast majority of foreign manufacturing investors are attracted by the infrastructure already in place, including the reserve army of what Tony Gonzales described as "very, very trainable" labor left by the departed American military economy. Clark's military infrastructure thus continues to mold its current incarnation as a special economic zone. From its labor pool, buildings, location, and airstrips encouraging the efficient flow of traffic and goods, Clark remains a pocket of American-style modernity in the Philippines. The main zone of more than 4,000 hectares contains most of the former Clark Air Base infrastructure. Lakeside, resort, and agricultural areas make up an additional 29,000 hectares.

The original area has now been expanded to 69,000 hectares to include Tarlac and Hacienda Luisita, the latter a large estate owned by former President Corazon Aquino's family. Under the management of the Clark Development Corporation (CDC), the modern facilities of the former Clark military reservation are a draw for investors. One of the CDC marketing staff states that the "nice thing" about Clark is that the infrastructure is already there: buildings are merely renovated by the tourist and manufacturing industries to fit their needs. Barracks and other buildings are turned into assembly-line factories and duty-free shops, while former officers' quarters are transformed into short- and long-term residential housing (for the managerial class) and tourist lodging.

In 2001, with little fanfare, Philippine president Gloria Macapagal-Arroyo changed the name of Clark Air Base's airport to Diosdado Macapagal International Airport, in honor of her late father, a former Philippine president. This seamless nominal transfer signaled Clark's shift from a former U.S. military outpost to a hub in the global network of capital, labor, and leisure. Built to accommodate modern wide-bodied aircraft, the airport was marketed as an ideal international node for capital and traffic, tourists, shoppers, and investors traveling from Hong Kong, Singapore, and Taiwan.

Yet it is not so much the economic significance of the special economic zone that interests me here but its cultural and social functions. The artifacts and cultures of empire do the work of persuasion and rationalization necessary to projects of domination, and those at Clark are prime examples. When the Philippines acquired control of the bases, a surprisingly wide range of political interests invested in a narrative about these former military reservations- one of desire for the symbolic modernity of the United States. With the official departure of the U.S. military, nostalgia for a safely absent, modern big brother overwrote a long history of colonial violence, war, and economic and political domination.

In the Philippines' struggles to establish itself as a developing and secure nation, the artifacts of American occupation were embraced as icons of modernity and stability. As one commentator mentioned of Clark's former counterpart, Subic Bay Naval Base, it "is an oasis in the middle of the Philippines. Things really do work here." The image of American modernness is the draw for this globalizing hub. Identification with modern power and control was carried out by means of road networks, barracks, airstrips, and the recreational facilities. The order and discipline of militarism promise an alternative narrative to the tumultuous economic and political reality of Philippine society today.

Through Clark's incarnation as a special economic zone, modern subjects of transnational capital and leisure are able to enter and exit the Philippines with ease, untouched by the bureaucracy of Manila and unencumbered by the federal government's rules for foreign investors. Clark accommodates the fluidity of transnational capital and its mobile subjects. These transnational subjects are joined by domestic elites who are also members of this international cadre. Chauffeured on the smooth concrete highways from their gated Manila suburbs, Filipino elites spend time and money in the leisure zones set aside for them, a custom reminiscent of the earlier colonial exodus of colonial elites from Manila to the cool mountain resorts.

At the entrance to the Clark Special Economic Zone, guards at the checkpoints allow private automobiles through, while those using public transportation must wait in the dusty area allotted for buses and jeepneys just outside the gates. The few jeepneys permitted inside carry mostly hotel and resort staff, groundskeepers, and factory workers. Clark's grounds are well tended, and the layout of the buildings follows the standardized organization of many American military campuses. This is modernity, American-style. The dark twin of this new American-style vision of modernity is Clark's old self.

Just outside Clark are older sites and sights of U.S. militarism: the ubiquitous twenty-four-hour-a-day girly bar catering to visiting servicemen and tourists, the significant numbers of fatherless mixed-race children around the bases, the quiet but deadly presence of HIV, and the radioactive and chemical waste slowly seeping into the land. Indeed, the "official" Clark, bounded by fences and closely watched by guards, is not so easily separable from these other spaces and scenes of former occupation. The celebration of modernity, U.S.-style capitalist democracy, and stability inside Clark is made possible by violent histories of U.S. colonial and neocolonial relations that are effaced by discourses of improvement, progress, and mobility.

Outside Clark, more overt relations of power reminiscent of Clark's air base days continue to shape material realities. Needless to say, with the continuing militarized relationship between the United States and the Philippines, Clark (inside and out) remains a highly militarized space. While the bases are officially in Philippine hands, "joint exercises" between Philippine and American militaries have taken their place, essentially locating the entire archipelago under a model of flexible and total militarization with less U.S. accountability. Despite the Philippines' continuing negotiations with its former colonial master, Clark, ostensibly free of its former occupants, continues to trade on its former association with "America" to succeed.

Within Clark itself, two interrelated sites perform the symbolic and material labour that produces narratives and structures of feeling about progressive American intervention. The first, Clark Museum, represents Clark's history through the display of photographs and manufactured commodities-what Campomanes might call the artifacts of colonial gratitude. The second is the golf and country club at the Mimosa Leisure Estate, where international and domestic tourists partaking in the pleasures made available at Clark can take advantage of colonial labor practices and established hierarchies of class, race, and gender as well as modern amenities of militarism. Clark Museum, in effect, constructs the history for the present that is lived out on the grounds of the Mimosa Leisure Estate.

Returning to the epigraphs, this history and lived materiality is made legible through gendered and racialized Filipina labor, labor that lies outside of, yet is intimately necessary to, the image of a modern Clark. Taken together as artifacts of empire, these two sites form an interconnected teleological narrative whose pedagogical function is an apologia for a long history of American colonialism. Clark Museum is an unassuming building (formerly officer's quarters) that occupies a corner near the former military parade grounds. It is a short walk from the office of the Clark Development Company's president's quarters (the post commander's headquarters in its previous life). The museum itself does not attract many visitors, but it is worth discussing here because of the way its exhibit authoritatively distills the overall feeling that permeates Clark.

The exhibit is modest but potent, tapping into and producing a familiar colonial history. Consisting mostly of wall panels of enlarged and captioned photographs from Clark's American era and supplemented by glass display cases of smaller military paraphernalia and other artifacts, dioramas, and poster-size photographs of contemporary investors, the exhibit taken as a whole produces a history of Philippine uplift, salvation, and modernity, made possible by its colonial steward. It is reminiscent of the world's fairs that first advertised the American colony's presence to the American public in the late 1800s.

Writing about the 1893 World's Columbian Exposition in Chicago, Curtis Hinsley describes the juxtaposition of Euro-American exhibits of progress with the display of various natives as heralding the arrival and shape of a modernity that "was in the final analysis a celebration of market flow." The origins and evolution of this market-based modernity are exhibited at Clark Museum in a way that erases the violence of imperial and postcolonial occupation. In particular, the developmental pictorial narrative deploying gendered and racialized logics reminiscent of colonial and military occupation is notable for the way it seamlessly transfers colonial ideologies onto a neoliberal agenda.

On the walls of the museum, the story of Clark runs along a familiar developmental narrative, beginning with the "pre-historic" occupation of the land by the Negritos and Aetas, here called "ancient" indigenous Filipinos. The abrupt disjuncture between Philippine "pre-history" and U.S. arrival and occupation is mediated by a story of contact and friendship, of mutual "service." This story of "first contact" is reassuringly familiar: white man brings civilization to the primitive savages. It also functions as a foil for the kind of progress that follows.

Upon the arrival of the American colonizers, as told by a diorama display, a "special relationship" was formed- leading to the recruitment of many indigenous peoples into the Philippine Scouts during the Philippine-American War. This special relationship elides the complicity of these Scouts in the eventual violent defeat of their fellow Filipinos. Instead, what is highlighted is the quasi-military service that resulted from their "primitive" status of knowing the land. Once the Philippine-American War was over, they were hired as menial labor inside the military camp, initiating their colonial tutelage as proper laborers under their American teachers.

Museum history then proceeds with archival photographic displays of Clark's growth and development in the intervening years, giving prominent space and attention to two pivotal wars in which U.S. military bases in the Philippines played crucial roles in the Pacific theater: World War II and Vietnam. The central display of World War II-era Japanese imperial materials successfully deflects the prior history of U.S. colonial violence onto more recent (and remembered) occupiers. Highlighting Japanese propaganda leaflets and posters, an alternative potential history of Japanese modernization and domination is alluded to, which in contrast makes U.S. colonialism a soft-core occupation and recasts U.S. militarism in the Philippines in a messianic role.

World War II is retold through a story of mutual American and Filipino suffering (the Bataan Death March) and ultimate triumph. By making reference to the Japanese, the display places a longer history of U.S. violence safely in the distant past, conjuring up the United States in its familiar role as liberator of Asia. The overall narrative of the display thus serves to highlight U.S.-Philippine special relations through a Cold War lens of uplift and united struggle rather than of violence and domination.

A 1948 speech that President Manuel Roxas made to officers at Clark Air Field captions a panel featuring American soldiers at "this field that is being rapidly built up so that it may be one of the strongest bastions of freedom and peace in our part of the world." Clark's role as the staging area for the Vietnam War's Operations Baby Lift and New Life likewise elides the imperialist Cold War politics that a U.S. military base in the Philippines both enabled and inflamed. Instead, a focus on the rescue of "orphans" and the surrogate parenthood of American military wives volunteering as foster parents to Vietnamese children rewrites a protracted and violent war into a narrative of salvaged and altruistic multicultural domesticity.

The rescue narrative about Filipina labor could not be told as successfully without the stage-setting function of these rescue narratives of colonial uplift and war. This historical and contemporary framing of Filipina labor in Clark is ultimately about relaying a pedagogical narrative about the exemplary subjects of benevolent colonialism. Two sets of visual displays in the Clark Museum demonstrate this point.

The first consists of the nostalgic black-and-white photographs that illustrate the "domestic" cultures of military occupation at Clark Air Field. American military families, after all, needed looking after. Documenting everyday life for American families who were part of the imperial project, these photographs are powerful artifacts of empire precisely because they do not show domination by military force. Instead, what we have is visual evidence of the banality of imperialism in the domestic sphere. One of the most eye-catching photographs is of a child's birthday party in 1940: white American children are arranged in rows, with their uniformed Filipina nannies stationed at the back.

These photographs of white American children with their Filipina nannies illustrate the "special relationship" between the United States and the Philippines, establishing colonial hierarchies of caretaking on a smaller scale. It seems that the white man's burden (as well as the white woman's) entailed hiring brown women to care for their families as part of the civilizing mission. As Ann Laura Stoler would argue, such techniques were part of the colonial society's need to structure the complex and intimate relationships of the colonial sphere into more clearly demarcated lines, producing the proper subjects of the colonial project. This early domestic arrangement is the foundation for the "royalty trip" of contemporary fantasy.

Colonial subjects practiced and lived out colonial ideologies and hierarchies in the intimacies of domestic life. Amy Kaplan, writing about the imperial ideologies of the "domestic" spaces of both home and nation, argues that the rhetoric of the feminine reproductive and familial space permeated the broader imperial project. In a sense, the domestic "education" of Filipinas as household servants demonstrates the success of the American civilizing project in the Philippines. These gendered artifacts of U.S. imperialism tell a story of the quotidian domesticity of military life, and not of its violence, producing U.S. Empire as a way of life worthy of nostalgia.

Rather than construct white modernity according to more overt codes of manliness and soldiering, the museum exhibit displays the products of benevolent imperial tutelage, giving the U.S. empire visual form. In that sense, the museum photographs continue to be both instrument and product of colonial ideology. The photograph's romanticization of American colonial occupation has a different message when articulated with Clark's mission as a special economic zone. The message of benevolent colonialism transforms to one of benign globalization. The photographs enable the understanding that colonial military occupation may be a necessary first step to Western-style modernity.

In this narrative, the Filipina nannies watching over their charges become apt pupils of ideologies of civilization and uplift.

Yet the photograph also reinforces the racial taxonomies of U.S. imperialism that continue to have currency today, particularly in the ways in which Filipina bodies are circulated as overseas domestics. The Filipina nannies in the photograph are part of the empire and essential to the American racial family, even as they stand at their margins. Continuing the arc of progress and development, the museum display also boasts artifacts of indigenous Filipino culture, such as baskets, weavings, coconut shells, beads, and arrows. These are juxtaposed with "an Industrial Exhibit of CSEZ Locators" that offers samples of the modern commodities produced in Clark's incarnation as special economic zone, such as computer components, textiles, and furniture.

The second set of images forms the backdrop to the manufactured commodities on display: photographs of productive Filipina workers in the various manufacturing and technology industries housed in Clark. In these poster-size photographs, former barracks and military equipment buildings are transformed into factory spaces. Instead of soldiers, the buildings house (usually) young Filipina workers in assembly-line manufacturing for electronics and garment industries. Here, the orderly management and production of these laborers represent the outsourcing of manufacturing to the underdeveloped world, one of the characteristics of globalization. Juxtaposed with the photographs of the Filipina nannies, these images of modern Filipina factory workers parallel the teleological arc showcased by the indigenous artifacts of primitivism and the displays of manufactured commodities.

Taken together, they reconfigure colonial violence into a story of development and modernity. Progress is marked by the shift from baskets to hard drives, from colonial service to manufacturing industry. Under the discipline and tutelage of colonial power- here nostalgically and lovingly remembered- the move to globalization is made simple. The display on the walls of the museum is a romantic narrative of a kinder, gentler imperialism that produced disciplined and docile workers in preparation for modern working and living, underpinning the story of modernity told by Clark's renovation.

The narrative encapsulated in the display at Clark Museum works in tandem with the actual lived reality of workers who make possible the various manufacturing and leisure corporations that occupy Clark today. One of the contradictions at Clark shows up under close scrutiny: the "feel" of modernity, indeed, its virtual achievement, is founded on the continuing unmodernity of human labor.

That is, the story of manufacturing and its ostensibly modern kinds of regulated labor has not displaced the colonial patterns of care giving that are now reappropriated by the tourism and leisure industry. Indeed, manufacturing labor itself rearticulates colonial hierarchies of labor. As Tony Gonzales points out in the epigraph, outside the museum, the former military golf course and clubhouse enacts embodied logics of imperial class and race that echo the museum photographs of the Filipina nannies in their uniforms, watching their young white American charges on the military base.

A leisure class formed by a white expatriate managerial class, elite Filipinos, and upwardly mobile Asian tourists circulates in Clark's former military golf course. A 250-hectare "tourism haven," Mimosa Leisure Estate (hereafter Mimosa) boasts vacation villas, a Holiday Inn, club houses, a convention center, and a twenty-seven-hole championship golf course, famous for having hosted Tiger Woods. Here, in a space segregated not only from the rest of the Philippines but also from Clark's manufacturing and commercial zones, the leisure class can indulge in and live out fantasies steeped in colonial romance. Clark's modern up-to-date facilities meet the high standards demanded by this cosmopolitan class, yet its colonial structures of labor continue to provide plentiful, cheap, and trained laborers to serve those at play.

At the Mimosa golf course and clubhouse, these colonial social hierarchies are most apparent. Golf courses, initially imported to the Philippines by imperial investors in the colonies, became spaces where colonial officials affirmed their status. In the Philippine colonial hill station of Baguio City, for instance, golf courses and country clubs were key to the spatial segregation of colonial administration and elite Filipinos from the unruly masses and enabled the social reproduction of the ruling class.

Today at Mimosa, the social function of the golf course and country club is deeply entrenched in these colonial practices. In tandem with this colonial history, the proliferation of golf courses in the Philippines during the 1990s was a result of Asia's emergence as a site for international, mostly Asian-based tourism during the economic boom. The renovation of Clark's military golf course as an exclusive, membership-only golf club is part of this larger trend to accommodate both colonial and modern desires. Originally a game of the elite colonial administrators, golf in the Philippines today manages to hold in tension nostalgic imperial desires and claims to modern, capitalism-friendly democracy.

In one of the Philippines' tourism poster campaigns, President Gloria Macapagal-Arroyo is shown teeing off in front of the former American colonial summer palace, selling the charms of Baguio City to tourists. Following in the footsteps of former presidents Fidel Ramos's and Joseph Estrada's sponsorship of golf tourism, Macapagal-Arroyo's public endorsement of golf as a symbol of Philippine modernity and competitiveness illustrates its international potency as a marker of democracy, a product of development gone right. Implicit in the poster is a message about an economy stable (yet desperate) enough for foreign capital investment, where the peso's poor foreign exchange rate can buy a cheap and spectacular round of golf.

The poster elides the fact that the tensions and contradictions between capitalism, development, and democracy in the Philippines are resolved only through the disciplined labor of its poorest citizens. In selling the pastime of golf to men who have disposable income, cultural capital and the time to play both the Philippine tourism industry and privately produced guidebooks such as the one quoted in the epigraph naturalize the gendered relations of leisure and labor in the country club. Claims for golf's democratic effects in the post-colony are taken up, repeated, and circulated in Golfing Asia's Golfing

Philippines: The Complete Guide to All the Golf in the Archipelago. An expensive paperback published by a regional corporation that promotes golf and golf courses, it is the first in a regional series of golf guides targeted at expatriate businessmen, local elites, and tourists.

The guide assumes a male cosmopolitan subject, one familiar with the gestures and cultures of country club life. It begins with a photo layout of several golf course landscapes in the Philippines. The high-quality photographs dominate the guidebook with images of vast expanses of groomed grass and rolling hills, referencing that trope of imperial civilization, the perfectly manicured English lawn, and evoking a tranquility that only exists in the imagination. The guidebook, while primarily enumerating the different golf courses available for play, is also a reference to how gendered labor works in the post-colonial golf course.

Tourists and locals alike who are privileged enough to circulate in the hallowed fairways and clubhouses of the Philippine golfing scene are positioned as consuming cosmopolitan subjects, marked as such in contrast to the representations of Filipina labor in the pages of the guidebook. Buddy Resurrection, a Filipino writer for the series, signals gender as a central mechanism of disciplining and controlling racialized, formerly colonial labor. His pedagogical narrative reinscribes a rigid, sexualized definition of gendered labor on Philippine golf courses. At the same time, it taps into the neoliberal discourses of uplift for labor that resonate both in colonial ideas of service as well as in globalizing narratives.

The first epigraph in this chapter comes from Resurrection's article on "Local Style: The Things that Make Philippine Golf ... so Filipino," which tellingly reveals the ways in which Filipinas are reduced to their much gendered, racialized laboring bodies as "retractable umbrellas." Illustrating Resurrection's insider look at how Filipina labor makes golfing in the Philippines a "royalty trip" is a cartoon of a shapely young Filipina in a bikini and beauty pageant sash, holding an umbrella over the golfer's head. For Resurrection, the Filipina "umbrella girls" who function as the "retractable roof[s]" allow domestic and international elites to experience the nostalgic desires of colonial fantasy as one part of the package of the modernizing landscape of Clark.

Regardless of whether these elites are Filipinos, Americans, Japanese, or Korean (the major client groups identified by Mimosa's management), they are all elevated to "royalty" through the labor of the umbrella girls. This kind of discursive labor on Resurrection's part serves not only to obliquely rationalize the logics of development but also to conceal the causal role it has in the production of the material asymmetries that make possible the "royalty trip." Discourses of paternalism and development- shored up by narratives like Resurrection's and Tony Gonzales's- are embraced by the Arroyo government in its antipoverty campaign.

That "there are a lot of women in the labor force" who are provided jobs like these by such development and modernization projects as those being undertaken at Clark misses the point that many of these women are in positions of poverty because of a long history of colonial and neocolonial dispossession. The latest incarnation of this history is being literally played out on the golf courses that they service. Framed as a benevolent project that provides much-needed jobs to unskilled workers, Clark's bid to enter the geographies of modern leisure turns on the disciplining of this largely female workforce.

Gender, as deployed in these narratives, is a regulatory mechanism that rationalizes the position of Filipinas as cheap service workers. On the other hand, it also symbolizes the "democratizing" opportunities created by tourism and globalization, as signaled by the Macapagal-Arroyo poster. That is, while representing tourist possibilities and desires, Macapagal-Arroyo's Filipina body conceals the overwhelmingly female workforce that caters to the mostly male transnational golf market.

The "royalty trip" is precisely the kind of fantasy that is served by both the historical representation of colonial labor (as epitomized by the Clark Museum display) and contemporary social inequalities that are exacerbated by globalization. Golf, in this case, also functions as a symbol of the foreign and domestic big business interests that flourish under Macapagal-

Arroyo's adherence to neoliberal policies of globalization, best characterized by her Medium-Term Philippine Development Plan, 2001-2004. Such neoliberal policies contribute to the growing poverty class in the Philippines, which is overwhelmingly represented by the growth in the overseas and domestic service sector.

Under the aegis of democracy and development that ostensibly go hand-in-hand in these special economic zones, Filipina labor is a symbol of and a material means to American-style economic and cultural modernity. At the Mimosa grounds, in particular, the state and the private sector regulate Filipina labor in various ways to produce Mimosa as a "world-class facility." As the exemplary subjects of globalized labor, Asian women, and in this case, Filipinas, are cast as docile, manageable, and replaceable.

This myth of the tractable Asian woman fuels not only the exploitation of the women's labor in export processing zones but also their employment in leisure and tourist industries. Laura Kang and Aihwa Ong have explored the ways Asian states, competing for foreign investment, promote their readily disciplined female workforces as valuable resources, tapping into both local and Orientalist patriarchies, as illustrated by Gonzales's observation about the "trainability" of labor at Clark. Thus, while smiling women figure dominantly in discourses of Philippine tourism, the actual playing grounds demand their loyal, uncomplaining, and invisible service.

Today, caddying is an overwhelmingly female occupation in the Philippines. The current management at Mimosa chooses Filipinas as caddies because they are widely perceived as more manageable, submissive, and hardworking than Filipinos. When Clark was under U.S. jurisdiction, the caddies were all Filipinos. In 1991, the phasing in of women into a historically male occupation was a major part of the clubs' arsenal of worker discipline. Docility and manageability were the two watchwords that golf club managers in the Philippines (not just at Mimosa) tout when describing their ideal unskilled labor force, and Orientalist patriarchies have bought into the belief that Asian women are culturally or naturally inclined to obey.

Managers cited male caddies' propensity for unionizing and being more vocal with their disagreements with management. As a club manager put it: "Women are more manageable. They seldom fight, while male caddies bet, drink, and fight." In addition, as golf became linked with the Philippines' tourism industry, women were increasingly preferred as representative bodies of the highly gendered tropes of hospitality. This choice played into the tightened budget of the management team, which is pressured to make consistent profits for the investors. Employing women also justified keeping the caddy fees low, as they are not seen as the main income earners of their families.

At Mimosa, a large majority of the male employees were regular, salaried workers with three-month contracts that in practice were always renewed. This meant that overwhelmingly, male employees received a regular salary, meal coupons (for free meals), health benefits, social security, on-the-job training, and, in some cases (such as the male groundskeepers), could work toward the cooperative ownership of machinery that they used. The female laborers, on the other hand, were not long-term contractual workers and did not enjoy benefits or regular salary. Despite this status, the female laborers at Mimosa do tasks similar to those done by the male laborers. With the exception of the operations of the grounds keeping machinery, the skill level and hours required of the female workers equals those expected of the male workers.

The caddies at Mimosa take charge of accompanying and assisting players on the course, including cleaning, carrying, and keeping track of the equipment. Like the umbrella girls, they tend to be younger than the groundskeepers, although umbrella girls tended to be, on average, the youngest group. Caddies receive some rudimentary training in an apprenticeship model from the golf manager or caddy master before being certified to work as a caddy at the club. Many had worked for the club for five to ten years and had regular patrons among the workers. Umbrella girls carry the umbrellas that shade golfers from the harsh tropical sun and are also expected, like the caddies, to provide a female audience to the masculine play and banter of the mostly male players.

There is no training required to be an umbrella girl, though it is often implicitly understood that one should be young, a "good sport," and not unattractive. Umbrella girls and caddies tend to be local Filipinas, but most do not belong to the displaced Aeta indigenous community, who make up the majority of the female groundskeepers. Unlike the caddies and umbrella girls, the female groundskeepers had a wider range of ages (20-38 for the women I interviewed). Their jobs were limited to thirty-day, non-renewable contracts and consisted of cleaning up the grounds debris produced by the machines, sweeping grass cuttings, weeding, and general upkeep of the golf greens.

According to the golf manager of the Mimosa Club, these groundskeepers are the "secret weapon" of the club's renaissance because they are cheap, plentiful, and hard-working. They are perceived as unskilled workers, the epitome of the "very trainable" labor force at Clark. The caddies and umbrella girls, like the women who work in the factories in the special economic zone, are overwhelmingly young Filipinas from the poorer classes whose only other way of earning a living is to go to factories of the export processing zones. Many support at least their immediate families with their small earnings.

Most have not finished high school because financial hardships force them to enter the workforce early. In contrast, according to Steven C. McKay's work on export processing zones in the Philippines, many of the young women who work in the manufacturing factories in export processing zones have some college education. Yet some caddies I interviewed had been former factory workers who traded in the assembly line for a rotation schedule service job, one they perceived as having more flexibility. Despite McKay's findings that most factory workers in export processing zones do not work under contract, many caddies and umbrella girls emphasized their relative freedom from long-term contractual obligations and a strictly enforced workday as an advantage in rationalizing their choice of employment, whether or not that was the actual case.

For many of these women, these low-paying jobs are a boon, because they do bring home some income, yet the numbers do not tell a simple story. Most caddies are paid two hundred to three hundred pesos for each eighteen-hole round of golf, which takes about four to six hours. That translates to about four to six dollars for a day's work, for many caddies barely enough to cover transportation and food costs. This wage, however, is a cheap golfing expense for the club member or tourist who hires the women.

The IBON Foundation, an independent research think-tank in the Philippines, notes that government figures of 34.2 percent of Filipino families living in poverty is woefully understated and is based on the Macapagal-Arroyo government's estimate of 38.13 pesos to meet a Filipino's daily basic needs, which even the poorest of the poor would deem insufficient. The two-to three-hundred-peso earnings could certainly be considered a living wage if earned daily, yet it should also be noted that caddies and umbrella girls have irregular hours subject to the whims of the tourist industry: they can work every day during tourist season, or once a month in rainy season.

How do these decidedly "unmodern" lives trouble Clark's claims to progress and modernity? Clark Museum's nostalgic framings of a paternalistic yet beneficent colonizer are crucial to smoothing over the lack of economic justice for the workers that development narratives claim to serve and uplift. The narratives that follow illustrate the ways in which Filipina workers frame themselves within the modernizing borders of Clark. These interviews of the service workers at the Mimosa golf and country club illustrate the complicities and contestations over the meanings and the roles attached to Filipina bodies in these postcolonial spaces.

These narratives are not meant to represent the "true" voices of gendered labor, but rather to begin to sketch out alternative understandings of how Filipina workers operate in complex ways on the uneven terrains of globalization. In what turned out to be ethnography of pragmatism, complicity, and survival, these narratives taken as whole trouble neo-liberal claims to uplift and progress as well as any kind of simple solution to the exploitation of gendered labor.

A tight network of diverse disciplinary techniques regulates and manages the bodies of Filipina labor, ranging from limiting contracts to short periods, withholding employee status, and institutionalizing rules on hygiene and behavior. The female groundskeepers see the thirty-day contract as a deterrent to any kind of self-determination and security as a worker. As one grounds-keeper put it: "Sana maging regular ako sa trabaho ko" ("I wish my work could become regular"). Even as she joked around about being grateful for the job as Christmas was coming up, she insisted that she needed money to support her family. The thirty-day contract also prevented feelings of entitlement to a regular wage and disciplined the workers through a layer of bureaucracy.

The management also placed the women in different "batches" every day that they worked, limiting worker solidarity. This is reflected in another groundskeeper's wish: "Sana, kaming mga babae magkakasama sa isang trabaho, at wala ng batches" ("I wish all of us women could be together in one job and that we didn't have the batch system anymore"). By mostly reserving groundskeeper work for Aeta women, the management also establishes an ethnic hierarchy of labor. This job requires the least amount of trained skill, and many of the workers perceived it as the most menial work available. Groundskeepers are paid at the end of the month for the time they work, putting much of the power in the hands of management.

The vast repository of reserve labor that produces the underpaid occupations of groundskeeper, umbrella girl, and caddy works in tandem with the refusal of golf club management to provide official employee status for these women, even though the caddy and umbrella girl are now officially written into the rulebooks. Every caddy I interviewed pointed out that as non-employees- for they are considered by the Mimosa to be independent contractors- they are not covered by insurance or benefits: as they say, "Kami lang talaga lahat" ("we have to take care of everything ourselves").

By disavowing employee status for the caddies, clubs avoid the paperwork of filing taxes and social security benefits. It is also a deterrent to union organizing, although some try. They have no regular kita or suweldo (salary), their livelihoods depending completely on the club members and tourists, as well as the weather. According to another caddy, "Ang player lang ... ang golfer lang ang nasusuweldo sa 'yo" ("It is only the player ... the golfer, who will be paying your salary"). Setting up the relationship between master and servant in this way makes the caddy's earning ability highly unpredictable, as the workers hope for tips that can supplement their meager earnings.

It also reinforces the paternalistic and patronizing dependent relationship between benevolent player and grateful caddy. This brings to mind the image evoked by the museum photograph of the nanny and her charges, with the nanny's employment subject to her employer's good graces. The caddies' dependence on an ongoing relationship with their patron can be disastrous, particularly if those patrons are tourists. In the aftermath of the 9/11 attacks in the United States, the damage to the tourist industry in the Philippines was compounded by media coverage of extremist Muslim groups kidnapping foreigners in the southern region of Mindanao.

During my field-work in the aftermath of the SARS epidemic of 2000-2001, caddies reported that the tourism downturn damaged their ability to make a living. Even with the small percentage of golfing tourists coming from abroad, caddies felt the pressure that results from not making a regular salary. Another caddy added that it is up to the manager to advocate for a higher rate for them, but she concluded that this was probably unlikely. As free agents and self-employed workers, they provide the clubs with a valuable and necessary service without the headaches and obligations of a payroll employee. In this extreme rationalization of employment, in which capitalists squeeze more labor from their workers while evading their own obligation to provide a secure working environment, the caddies are among the most vulnerable parties.

Moreover, while denying employee status and its protections to caddies and umbrella girls, the club exercises employer authority through rules and regulations. "Job security" (insofar that they have jobs but are not employees) exists as long as they have committed no "kasalanan" (literally, sins, or wrongs), which are assiduously recorded by a caddy master (usually a longtime former caddy who is hired by the club to manage her fellow caddies). For these, a caddy can be suspended. To add insult to injury, caddy and umbrella girl duties usually include caring for the golf course whose operator does not recognize them as official employees. Caddies are often assigned an unpaid "work day," during which they walk through the course to repair divots and other damage caused by golfers. In addition, Mimosa requires its caddies to purchase their own uniforms and participate in training exercises. Thus, even as they are not considered employees, they are disciplined as such.

Yet the female freelance workers, constituting the "secret weapon" of the golf course's successful makeover, also consider the job as at least a partial answer to their own survival. In our conversations, many caddies and umbrella girls chose to highlight the choices and benefits of this kind of quasi-employment status. Characterizing the caddy or umbrella girl position as "easy money," some women claimed that "Pag uwi mo ditto, may pera ka na" ("When you go home, you've already got money"). Though not a large salary, the immediacy (if not the dependability) of the pay was gratifying. Rather than the regular factory salary (and fixed working schedule), many umbrella girls and caddies preferred the instant gratification of being paid the day that they worked.

Most also cited the flexibility of the job as a positive attribute, particularly those with families, even as they noted that if they didn't show up, they would not be paid. Thus while they are economically dependent on the players and the club for their livelihoods, they also find ways to rationalize the existing inequities by claiming that they are their own bosses. One could argue that these statements illustrate that the workers are being duped by the management into tolerating such low wages. Many of the workers were part of a household wage economy in which their wages supplemented that of parents or spouses and so had become accustomed to and justified the unpredictable employment.

Yet judging from the income bracket the workers occupied, any wage, no matter how limited, would be important additions to the family income. These economic straits leave little room to think about "freedom," yet many of the caddies and umbrella girls insist on framing their jobs in terms of ease and flexibility. To some extent, given their socioeconomic constraints, this kind of "freedom" is preferable to the alternative- working at an export processing zone factory and being under the scrutiny of what would be a more institutionalized workday. For them, this job means owning their own labor and controlling their hours. While in the United States health insurance provided to one partner may cover the family and allow for the other partner to work as an independent contractor, such is not the case in the Philippines.

Workers who were married had spouses who worked in similar contract labor conditions, as jeepney drivers, for example. Working in the factories would not guarantee health insurance for the women either, so the "freedom" and "flexibility" of their hours as independent contractors on the golf course is their main rationale. Even if this is a questionable claim, such rationales demonstrate that these women exercise some decision-making within the larger socioeconomic structures that constrain their life choices. Other workers, highly aware of the deeply gendered colonial relationship playing out on in the club and on the greens, choose to play along. For instance, many women were aware that they could use their gender and the gendered relationship between player and caddy or umbrella girl as a way to generate more income.

The caddies and umbrella girls interviewed in this study understood that their behavior has consequences on the tips they receive and on their opportunities for repeat employment with a particular golfer. They agreed that one must act a particular way-being subservient, adapting and adjusting to the individual needs of each temporary boss-to coax more substantial tips and repeat clientele: "Maging mabuti kang caddy para magustuhan ka. Kahit gaano siya ka-suplado, paki-samahan mo siya ng maayos. Kasi player yun, eh. Diyan ka kukuha ng mga kailangan mo" ("Be a good caddy so you'll be liked. However arrogant he may be, try to get along with him. He is the player, after all. You get the things you need from him.")

While the gendered service relationship between player and caddy plays neatly into various fixed hierarchies (male-female, older-younger, wealthy-poor), many caddies and umbrella girls also consciously appealed to gendered behaviors meant to elicit feelings of protection, chivalry, and attraction to generate more substantial tips and perhaps solicit a player as a regular customer. Playing into the kinds of gendered and racialized stereotypes that also constrain and discipline them, these women find ways to make these discourses work for their own benefit.

The women's value as golf "accessories" and their potential for income unofficially rests on their looks and their youth. This is particularly true for umbrella girls, who have no practical role on the golf course. The women understand this, even as they question it. As one umbrella girl explains, "Okay lang ang trabahong ito habang bata ka pa. Pag matanda ka na, sino pa ang mag-papa-assist sa 'yo?" ("This job is only good while you are still young. When you are already old, who is going to ask you to assist them?")

Hired on the basis of their youth, which translates to their perceived availability and malleability, and their looks, which add to their desirability as golfer accessories, umbrella girls have a short working life. The women tacitly understand that youthful looks translate to higher income potential: "Kahit hindi marunong, basta maganda," says another umbrella girl, explaining that looks matter even if the umbrella girl knows little about the game. Many of the umbrella girls use the universal acceptance of youth and beauty as leverage to camouflage their sub-par understanding of the game, whereas caddies need to know the game as a requisite to work.

Understood by Resurrection and others as the sexy "retractable roof" that is the incarnation of gendered colonial servitude and availability, umbrella girls are seen as potential unofficial sex workers and tend to receive the brunt of sexual advances from golfers. As one umbrella girl put it: "Minsan, may nag-cha-chancing, mga turista. Pero sinasabihan namin bawal yun. Humihinto naman. Kung mang-hihipo sila, puwede namang iwanan yun!" ("Sometimes, there are tourists who try to take advantage and harass us, but we tell them that are not allowed. They stop. If they touch us, we can leave them!")

Many incidents of sexual harassment, however, go unreported or unchecked because the player is the sole source of income and holds membership in the club. Should the umbrella girl leave an abusive player, she also risks foregoing much-needed monetary compensation that she has already earned. She might also build a reputation for not being a "good sport." Behind her, after all, are countless other pretty faces just waiting for the chance to make some money. Player- umbrella girl relationships are usually frowned upon, at least in official club policy. If found out, however, the umbrella girl may lose her job, while the club member usually gets a slap on the wrist.

Even as they might compete with each other for clients, however, these women find ways to make the system work for them, and to create fleeting communities centered on gender concerns. In light of reports of sexual harassment during their commute, twenty-five groundskeepers organized to pay for a commute vehicle to take them to work in the mornings. Guaranteed a safe ride in the early morning, they can share time as a community outside of work, even if that community might be short-lived. Yet they do provide evidence that even within the patriarchal structures of militarism and global capital, the members of the overwhelmingly feminized labor force managed and deployed by the state and private agencies find ways of negotiating their positions.

In these jobs, groundskeepers, umbrella girls, and caddies alike consciously work within and against different disciplinary technologies to eke out uncertain but vital earnings. Subjecting themselves to an unpredictable income that depends on the largesse of golfers, they substitute one kind of gendered discipline for another. Outside the special economic zone, these young women are subjected to a number of overlapping patriarchies- at church, at home, and in their communities. At work, male golfers continue the seamless flow of these patriarchies into what is leisure for the golfer and labor for the Filipina worker, again evoking the nostalgic colonial caretaking imagery that undergirds the display at Clark Museum. In many ways, this closer look at the lives of Filipina workers at Clark's golf and country club forms a layer of a larger colonial palimpsest of gendered and racialized labour. The colonial photographs, the modern factory displays of disciplined workers, the guidebook texts, and the workers' own assessment of their working conditions make up the uneven cultural countergeographics at work in this story of globalization.

8

MNC
The Profits that Kill

After many years in which developed countries were more part of the problem than the solution, the United Nations Conference on Population and Development, held in Cairo in 1994, established some goals to begin reversing this pattern. Unfortunately, although the developed nations paid lip service to this reversal, they've done little to bring it about. In truth, what action there has been has weakened accomplishments at Cairo. For example, within only a few months, the United States agreed to pay some of its back dues to the UN in a so-called compromise that inhibits the ability of family-planning groups around the world to provide reproductive health services. More recently, Vice-President Al Gore told delegates at the first UN Security Council session on a global health issue that "the number of people who will die of AIDS in the first decade of the twenty-first century will rival the number that died in all the wars in all the decades of the twentieth century." Calling this- reasonably enough- a "threat of the greatest magnitude," he added proudly that the United States hoped to increase its overseas spending on AIDS by $150 million.

Ironically, however, according to testimony before a congressional subcommittee by Dr. Peter Lurie of Public Citizen's Health Research Group, the United States could increase poor nations' access to critical medications "without spending a penny." Mechanisms called compulsory licensing and parallel import- perfectly legal even under World Trade Organization rules- could substantially lower the price of needed life-saving drugs. Instead, the U.S. government has pressured developing countries not to implement these mechanisms, placing, said Lurie, "the profit motive of multinational drug companies over the public health needs of desperately ill patients." In fact, the aid programs of foreign elites have often benefited donors more than the needy for which the programs were designated.

The 1954 bill establishing the Food for Peace program- the main avenue of U.S. food aid- was designed to "improve the foreign relations of the United States" and "to provide the economic stability of American agriculture and the national welfare." It wasn't until 1961 that "to control hunger and malnutrition and to encourage economic development in developing countries" was added to the statement of purpose, although Food for Peace continued as a political rather than humanitarian instrument. Finally, in 1975, Democratic Senator Hubert Humphrey introduced legislation to make disaster relief the first priority of the program. Aid programs are also frequently tied to the construction of unwieldy, even useless projects. What analysts' call "aid monstrosities" rely on complex technology and costly expertise that mostly benefit those companies that design and construct the projects?

There is the mango canning plant in Ghana that has never run anywhere near capacity because its capacity is greater than the entire world trade in mangos. There is the milk bottling plant in Sudan that has never produced a bottle of milk because the Sudanese like to drink it fresh from the animal. And there are the giant grain storage silos in Senegal that have remained empty because they're built in places where Senegalese peasants never go. Even when such aid monstrosities are benign instead of pure self-interest, this path of development often debases local living conditions, aggravating rather than relieving poverty. Worse yet, ruling local elites, often kept in power by industrial nations- the names Marcos, Mobutu, and Suharto immediately come to mind - have copied this style of development, taking out huge loans to build showcase projects or to buy tanks and fighter planes. The result is a developing-world debt crisis that's been growing bigger every year for decades.

The price imposed for relief from this backbreaking debt is "structural adjustment": cuts in wages and in public spending, currency devaluation, and in some cases swapping debt for shares in profitable developing-world companies. The consequences have been increased hunger and poverty and decreased funding for education and health services. Alternatively, as Lisa Mastny of the Worldwatch Institute reported recently, outright cancellation of payments from the most indebted countries "could lead to investments that in Africa alone would save the lives of 7 million children per year ... and provide 90 million females with access to basic education."

It costs nothing to involve the participation of local people rather than promoting only the interest of elites. A good guiding principle repeatedly revealed in the work of Nobel laureate Amartya Sen, is that it is the synergy among personal, social, and economic improvement that constitutes genuine development. As Sen and some demographers who bothered to look have observed, people choose to have smaller families as they edge closer to decent living conditions. Significantly- as much as nutritious food, adequate housing, clean water, and access to health care- this means more education, broader opportunity, and greater empowerment for both women and men. These traditionally have not been high priorities for the foreign elites who dominated, d still dominate, the underdeveloped world. Africa provides a chilling illustration. Its current image is of mostly poor countries growing too little food to feed populations growing too fast. This is in striking contrast to the view held by the colonial powers when, in 1884-1885, they held the Berlin Conference to lay ground rules for dividing up the African cake.

African political scientist Ali Mazrui observes that economies emerged in the colonies "disproportionately focussed on producing some beverage or dessert" for Europe's dining tables- "cocoa (from Ghana), coffee (from Uganda) and tea (from Kenya)." The priority placed on exports determined how the richest soils would be allocated and where investments would be made. Traditional food crops were relegated to the poorest, least productive land. Equally important, the same priority shaped the infrastructure. Roads, like the best land, were to serve the needs of export, not those of the local people. It's not surprising then that, during post-colonial food shortages, often a bigger problem than getting food aid to a country's border was moving it inland to the hungry.

The Berlin Conference, claiming as one of its goals to end the "Arab" slave trade, was a classic case of the contradictions of colonial exploitation. No one personified this hypocrisy better than King Leopold II of Belgium, even if his country never ranked among the leading imperial powers. Condemning the slave trade and advocating formation of a "Congo Free State," his stated plans were praised as "the greatest humanitarian work" of the time. But his unspoken goal was to turn the Congo into a huge rubber plantation. Mazrui describes some of the punishment Leopold had for workers "who did not deliver: unrelenting forced labour, mutilated limbs, villages razed to the ground because of the `offence' of a single individual. Populations were decimated."

A similar pattern prevailed elsewhere, starting earlier in the Western Hemisphere. Columbus, too, used amputation to control native labor, but that was only symbolic of the more basic change that he brought. As the Europeans spread out, the native peoples quickly learned who had the power and who had lost it. For example, when the Spanish arrived in Peru, the Incas were cultivating about eighty species of food crops, most unknown to the Europeans. One, the potato, was taken back to the Old World. But most were lost, along with the agricultural methods that successfully fed twelve million people of the Inca Empire, because the new rulers forced cultivation of wheat, barley, and other European crops instead.

When colonial domination finally declined, transnational conglomerates, operating through international markets, took control virtually as complete. Clearing of tropical forests is an exceptional illustration because its implications reach so far. Norman Myers, one of the world's leading experts on the subject, notes that these forests are essential to the climatic and ecological stability not only of their region but of the entire planet. Often this disastrous clearing doesn't hold even short-term benefits for local people. Throughout Central America, forests were cleared to raise beef for export. According to Myers, in Costa Rica "between 1960 and 1980, beef production almost quadrupled yet during that same period local consumption of beef actually declined by more than 40 percent." Guatemala, Honduras, and Nicaragua followed much the same course.

Perhaps nowhere have transnational corporations, working with a corrupt local power structure, done more damage than in Indonesia. Periodically over two decades, fires attributable to destructive logging in Borneo, Sumatra, Sulawesi, and Java have shrouded those regions in dense smoke, with winds carrying the choking smog to places like Malaysia and Singapore, hundreds of miles away. During months of burning in the most recent disaster, more than a thousand people died and more than twenty million suffered smoke-related respiratory problems. It is against this backdrop that most underdeveloped countries remain impoverished. High birth rates in these countries drive rapid growth in population, which further strains usually limited local resources. In some nations, poverty combines with and is sometimes aggravated by cultural factors to bring about new misery.

As a matter of simple justice, rich nations have an obligation to reverse the tragic course often followed in the past, as a means of preventing a more tragic future. Anyone still unconvinced should consider how the underdevelopment-population connection, in this era of rampant globalization, is affecting virtually everyone on the planet. The wanton destruction of forests- whether by transnationals for export materials or by local people for subsistence- is a major contributor to global warming, arguably the greatest threat to Earth's environment. Ravaging diseases like tuberculosis are at their worst in conditions of poverty and overcrowding, but in this time of high mobility, borders haven't blocked penetration into the wealthiest nations. And one consequence of the UN's estimate that about one-third of the world's labor force is unemployed or underemployed is that labor's power is weakened everywhere.

As the twentieth century drew to a close, decades of indifference to development created threats worldwide in scope. It would be an achievement of incomparable importance if at the beginning of the twenty-first century we finally overcame that indifference, converting global threats into global successes from the five million children working in Thailand's unregulated factories to girls working for less than 9 US cents per hour for multinationals in Bangladesh the popular image portrayed by developing country industrialisation is one reminiscent of early industrial Dickensian Britain.

Traditionally the finger of blame has been pointed at the nefarious activities of multinational capitalists seeking to maximise profits by exploiting third world workforces. Increasingly however it seems that governments in a number of these countries have been deliberately attracting such capital by offering up their own citizens as an exploitable resource. In a number of countries the absence of stringent labour and environmental legislation, the repression of trade union activities, and authoritarianism are all seen as enhancing international competitiveness. Perhaps nowhere are such images more evident than in the Export Processing Zones (EPZs) that have proliferated across the developing world.

While a whole host of different names are given to describe EPZs (maquiladoras, special economic zones etc.) an Export Processing Zone can be defined as: a relatively small, geographically spread area within a country, the purpose of which is to attract export-orientated industries, by offering them especially favourable investment and trade conditions as compared with the remainder of the host country. In particular, the EPZs provide for the importation of goods to be used in the production of exports on a duty free basis.

EPZs are therefore export enclaves within which special economic concessions apply including an extensive package of incentives and very often exemption from certain kinds of legislation which do apply outside the zones. Among the most common of such exceptions is that EPZs generally allow the duty free entry of goods for re-exports. Within the zone the physical infrastructure and all services necessary for manufacturing are provided: roads, power supplies, transport facilities, low-cost/ rent buildings.

In a number of cases restrictions on foreign ownership which apply in the country as a whole are waved for foreign firms locating in the zone. Furthermore the industry usually requires a relatively unskilled workforce with the goods produced relatively light to ensure a high added value. Consequently most EPZs concentrate on the production of textiles, clothing and electronics for the mass market. By 1995 there were in excess of 230 EPZs across 70 countries employing nearly 4.5 million workers. Add to these figures China's 'special economic zones' and the figure soars to 44 million. The overwhelming majority of these zones were located in the Caribbean (43 per cent) and East Asia (28 per cent). However, over 60 per cent of those employed in EPZs globally are concentrated in Asia, where the majority of such zones are located in Singapore and Hong Kong.

Almost invariably the linchpin of economic activity in EPZs is young single women. The simple reason for this is that for both foreign multinationals and local subcontractors women can be hired at wage levels below their male counterparts. For example, in Taiwan wages for female workers are actually fixed at 10-20 per cent below male wages in the EPZs. In addition to the wage discrimination, many managers of firms in EPZs argue that female workers are more docile and less unruly and possess greater manual dexterity ('nimble fingers') than their male counterparts. Their preference for single women is also considered to stem from the fact that such employees will often live either in the parental home or in dormitories and are therefore less likely to demand high wages.

For those women who live in factory dormitories, however, sexual harassment and squalid conditions are common. Despite this such harassment invariably goes unreported because any complaints automatically lead to the dismissal of the woman who has virtually no chance of having her case heard at a tribunal. Elsewhere management in EPZs have been accused of distributing contraceptive pills among workers to prevent pregnancy as well as forcing workers who are pregnant to have abortions. Although some legislative protection may exist for such workers, most are unaware that they have any rights. Indeed most women remain subservient for fear that they may be added to a 'blacklist' of troublesome employees that will often be circulated among firms operating in the EPZs.

Even when attempts to raise cases of harassment and expose poor conditions occur, labour movements in Asia are often confronted with draconian restrictions on activities. In South Korea, for example, between 1962 and 1979 the Hee regime systematically demobilised labour. Strikes and independent trade unions were outlawed; a state ideology that identified production objectives with the struggle against communism was promoted and a sophisticated internal security apparatus was created to monitor labour and repress it when and where necessary. This organisation, the KCIA, infiltrated factories with hundreds of agents, using intimidation and forces to get their candidates elected in union ballots and when necessary also resorted to mass imprisonment, torture and assassination. Although much has changed with democratisation in Korea, the recent stand-off between the government and trade unions, in which harassment and false imprisonment once again took place, vividly demonstrates that Korea still has a long way to go to meet internationally accepted labour standards.

Similar stories can be found in the so-called 'second-wave' of Newly Industrialising Economies. In Malaysia, for example, during the early phase of industrialisation there were no unions in the Free Trade Zones that were established in order to attract foreign investment. This proved to be 'a major plus factor that helped attract large American electronics firms to Malaysia'. Although unionisation has grown throughout the 1980s, the electronics industry to date remains by and large free from unionisation. Indeed while Japanese firms have allowed the creation of in-house unions broadly in line with the situation in mainland Japan, American firms have stubbornly resisted any worker representation, indeed 'nine managing directors of American component firms in the ... FTZs ... stressed that their presence in Malaysia would be seriously undermined if unions were allowed in their firms'.

It was in response to such restrictions that the American Federation of Labour and the Congress of Industrial Organisations (AFL-CIO) petitioned the US Trade Representative in 1988 to remove the preferential trade privileges that Malaysia enjoys under the Generalised System of Preferences. Across the developing world governments openly publicise the fact that export processing zones are very often anti-union zones in order to attract foreign capital. The magazine Business India, for example, referring to the Santa Cruz EPZ to the north of Bombay, stated, 'fortunately for the employers, most of the workers are not organised, a factor which according to the employers has helped them stay competitive at the international level'. Similarly on a trip to Tokyo the federal Finance Minister of Pakistan, Sartaj Aziz, assured a group of Japanese businessmen that 'the labour laws of Pakistan will not be applicable in the special industrial zones created by the government'.

However, labour is not only directly repressed by government action. Increasingly labour is being effectively indirectly repressed by the failure of governments to enforce social legislation. This lack of law enforcement may in some cases be the result of insufficient government funds to provide the necessary regulatory authorities, however in other cases it is nothing less than a conscious decision taken by central and/ or local authorities in order to provide additional incentives to capital. As The Organizer reports, 'In the Tijuana maquiladoras, it is standard procedure to assign difficult and dangerous work tasks to pregnant women so that they will quit before the companies are obligated to pay maternity benefits.'

In recent years there have been a number of well documented cases of fires that have gutted the dormitories of EPZ workers because the enforcement of health and safety regulations has been lacking. In 1993 alone, 2500 workers were burned to death in dormitory fires across China. (Indeed, despite the death of Deng Xiaoping, the architect of China's economic reform programme, such incidents are likely to continue given the regime's steadfast commitment to continuity in economic policy.) Similar evidence of official negligence/compliance can be found with respect to child labour. In Bangladesh for example, the myriad of regulations to improve the status of children is confusing and frustrated by a lack of enforcement, while in Nepal there are an estimated three million children working in agriculture, carpets, and garment and handicraft industries despite a minimum legal employment age of 14.

In addition to legislation and indifference, attempts to mobilise labour among the workers in the EPZs are often met with violence by security guards and/or paramilitary groups employed by the factory owners; protesters are regularly attacked by guards using batons and tear gas, while trade union activists are 'visited' personally in order to persuade them to halt unionisation. Such acts of persuasion have according to the ICFTU included abduction, torture and even in a number of cases in the Philippines and Guatemala, murder.

On the economic front although Export Processing Zones may have become the nucleus for export-led growth, and employment in these zones has increased, as a proportion of the total workforce their impact is still minimal. In Sri Lanka only 10 per cent of the industrial workforce can be found in such zones, falling to a paltry 1 per cent in the nation at large. In Malaysia they account for 8.5 per cent of manufacturing employment and 1.7 per cent of total employment. Nonetheless it is usually estimated that for every job created in an EPZ another job is created outside the zone, consequently EPZs can have an important multiplier effect in a local or regional context.

In contradistinction, EPZs have made an impressive impact in terms of their contribution to total manufactured exports. For example, Sri Lanka launched its economic liberalisation in 1978 after decades of protectionism. At the heart of this policy was the promotion of export-led industrialisation using EPZs as the means for attracting foreign investment. To this end the strategy has been successful. EPZs' share of manufactured goods rose from 8.8. per cent in 1980 to 44 per cent in 1991, while the zones have attracted considerable foreign capital: investment went up from 208 million rupees in 1978 to 3,016 million rupees in 1991. Similarly in Malaysia EPZs' share of exports rose from 1 per cent in 1972 to 57.5 per cent in 1990, while total foreign investment rose from $94 million to $4,073 million in 1991.

Nonetheless, despite the fact that in a number of cases local small and medium-sized firms have become engaged in sub-contracting activities with the multinationals, the linkages between EPZ firms and the domestic economy have remained for the most part weak. In Malaysia, apart from rubber products, the overwhelming proportion of raw material and capital goods for industries in the EPZs are imported, ranging from 96 per cent for scientific goods and 93.7 per cent for electrical/electronic goods to 62 per cent in the textile and garments industry. One of the main reasons for this lack of forward and/or backward linkage is because most EPZs allow for duty-free imports to firms located in the EPZs as an incentive for location.

As expected the vast majority of technology transferred to such states is mainly by wholly foreign-owned firms and joint venture multinationals. Most of this technology, particularly in the electronics industry, is bundled or packaged. This means that it is protected by a whole host of trademarks and patents. Where transfer does occur it is usually limited to contracts between foreign and local firms such as in the produce of designer garments under license (e.g. Nike shoes, Yves St Lauren shirts etc.). Indeed sub-contracting and 'name-borrowing' only complicates any assessment of the impact of EPZs since 'behind the supposedly local owned enterprises there are often enterprises from the North who have decided they don't want to get their hands dirty'. Without greater backward linkage and technology transfer there is a real danger that EPZs will remain isolated enclaves of economic activity. Without technology diffusing into the local economy foreign enterprises will find the gap in corporate cultures and skills to great for enhanced cooperation.

Few governments in the developing world today refuse to accept that in order to industrialise foreign capital is vital. However, although EPZs have been successful in attracting such capital, bringing with it employment and some degree of stimulus to the domestic economy, they have their price and one has to ask whether the super exploitation of workers within the zones might be a price too high.

Indeed the future of workers in EPZs across the developing world seems likely to deteriorate rather than improve as it is highly probable that EPZs will become victims of the very success that has precipitated their proliferation. Such an observation is based on three developments that highlight the most salient dangers facing developing countries embarking on an EPZ-led strategy of export oriented growth.

Firstly, international investors are fickle characters; the slightest change in policy or in the political situation of a developing country can lead to a massive flight of capital to relocate elsewhere. Examples of capital flight serve to illustrate this point: the enacting of the Industrial Co-ordination Act in Malaysia during 1974-5 saw foreign investment fall by nearly 62 per cent; in Sri Lanka a sharp drop in investment in 1983 is attributable to ethnic and civil unrest; or in more recent memory a massive flight of capital out of Mexico followed the Chiapas revolt and subsequent Peso Crisis. (Similarly, it can be argued that the fear of capital flight, as much as anything else, will deter the Post-Deng Leadership in China from abandoning the reform process.)

Secondly, with an ever increasing number of developing countries embarking on similar export orientated development programmes, exploiting their comparative advantage in labour, the battle for foreign investment becomes increasingly fierce. The danger therefore is that competitive outbidding between sites will take place, and that such a 'race to the bottom' will ensure that potential for recovering the capital costs of creating EPZs and the fiscal incentives of attracting FDI will be eroded. Finally, the above dangers are further exacerbated by the very international capital that the strategy seeks to attract. In taking advantage of the increased mobility of multinational corporations these very states are vulnerable to this mobility.

Not only are multinationals able to use the threat of relocation to wrestle further concessions out of host governments, but because of the proliferation of EPZs among developing countries multinationals are increasingly able to bargain and counter-bargain between prospective hosts. Indeed interviews conducted with civil servants in Malaysia and Thailand during 1996 confirmed that both the threat 'from below' (i.e. from regimes providing less regulatory environments and/or more generous fiscal incentives) and from multinational (counter) bargaining already exist. For example, in the case of Thailand the textile industry is particularly concerned by the challenge presented by the Doi Moi reforms in Vietnam - which by opening the Vietnamese economy to the world market provide a labour force that can undercut Thailand's.

In the final analysis the proliferation of EPZs appears only to facilitate the nefarious activities of the worst type of capitalists. Challenging such practices requires concerted action to force multinationals to abandon such policies or pressure their sub-contractors to act more ethically. Although ultimately campaigns for better working conditions in the EPZs depend upon the success of local social movements, because EPZs are a global phenomenon there must be action at the global level. Activism in the Dominican Republic between local groups and union organisations such as the American Institute for Free Labour Development (AIFLD), the International Ladies Garment Workers' Union (ILGWU) and the International Textile Workers' Federation, succeeded in 1994 in pressuring the client companies of a particularly pernicious factory to suspend their orders if abuses continued. To exert further pressure on the government of the Dominican Republic, the AFL-CIO petitioned the US Congress to remove the country from the GSP.

The result was a victory for the labour movement with the government eventually recognising the right of workers to unionise. Detractors of such action respond by arguing that the campaign for universal social standards represents nothing more than a new form of protectionism against developing country exports. Such claims fail to recognise the role of local social movements, exaggerate and conflate the objectives of organisations such as the International Labour Organisation (ILO) and the ICFTU, and serve as an apology for authoritarian and exclusionary political regimes.

Sheila Rowbotham is an active British socialist feminist as well as a political-historical writer. Growing up intellectually and politically in the Marxist tradition as shaped by Edward and Dorothy Thompson, growing and changing in struggles lost and won, Rowbotham continues to base her analyses in history. Her personal history and memory contribute significant details to the political analyses she offers, especially of grassroots movements.

Rowbotham lives the life of a politically committed activist and an historical reporter, while a single mother actively engaged in her community. She has written fifteen books, innumerable articles, introductions, essays, poems, films, record jackets, reports, reviews, and interviews. Her first book, Women, Resistance and Revolution: A History of Women and Revolution in the Modern World (New York: Pantheon), created a major stir when first published in 1972. Her writing is a product of her own experience as a teacher of apprentices in continuing education (where she has taught hairdressers and typists), her efforts to organize night cleaners, of marching with coal miners and their wives, and of years of active engagement in the Trotskyist movement and in the world of left publications.

In the later 1970s and the early 1980s she helped organize a movement inspired by her pamphlet Beyond the Fragments: Feminism and the Making of Socialism (Islington Community Press), published in 1979. Later it was published in book form in both America and Britain. The pamphlet acted as a springboard and inspired a small social movement that brought together people in traditional workers' organizations, the Leninist left, local community initiatives, women, gays, blacks, and youth. Beyond the Fragments groups appeared throughout England in the early eighties. These were not only political forums, but also social networks, part of people's everyday life and leisure, connected to looking after children, having fun, being active on the job and in the community.

Sheila carried the politics of the Beyond the Fragments groups into the government itself. In 1982 she went to work for the Greater London Council (GLC), the then popularly elected governing body of the city of London in which the Labour left had a majority. It sought to mobilize people usually excluded by the formal political process, and to organize them in informal ways combining participatory democracy and representative government. She also edited Jobs for Change, a widely distributed photo magazine about economic policy and projects. Margaret Thatcher abolished the GLC in 1986, a sort of tribute to the success of its programs. After working for the GLC, Sheila has returned to supporting herself and her son by her writing.

This has not been easy in the depressed political atmosphere of the late eighties and early nineties. She has never retreated into academia or become cynical about the power of working people. She lives both her scholarship and active left feminist politics, which has made her a true public intellectual. Movements develop in the process of communicating themselves.... We have not even words for ourselves. Thinking is difficult when the words are not your own. Borrowed concepts are like passed down clothes; they fit badly and do not give confidence.... We walk and talk and think in living contradiction.

Sheila Rowbotham wrote these lines in the context of feminists using male-centered language and concepts. But these lines also useful to explain my dilemma as a "Third World" woman using the English language, as well as using Western feminist concepts and categories. This dilemma started back in India, where the English language has long been a status symbol as well as a vehicle for social mobility. The position of the English language within India as well as in the world today is a tacit mark of the continuing vigor of Western imperialism.

These notions have been put to dubious use, as has the slogan of "multiculturalism."

The notion of multiculturalism was interpreted as promotion of "differences" and separation among various ethnic and national groups within the United States as well as in the world at large. Such interpretation of the concept of "multiculturalism" came at a time when the Cold War was ending and large areas previously beyond the direct reach of the multinational companies (particularly the former "Eastern Bloc," but also India and to some degree China as well) were being ripped open for exploitation under the banner of "liberalization." The promotion of segregation of identifies among various ethnic and national groups within these states led inevitably to political conflicts and to the weakening of potential resistance to imperialism. Such ethnic and nationality group conflicts in turn further ensured global domination by the First World in the name of "maintaining the peace" in the post-Cold War era.

It is in this historical context (and while reading Sheila Rowbotham) that I found myself thinking of building bridges among women, rather than promoting the idea of "differences" according to the prevailing fashion of academic and political discourse. But I am also aware that I shall be misunderstood if I claim to agree with Sheila without examining the relevance of the fact that she is a white British feminist and I am an Indian (problematic concept) "colored" woman. This threshold dilemma arises because postmodernism in the academy does not allow me any other voice except standing against the West as "different."

Indeed, it is generally found very difficult to communicate with Western feminists (with a few exceptions of course) because when not feeling guilty for not "understanding" me, their predominant mode has been that of condescension. These experiences made aware that to remain comfortably "different" and alien in U.S. society or find support from the Indian community (which has its own oppressive mechanism to control their women) for the rest of my life and cannot accept this imposed reality because to constantly define myself in opposition to the constructs of "otherness" thrust on me, then that would be the surest way to "othering" myself. The moment one allows oneself to be subsumed within categories of "otherness" one automatically empowers what one is set against. What I seek instead is the creation of voices of dissent, of multiple points of attack and defense, sharply individuated yet linked.

Any theory, if it is to be of some practical use in the material world, must be capable not only of explaining material reality but also of providing a tool to act upon that reality. All of us know that today no country is formally a colony, but this does not mean that we are living in a post-colonial era. It only means that relations between First and Third World now take a more concealed form. We are well aware of the debt-dependency of Third World economies, of the no longer subtle means of control exercised by the World Bank and the IMF. It is in this wider context that the link between the micro-politics of the academy and the macro-politics of imperialism exists.

Therefore, it becomes imperative that scholars both from First and Third Worlds should be aware of the ways in which their investigative and interpretive studies promote or serve the designs of imperialism. As scholars our concern should be to find the lived truth of specific human relationships in specific historical circumstances and not the theories of inevitable incomprehension, of convenient relativism, that now flourish in the Anglo-Saxon academy. Therefore, in order to understand the issue of "differences" as promoted in the United States, and searching for ways to live with respect, independence, and human dignity, I started asking the following question of myself: Why should I always see myself as "different" in U.S. society when I have become a typical part of the historical process of this country?

Moreover, my arrival in the United States is not simply a personal decision on my part but also a product of a complex historical process of capitalism, colonialism, and imperialism in which the histories of Britain, the United States, and India are intertwined. With this understanding of the historical process of the world capitalist system I do not see myself as "different" from Western women.

Today, all of us (Third and First Worlds alike) experience the pressure of unrestrained global capitalism. In this perspective and context it seems illogical and unrealistic to interpret and analyze the experiences of people and societies as only a process of internal (therefore, different) conditions. Instead, we should try to understand the contemporary hegemonic powers and forces, their ideological and other mechanisms of control, and explore how they interact with different societies and how they shape peoples' views and consciousness. International feminist scholarship has begun the task of understanding the connections between First and Third World economies and their effect on the lives of women in all countries. This work is essential if links are to be forged between women's political struggles all over the world. The idea of creating bridges has caught up many women in the world in recent years, and Sheila's writings have been a contribution to that healthy trend.

The massive migration of ex-colonial populations to the industrial cities of Europe and the United States (due to the demand for cheap labor) has created new kinds of multiethnic and multiracial social formations. Keeping these new realities of the contemporary world in mind Sheila explains in her recent book *Homeworkers Worldwide* the growth "of a Third World within the First." She also highlights an important fact that "several organizing initiatives among Third World women workers outside the conventional situation of highly organized western trade unionists have challenged the fatalism which assumed that poor women were not organizable."

She correctly saw the home workers phenomenon in Britain and in India as a product of a global process of capitalist relations and not a problem of women of the "Third World" separately. Soon the home workers themselves began to make global links. This process raises the hope of a new kind of labor movement which is a contribution to a new kind of internationalism. Moreover, these women home workers are not just Chinese, Indian, Pakistani, Filipina but also include white women. "Home working groups in Britain and Holland now are lobbying the EEC to recognize home workers' conditions and make legislation in the different European countries more similar." These new types of associations have shown the capacity to cross over the boundaries of production and reproduction, of labor and community, of the economic and social. The account in this book urges women of the West to learn from the experiences of Third World poor women who are resisting the exploitation of the multinational corporations. She notes that home workers organizations have had an important international role in Europe and Canada as well as in the Third World, where organization of casual workers is emerging in countries like the Philippines. "Synthesizing old and new forms of organizing will be the work of the future - that future whose outline we can as yet barely discern."

While pointing both at the international links between women's movements and the interaction of ideas, Sheila Rowbotham also brings to our attention that the development of ideas itself is an integral part of the movements. One cannot develop without the other. The relationship between collective action and women's emancipation is of special significance because a lone voice claiming liberation is no threat. Sheila is aware that none of us can know exactly how new struggles will emerge, what interpretations will be given to women's movements, or what ultimate form they will take. Women join collective actions for different reasons at different times and places.

Many women have participated in social protest action due to historical reasons particular to their own situation, and not simply in response to ideas taken from the outside. In this process of struggle each group of women developed their own strategies, and their own interpretations of the questions of equality. Moreover, all women do not use the demand of equality in the same way. In many cases "women demand peace sometimes as 'mothers,' sometimes as 'human beings.'" The process of liberation is obscured when mothers can be at once revered and marginalized as happened in the mobilization of women in nationalist and sometimes in socialist movements.

These various factors that color women's actions and the nature of their demands is a reason why many women's movements not revolutionary as normally understood. It is a continuous and central insight of the work of Sheila Rowbotham that even when these womens' movements are not revolutionary, the demands they make require such a fundamental change in society that they are completely inconceivable without revolution. Sheila Rowbotham's work emphasizes the relationship between the making of feminist theory and women's life experiences, because theories evolve in the process of interaction between these two.

It means there cannot be one theory only or any universal model for women's movements to follow. "Thought of a social movement is not packaged neatly between two covers.... Anyone who has been an active participant in politics knows people do not sit solemnly reading a book and then march off to make strategies and programmes." Earlier, Sheila wrote on this issue that every new movement assumes a different shape and in the process women's movements all over the world look as if "thousands and thousands of women were busy making a gigantic garment in which they all borrow themes from one another but create their own patterns." These specific "patterns" in women's movements emerge due to the specific social, cultural, political and economic conditions of the countries where these women live in a particular historical time.

For example, modern inventions in information technology have been used to create a large pool of women workers in the developing countries. This is a phenomenon that cannot be understood at a journalistic glance, but requires study. Each region is incorporated in the global economic network as a specific component of the international division of labor. Sheila Rowbotham and the Indian scholar Swasti Mitter have explored this phenomenon in the recent anthology they edited, Women Encounter Technology: Changing Patterns of Employment in the Third World.

In raising the issue of the impact of technology the editors are able to challenge the existing definition of the term "Third World" as including only the underdeveloped nations. These studies include as subjects non-affluent communities and nations and immigrant groups residing in technologically and economically developed nations as well, while continuing to use the term "Third World." This strategy allows the possibility of an alternative perspective that links the struggles of poor people from different regions of the world, in the context of the links that integrate their regions in global capitalism. Various accounts in this volume show that a consequence of urban employment in the new technology is to give women social power and control (albeit contested) over their fertility.

This is an instance where the contest itself is proof of a progressive change. Most of all, women all over the world are able to become aware of their connection with one another by means of the same information technology. The editors urge that women need to use this awareness of their connection with other women in the world to share experiences and to collect data about common problems and issues. For instance, very little is known about the effects of new technologies on the health of women workers. Most of the concerned governments give priority to the question of creating jobs and economic growth, but little or no attention to the issue of the health hazards in the new work environment.

Postmodernist discourse has tended to be an obstacle to taking up the research that might best serve to promote internationalism in matters of women's economic empowerment. The editors write that "in our current intellectual climate, women of the Third World have become the subject of research in connection with the 'other.' It is the 'differences' rather than the issues of economic liberation that has assumed a central position in academic analysis." Postmodernist discourse of "Eurocentric bias" has had the odd result of discouraging the interest of women academics in the developing world in research that deals with the life and work of women with different heritages than their own.

The work in this collection explains that this trend coincided with the ascendant ideologies of the 1980s which fetishize the market mechanism and glorify self help and individual entrepreneurship. In such an atmosphere people will readily shun collective responsibility for vulnerable or marginal groups even within the boundaries of their own nation, let alone beyond the boundaries (cultural or political) of their own community. The problem is compounded by those Ecofeminists who consider research on new technology and its impact on women to be irrelevant and unproductive.

According to such Ecofeminists, technology itself incorporates and reproduces values harmful to the poor people of the world. With logical consistency but little sense, they promote the goal of the subsistence economy. This entire volume argues that appeals for subsistence economy are a diversion from the central question of how to alter the material conditions that determine relations of power both nationally and internationally. The editors argue persuasively that both postmodernist and Ecofeminist approaches lead to the erosion of any belief in the power of collective action, of course without in any way diminishing the rate of feminist publications. One can find "shelves and shelves of poetry and fiction, books about sexuality, about race, about health, about housing, about violence, about psychology."

But the very few books that attempt to put these concerns in the context of women's changing economic relation with technology are "heavily outnumber[ed] by 'how to' books about computing " It seems that feminist attention has shifted away from the previously central concern of women's economic place in the system and of women's work, both paid and unpaid. This change in the focus of feminist academic attention is linked to a radical shift of emphasis from the collective to the individual. Rowbotham and Mitter point out that the "language of 'difference,' and anti-modernity ironically gives the politics of exclusiveness and Eurocentrism a new lease of life." The feminist critique of the Enlightenment devalues the different needs of women of non-European origins which are best expressed in precisely those same despised universal Enlightenment values of equality, reason, and autonomy.

Sheila Rowbotham has taken pains to remind us that "women studies after all had its origin not only in the desire to extend what was studied but to transform the power relationship in how knowledge was constructed and communicated." To this end our attention must focus on the question of organization for collective action. Rowbotham and Mitter have developed their ideas on the process of organization and collective action in a second recent collection entitled Dignity and Daily Bread: New Forms of Economic Organizing Among Poor Women in the Third World and the First.

This book is a valuable effort to open as an area of inquiry the new kinds of organizing emerging among poor women around questions directly concerned with the process of production. But the actions and consciousness of poor women workers of the Third World, generally unable to use traditional methods of labor organizing in the teeth of fiercely repressive local regimes, cannot satisfactorily be explained under narrow and constricted definitions of class consciousness and resistance.

These workers are creating novel democratic organizing processes in the most varied contexts in the poor countries, with consequences in the Western countries as well. The accounts in the book reveal the true interconnection of class with gender and race by insisting on the basic Marxist notion of situating work and class centrally within social existence as a whole, while also subverting the assumption that new cultural forms and their theorizing originate only in the North. Again by including studies spanning both Third and First Worlds, the editors are able to challenge the prevailing separation between studies focused on "women and development" issues in the Third World and work done on the economic and social circumstances of class, gender, race, and ethnicity in the First World.

This division of scholarly inquiry obscures the importance of multinational capital, which does not fail to exercise influence over "women's studies" in line with its influence in society more generally. We are then diverted from the task of finding patterns in the multiple forms of global events affecting women. Our problem is that these patterns are complex, variable, and far from readily predictable in their development. Instead of giving up efforts to find commonalities amongst working women, our aim must be to understand these complex patterns by starting with inquiry into what is happening.

This is the only way we can assess the odds which are stacked against poor working women. For example, one can find patterns in the history of nineteenth century textile mill women workers in Britain and the United States, and in late nineteenth and early twentieth century Japan, which are parallel with conditions within the modern Free Trade Zone (FTZ) found in the Third World. For instance, the employers in all these cases sought influence over the attitudes of the new mostly female work force through providing accommodation. The historical study of these lodging houses showed interesting unintended effects when women by sharing living space with other women also able to share their experiences at the workplace as well, and derive strength from one another, which frequently, developed into militant consciousness.

The study of women's current parallel experience in the FTZs is the type of task that Rowbotham and Mitter rightly demand is taken up by the feminist scholarship of today. "Big Pharma did not invent these lifesaving drugs that they have patented and arbitrarily overpriced. Anti-retrovirals were for the most pars discovered by publicly-funded US research projects into other diseases, and only later entrusted to pharmaceutical companies for marketing and exploitation." In a recent major series that ran over four days titled "Dying For Drugs", the British daily, The Guardian, exposed how the West's pharmaceutical giants are capitalising on "intellectual property agreements" and "making too much money for the West". They are even selling the new anti-retroviral Aids drugs at a higher price in Africa than in the West. New African asked Osei Boateng to summarise The Guardian's series for our readers who may not have seen it.

John le Carre, the famous novelist, was one of the giants wheeled our by The Guardian to write in support of the campaign to expose the excessive profits being made by what Le Carre calls "Big Pharma" at the expense of Africa and the developing world. Le Carre's new book, The Constant Gardener, portrays Big Pharma as an industry devoid of morality. And the charge was proved beyond reasonable doubt by The Guardian in the four days that the series lasted. Yet Oxfam accused GSK and the other drug giants of abuse of patents. It said they were "systematically using parent rules to squeeze low-cost copies of branded medicines off the market."

In fact, the origins of the campaign should be credited to Oxfam, the British NGO, which is now fed up to the teeth with the immorality of Big Pharma. Oxfam singled out the British multinational, Glaxo SmithKline, the world's leader in pharmaceuticals (with annual sales of $22.8bn, Research and Development costs of $3.75bn, and profits of $7.6bn) for censure. Oxfam (based in Oxford, England), interestingly, has part of its pension funds invested in Glaxo SmithKline (GSK). A recent successful attempt by Big Pharma to block the importation of inexpensive copies of the Aids drugs by Ghana and Uganda from an Indian company, Cipla, and the decision by 39 drug companies to sue South Africa in an attempt to stop it from acquiring the generic drugs cheaply, were cited by Oxfam as the last straw that broke its back.

The Guardian appeared to have benefited immensely from Oxfam's research, and justifiably went for Big Pharma's throat in a big way. John Le Carre was one of the casts for the opening day of The Guardian's series. He wrote:

"I had not been exploring Big Pharma for more than a couple of days before I was hearing of the frantic recruitment of Third World 'volunteers as cheap guinea pigs. "Their role, though they may not ever know this, is to test drugs, not yet approved for testing in the US, which they themselves will never be able to afford even if the tests turn out reasonably safe. And then to disappear. "In the US, it costs on average $10,000 per patient to conduct a clinical trial, in Russia $3,000, and in the poorest parts of the world, still less. "I learned also of how Big Pharma in the US had persuaded the State Department to threaten poor countries with trade sanctions to prevent them making their own cheap forms of the patented lifesaving drugs that could ease the agony of 35 million men, women and children in the Third World who are HIV-positive..."

The big question that immediately arises here is: Why does the State Department, an important organ of an American government which is supposedly at the forefront of the fight against Aids, and whose immediate past vice president, Al Gore, chaired last year's big United Nations meeting in New York that declared Aids a "national security" issue, allow itself to be used in this way by Big Pharma? Is the American "concern" about Aids all a gimmick? Le Carre's next paragraph was even more disturbing: "Big Pharma did not invent these lifesaving drugs that they have patented and arbitrarily overpriced," he wrote. "Anti-retrovirals were for the most part discovered by publicly-funded US research projects into other diseases, and only later entrusted to pharmaceutical companies for marketing and exploitation."

The question that logically flows from this paragraph is: Why did the American government do that? For an answer, we have to continue reading Le Carre. "Once the pharmals had the patent," he explained, "they charged whatever they thought an Aids-desperate Western marker would stand: $12,000 to $15,000 a year for compounds that cost a few hundred to run up... Nobody said it was a massive confidence trick. Nobody remarked that, while Africa has 80% of the world's Aids patients, it comprises 1% of Big Pharma's market." Some of the HIV-Aids drugs are 20% more expensive in Africa than in the West.

On the second day of The Guardian's series, the paper's correspondent in Washington, Julian Borger, expanded on John le Carre's revelations. Borger wrote: "In fact, much of the R&D [research and development] work on new drugs is government-funded. A study by the Boston Globe newspaper in 1998, found the [US government's] National Institutes of Health (NIH) laboratories spent $1bn on drug and vaccine development in the 1996 tax year [alone], but only took in $27m in royalties. "In September 1999, it was pointed out to the director of the NIH, Harold Varmus, that six HIV/Aids drugs, as well as anti-malarial treatments and other medicines of vital interest to the developing countries, had been invented with [US] public funds. The [US] government, therefore, had the right under US law to use the drugs in public health initiatives.

"James Love, who runs a Washington-based group, called the Consumer Project on Technology, sees the responses [by Big Pharma that it has to charge more to offset R&D costs] as nonsensical because it was the NIH which did the hard work of discovering and synthesising the drugs in question."The rest of the world will have to go many years more of paying an astronomical sum for something invented by the United States government. How can we expect Glaxo to share its intellectual property if the US government won't share its intellectual property to save millions of people? What does that say about the moral character of the American public? We are responsible."

This should come as a shock to the peoples of the world. Why did the American government hand the Aids drugs over to Big Pharma after discovering and synthesising them? Was Washington afraid that critics and so-called "conspiracy theorists" would link the invention of the drugs to the still unsubstantiated claim that HIV was invented as part of the US government's germ warfare programme - a kind of "they invented the virus in the first place and so know how to fight it?" On paper, America appears so concerned about fighting Aids. So why didn't Washington just donate the patents of the drugs to the world, so that any country able to manufacture them locally could do so cheaply? Wouldn't that have gone to enhance even more America's "leadership" of the world?

Madeleine Bunting, one of the casts on the first day of The Guardian campaign, tried to explain the American ambivalence. She wrote:

"The impetus for an international system of intellectual property protection was the rise of the knowledge economy.

Countries such as the US wanted to maximise their returns on knowledge through licences on their patents across the globe.

"Seventy per cent of US export earnings are now linked to intellectual property - on everything from Aids drugs to brands such as Disney, McDonald's and Microsoft. "The US needed an international regulatory regime to reap the benefits of its economic and cultural hegemony, and it is working: Between 1991 and 1997, the value of royalties to the US doubled to more than $33bn a year... "It becomes harder and harder for developing countries to catch up. They can't copy - they have to import the technology and pay royalties on the licences. The flow of revenue is one way, from poor to rich."

And the vehicle facilitating the flow "from poor to rich" is the World Trade Organisation (WTO). Larry Elliott, another member of The Guardian cast shows how. He wrote:

"The financial muscle of the pharmaceutical companies also gives them enormous political leverage. So, during the Uruguay Round of trade talks, they lobbied hard for tougher rules protecting intellectual property, which provided patent protection for a minimum of 20 years for 'new and inventive' products.

"Where previously around 50 developing countries and several developed countries had excluded medicines from being patented, the Trade Related Intellectual Property Rights (Trips) deal made both pharmaceuticals and biotechnology part of the global regime."Infringements of the Trips agreement are heard by a WTO disputes panel, and unlike a criminal trial, the burden of proof is put on the defendant country. "In itself, the Trips - a protectionist clause in what was supposed to be a free trade agreement, roused suspicions about the way in which the rules were being skewed to suit powerful interest groups in rich countries. [However], countries could cite a national emergency as a reason to infringe the Trips agreement.

"Effectively, this provided two loopholes. Countries could either manufacture cheap drugs themselves, using what are known as compulsory licences to override patents, which is what Brazil is trying to do, or they could import a patented drug from wherever it was sold cheapest, the method favoured by

South Africa. "All quite simple, you might think. If the HIV/ Aids pandemic does not constitute an emergency, it is hard to know... [But] what is happening now is that the US is using every available means to close the WTO loopholes... "For example, the US offers a special deal to the Dominican Republic for exports of textiles. It is now threatening to withdraw this privilege unless the country scraps plans for compulsory licensing and parallel importing [of drugs]. Brazil and India have been warned that they could face sanctions under America's bilateral 'Super 301' legislation."

In effect, as Larry Elliot says, "the dirty work for the drug companies is being done by the US government, although there is little doubt who is really behind it all." Big Pharma runs the show Julian Borger took up the story from Washington. He wrote on the second day of The Guardian's campaign:

"There was a time not long ago when the corporate giants that PhRMA represents were merely the size of nations. [PhRMA is the Pharmaceutical Association of America]. Now, after a frenzied two-year period of pharmaceutical mega-mergers, they are behemoths that outweigh entire continents.

"Until recently, the industry hedged its political bets, backing the Democrats and Republicans more or less evenly at election time. But at the [recent] election [won controversially by George Bush The Son], PhRMA gambled. With billions at stake in a heated debate over prescription drug prices at home and a growing number of patent disputes abroad, the drug makers stacked their chips disproportionately behind George Bush. The industry spent nearly 70% of its unprecedented $24.4m campaign war chest on the Republicans." Borger went on to show that the industry played a significant role in the drafting of the WTO's Trips. PhRMA has also made it a priority to ensure that the US government enforced the Trips rules in a manner beneficial to its neighbours.

"In 1998, for example, it was revealed that A1 Gore had bullied the South African government with threats of sanctions if it bought cheaper generic alternatives to brand-name Aids drugs, even though South Africa had the right to do so under

Trips," Borger wrote. He quoted the Democratic congresswoman, Sherwood Brown, as saying in a recent memo to her staff: "PhRMA doesn't need to lobby. The industry is in the White House already." The worrying aspect of the US government-Big Pharma relationship was unwittingly laid bare in a letter by one Dick Bentley of Southampton (England) who wrote to The Guardian on the second day of the campaign, defending the drug companies. Bentley said matter-of-factly:

"Drug companies are lust that - companies formed to invent and market medicines. Their boundaries are defined by commercial law; they exist to make profits for their shareholders, not to save the world."

It may well be so, but why then, in that case, do the drug companies use people from the developing world as guinea pigs (and not their shareholders) in the testing of the drugs? On the third day of The Guardian campaign, Julian Borger, again, showed how one of the drug giants "tested 590 patients in 1994 across Africa, the Middle East and Central & Eastern Europe. This year [2001] the company expects to run tests in those regions on 7,309 patients.

"There are fears that this mushrooming of Third World trials is leading to a loosening of the tight regulations that exist in the West. Recent US-government funded studies in Africa designed to show the effectiveness of the anti-Aids drug, AZT, in preventing the transmission of HIV from mother to infant during pregnancy, included a placebo group - a practice that would have been unacceptable in the US or Europe."

The Guardian's expose forced Jean-Pierre Garnier, chief executive of Glaxo SmithKline, to rise in defence of his company and its competitors. He wrote to The Guardian on the third day of the campaign, explaining that "patent protection fundamentally underpins the continued research and development for new and better medicines... Undermining intellectual property rights could have serious implications for the flow of new treatments and vaccines." He said GSK had been "offering preferential prices for HIV/Aids medicines in Africa since 1997 and last year increased the price reduction offers as part of the UN-led 'accelerating access initiative'.

"Our prices in Africa are at a level with, if not better than, those offered by generic manufacturers... Senegal, Uganda and Rwanda are already obtaining anti-retroviral treatments from us under the initiative at very substantially discounted prices, and others will follow." Tactically, Garnier refused to add that only 130 of an estimated 80,000 HIV-positive people in Senegal have access to GSK's "price reduction offers". If GSK scores 130 marks out of 80,000 in an exam, Garnier, for sure, will not be proud of it. In effect, the "UN-led accelerating access initiative" is not something to write home about.

As The Guardian's Malcolm Dean showed in his piece published on the same day as Garnier's article, while the drug companies "exaggerate" their R&D costs, they "underplay the role that public institutions such as the [US] National Institutes of Health (NIH) have made in drug breakthroughs."Two of the key drugs in the triple therapy for Aids were invented by the NIH, and several other [drugs] relied on NIH clinical trials."

Another worrying aspect of the drugs saga is the money paid to doctors by drug companies to act as salesmen for their products. Sarah Boseley, health editor of The Guardian, wrote on the last day of the campaign that throughout the Western world, doctors are paid handsome fees by drug companies to speak at conferences and in their daily encounters with patients, to put in a good word for the products of the drug companies that pay them the fees. Boseley cited one incident in Britain where a new drug for the treatment of heart failure was tried in a London hospital and elsewhere by doctors paid by the drug manufacturer. During the trial, "some patients suffered gastrointestinal disturbances, liver failure and problems with their immune system.

"The company asked us not to publish our adverse findings," one of the doctors in the trial told Boseley. "Then when we said we had to publish, they threatened us with legal action. When you are threatened by a multinational with infinite amounts of money, some people might find that a good reason not to go ahead." Boseley says the doctor's "team published. Others with similar results did not, after senior cardiologists told them their findings were out of line with everyone else's. The drug was withdrawn [in Britain] on safety grounds in 1984, but was sold over the counter in the Philippines and Africa until 1986."

Boseley quoted from the latest declaration of interests by doctors to the British government's advisory body responsible for drug safety, the Committee on the Safety of Drugs, which shows that 15 of the 36 doctors who so declared their interests had "either shareholdings, fees or paid consultancies from drug companies".

Not to save the world? The Guardian rounded off its remarkable campaign with a leader comment on 15 February headlined, "Millions of lives at risk - Drug companies must temper their power". Among other things, the paper said: "Equally disturbing is the way the US government blatantly disregards Trips when it chooses. There are now 16 countries being threatened by the notorious "301" legislative clause under which the US can impose trade sanctions without going through the WTO. All the disputes involve drug patenting.

"The reason for this aggression on the part of the US government is not difficult to discern. The pharmaceutical industry, as we reported earlier this week, is a powerful operator within the Washington establishment. In just two years, members of the US pharmaceutical association spent a staggering $236m on lobbyists and a further $14m went to political parties. This is likely to get still worse under a Bush administration, which includes several members with dose links to the drug companies... "Jean Pierre Garnier, the president of Glaxo SmithKline, pointed out yesterday, that drug companies cannot solve the problem of global poverty. True. But what he can certainly do is to pull out of the lawsuit against South Africa."

Glaxo SmithKline has since announced that it would make "price reduction" a priority. Under intense pressure from its institutional investors after The Guardian and Oxfam's campaign, the company promised on 21 February "to present a new policy framework outlining its stance on affordable medicines by the end of June." Oxfam said: "It's a welcome step in the right direction. It's a very public recognition by a world drugs leader that prices are a key issue to millions of sick people." The Guardian quoted Jean-Pierre Garnier as saying on 21 February: "Glaxo SmithKline is a new company. I have made it a priority from day one to urgently review what more we can do to significantly help in [the Aids] epidemic."

Glaxo sells four of the 10 Aids drugs currently in use. On the same day as Garnier promised to "review what more" the company could do, Glaxo revealed annual profits of [pounds sterling]5.32bn - "equivalent to more than [pounds sterling]14m a day", said The Guardian. "Glaxo's sales of Aids drugs rose 14% to [pounds sterling] 1.15bn, although this included only [pounds sterling] 114m from countries outside Europe and the US."

The Guardian's Letters Page had the last word. Phil Bloomer, Oxfam's head of advocacy wrote on 15 February: "According to Jean-Pierre Garnier, patents do not have the effect of increasing prices. In which case, why until recently, was his company selling the anti-Aids drug Combivir in developing countries at twice the price of a generic equivalent? Anne Alexander, writing from Liverpool, provided the coup de grace: "Let's get a few things straight. The pharmaceutical companies did not fund the initial trials into anti-HIV drugs. It was left to cash-starved public health laboratories and radical campaigners to wring research grants from the US Food and Drugs Administration, which was afraid to release funds to study a 'gay disease'.

"It is largely thanks to a courageous and determined campaign by early Aids activists that anti-HIV drugs are available in the US and Europe at all. The drug companies were prepared to write off the lives of thousands of people infected with HIV in the 1980s because they were either gay or injecting drug users. We must not allow them to do the same in 2001 because this time those who are ill are too poor to be profitable."

It gives me great pleasure to return to my alma mater, the Institute of Development Studies at the University of Sussex, an institution from which I graduated in 1970. My studies at the Institute of Development Studies, and subsequent interactions in the course of my work with faculty members and other alumni, have contributed to my professional growth as a development practitioner. For the benefit of those who may not be familiar with my country, Botswana is a landlocked, semiarid country of some 582,000 sq km in size, which is about the size of Kenya or France or Texas, and hosts a population of just fewer than two million people. It shares borders with Zimbabwe, South Africa, Namibia and Zambia.

The country attained self-governance in 1965 and independence in September 1966 after 80 years as a British protectorate. In 1966, the total population was estimated at just fewer than 600,000. From independence, Botswana has been a non-racial multi-party democracy operating within the framework of a democratic constitution, which enshrines freedom of speech, of association, and of worship, and affords all citizens equal rights. At the time of independence, Botswana was one of the least developed and poorest nations in the world, with a per capita income estimated at between US$70 and $90. The majority of the population was dependent on subsistence agriculture with beef production as the mainstay of the economy, amidst a series of recurring prolonged droughts.

There were 29,000 people in salaried employment and 30,500 migrant workers, of which 18,000 were employed in South African mines. Remittances of migrant labour were about 17% of total exports. The literacy rate was low and access to health, sanitation, water, telephone, electricity, public transportation and other services was negligible. There was virtually no infrastructure, apart from Cecil Rhodes' railway line completed in 1897.

There was less than 10km of tarmac road in the entire country. Availability of skilled and professional personnel was no better, with the country having less than 50 university graduates. The institutional machinery to run the operations of government was weak. Almost everything had to be started from scratch. Prospects for rapid development were bleak given the fact that for all its capital budget and even a major portion of the recurrent budget, Botswana depended on British foreign aid. This posed a major developmental challenge for the newly independent nation. At the time there was a lot of scepticism on the wisdom of this territory seeking self-government and independence.

In Botswana, everyone is free to air their opinions, no matter how different, something deeply embedded in our cultural heritage. Post-independence leaders built on this heritage. Botswana prides herself in that to this day, the country has never had a single interruption to democratic rule or a political prisoner! The opposition conducts its business freely and without hindrance. Typical of opposition parties, they are kept out of power increasingly by their own fragmentation.

Botswana has had nine multi-party elections since 1965 and the Botswana Democratic Party, the party that I lead, has been returned to power on all occasions. Although independent election observers have always pronounced the elections free and fair, some critics consider uninterrupted rule by one party as detracting from a true democracy. I must say, I am quite happy that my party has earned the enduring trust of the electorate to be returned to power with comfortable majorities, at each general election. But even then, we have not been complacent. Indeed, the very existence of the opposition has kept the government on its toes.

Over time, we have introduced changes to our constitution to solidify and adapt our multi-party democracy to suit changing circumstances. Some of the changes include a two-term (10 years) presidential term limit, extending the franchise to 18-year-olds and removing discrimination against women, establishing an Independent Electoral Commission. Botswana's stable democratic process has been further evidenced by the peaceful and smooth transition of power between the first president, Sir Seretse Khama, and his successor Sir Ketumile Masire in 1980 following the death of Sir Seretse Khama.

Between independence in 1966 and 1999, real GDP grew on average by 9.2% and per capita GDP by 7%. GDP per capita is now over US$3,500. The national budget has grown from under $3m to $3bn in 2004. Exports have grown from about $2m to $2bn in 2002, and imports from $3m to $2bn. Formal sector employment have risen from 29,000 people to 296,387 in 2004. In addition, life expectancy at birth rose from 48 years in 1966 to 65.3 years in 1991 before declining to 55.7 years in 2001, largely as a result of the HIV/Aids pandemic. The Infant Mortality Rate has declined from 100 per 1,000 live births in 1971 to 55 in 2001.

Primary school enrolment rose from 66,100 in 1966 to 327,600 in 2000, representing an average compound growth of 4.8% per annum. Tarmac roads have gone up from less than 10km in 1966 to over 10,000km in 2003. Access to health, education, transport, telecommunication and other services has increased. The structure of the Botswana economy has also changed significantly since independence. Agriculture accounted for 40% of GDP in 1966 and now accounts for less than 3% of GDP. Mining at just over 33%, is now the largest contributor to GDP. The Botswana economy is very open with exports plus imports constituting 79% of GDP. At independence, exports primarily consisted of beef, but diamond exports accounted for over 80% of total exports in 2003. Mineral revenues accounted for 45% of total government revenue in 2004.

Because of progress made, Botswana graduated from the list of 24 least developed countries in 1992. Furthermore, Botswana introduced appropriate macroeconomic and sectoral policies and also established institutions to service a modern-day economy, such as the Stock Exchange in 1994. Exchange controls were totally eliminated in 1999, a year after my accession to power. As a further attestation of the progress Botswana has made, Standard and Poor's and Moody's Investors Service have assigned Botswana better than investment grade sovereign credit ratings since 2001. Although some development experts attribute Botswana's relative success to the exploitation of diamond deposits in the late 1970s and the early 1980s, this is only part of the story.

I must say I do not agree with the characterisation of Botswana's development experience as a miracle- somehow suggesting some divine intervention or inexplicable reason for what was achieved. Natural resources, no matter how lucrative, cannot develop a country without political stability, sound economic management and prudent financial husbandry. What explains Botswana's success? In my view, many factors were responsible for the success. These include the political leadership at the time of independence. The leadership was genuinely committed to development and was responsive to the needs of the people through an inclusive political process.

There was national cohesion around the development agenda. In a way, the priorities were pre-determined as skilled human resources, physical infrastructure, such as roads and telecommunications; social infrastructure, such as water, health and education; and appropriate institutional infrastructure were almost non-existent. Botswana developed an elaborate system of planning and produced five-year National Development Plans to articulate government policies and development priorities. These Plans are enshrined in a law and approved by Parliament. As a result, a development project cannot be implemented if it is not in the Plan, and any periodic modifications, which have to be fully justified, also have to be approved by Parliament.

Botswana was consistent in its application of free market principles and practices and pro-growth policies and strategies in minerals, land, agricultural and social development. The Plans, coupled with transparency, accountability and commitment to abide by the Plans, helped the government to access significant levels of Official Development Assistance (ODA) and technical assistance. In fact, in the early 1980s, Botswana was one of the largest aid recipients on a per capita basis among the developing countries. The generous technical assistance we received, including from the Institute of Development Studies, enabled us to make effective use, not only of the capital assistance at our disposal, but also and above all, of our own financial resources when they became available as a result of mining activities.

Botswana also pursued pragmatic economic policies in the light of its geo-political situation. Although Botswana disagreed fundamentally with the racist policies of the then Apartheid South Africa, South West Africa and Rhodesia, trade and business relations were maintained. Botswana continued to be a member of the Southern African Customs Union and the Rand Monetary Area, in spite of several military attacks on, and other punitive measures against, us for our support of the liberation movements, which were dubbed terrorist organisations. Regarding the Rand Monetary Area, membership continued until 1976 when the then recently established Bank of Botswana issued the Pula, enabling the country to pursue independent monetary and exchange rate policies.

Because of Botswana's open market economic system, as well as limited domestic market, trade and exchange rate policies were, and continue to be, critical policies in order to promote the international competitiveness of our goods and services. For this reason, Botswana has been a member of the Southern African Customs Union, Southern African Development Community and the European Union/African, Caribbean and Pacific Group of countries under the Lome Convention, now the Cotonou Agreement. Under the Cotonou Agreement, Botswana beef enters the European Union market with a 90% rebate of the EU import levy.

The exchange rate policy has been managed to keep the value of the Pula, our currency, competitive with those of major trading partners. Of course, trade and exchange rate policies were pursued consistent with interest rate, monetary and fiscal policies. It is a well-documented fact that the exploitation of diamonds, beginning in 1971, with a further significant mine coming into operation in 1982, changed the economic landscape of Botswana. The country is now the world's largest producer of gem diamonds by value, accounting for about 30% of world output. In 2004, the diamond output was 31 million carats valued at over US$2bn.

Diamond mining is done in partnership with De Beers Mining Company and the government earns revenue through taxation, dividends and royalties. Diamond revenues now constitute about 45% of total government revenues. Revenues derived from diamonds have contributed significantly to Botswana's economic development because of appropriate political and economic policy environment as well as institutional framework. Diamond revenues have been invested in the development of human capital, social and physical infrastructure. For many years, especially when the value of the US dollar (the currency in which diamonds are traded) was high, the government accumulated substantial cash balances and foreign exchange reserves.

The thrust of fiscal and expenditure policy was to invest diamond revenues in productive assets rather than consumption.

Given Botswana's vulnerability to drought, other natural hazards and fluctuations in the international diamond markets, the accumulation of savings to smooth out the effects of the negative impact of these on our domestic economy was a prime consideration. Botswana is also a country largely dependent on food imports and with weak manufacturing capacity and at the same time currently hard hit by HIV and Aids.

Our policy has also sought to manage government demand in the economy so as not to crowd out the private sector or cause inflationary pressures as well as to keep a judicious balance between capital expenditure and future recurrent expenditure. Because of relative openness in economic policy making, national development planning formulation and priority setting, and the constitutionally-entrenched role of the auditor general, the attorney general, the Directorate on Corruption and Economic Crime and the independent judiciary, corruption has been kept in check. A democratic political dispensation, with a free but abusive press and vibrant civil society is also a good check against corruption.

Another important aspect of Botswana's development strategy has been to avoid the accumulation of excessive debt, both internal and external. Throughout the post-independence period, our debt service ratio has been kept below 5% of exports of goods and services. External borrowing was undertaken after careful assessment of projects to be financed as well as realistic assessment of ability to pay back. In addition, Botswana took advantage of concessionary international finance and resisted borrowing at high costs from private capital markets and multilateral development institutions.

Botswana has had limited success in a number of areas. Attempts to industrialise have not been totally successful. Import substitution proved difficult because of the limited domestic market, among others. Extension of time limited subsidies, to promote industrialisation through the Financial Assistance Policy, attracted foot-loose enterprises. Although manufacturing has increased, its contribution to GDP has remained at about 5% on account of GDP growing rapidly because of diamonds.

In the mid-1980s, government expenditure grew excessively causing the economy to overheat, especially in the construction sector. The cost of construction increased as a consequence. This was further exacerbated by negative real interest rates at the time. But we have learned from that experience. Real interest rates have been kept positive, and in spite of revenue fluctuations due to cross exchange rate movements, the ratio of government expenditure to GDP has been relatively stable at around 45%. Government has promoted growth across the economy, especially agriculture, through targeted subsidies. Some of the subsidy programmes generated little, if any, additional output and led to over-dependence on the government.

Botswana is often criticised for high levels of income inequality and rates of poverty. According to most recent data, the number of people living under the Poverty Datum Line decreased from 47% in 1993/94 to 30.3% in 2002/03. Government provision of health, education, school feeding, etc, has helped mitigate the effects of poverty. In the last two years, the government budget has come under stress because of the depreciation of the US dollar against the Pula as well as the South African rand in which our customs union revenues are denominated. Diversification of the economy as well as government revenue base has to be pursued with more vigour.

Whilst Botswana has made appreciable progress in economic development, many challenges remain. These include sustained improvement in living standards. Our national Vision 2016 is targeting a real GDP growth of 8% per annum up to year 2016. This can be achieved through economic diversification, especially into services such as tourism and international financial services, to reduce dependence on diamonds. Furthermore, concerted efforts are necessary for poverty eradication, sustainable environmental management, employment creation, macroeconomic stability, as well as sustaining high levels of transparency, accountability and good governance.

Botswana also has to optimise opportunities arising from globalisation. In this regard, the realisation of objectives underpinning the New Partnership for Africa's Development (Nepad) should assist the integration of our economy into the global economy as well as intra-African cooperation. And as you may know, one of the greatest single challenges the nation faces is the HIV/Aids pandemic. Preliminary survey results, released in December 2004, indicate that 17.1% of the total population over 18 months of age is estimated to be infected with the HIV virus. A worrying statistic is that the population aged 15-49 years is hardest hit with an infection rate of 34.4%.

In 2004, the government spent about US$130m in direct costs on HIV/Aids prevention, treatment, mitigation, support and care programmes. About 30,600 people are on anti-retroviral therapy in public health facilities and 7,000 in private facilities out of an estimated 110,000 most in need of immediate care. Other programmes include capacity building (infrastructure and human resources), prevention of mother to child transmission, orphan care, routine HIV testing, community-based home care and extensive information, education and communication campaign.

Although the various programmes are generously financed by multinational companies, multilateral agencies and some donor countries, the government of Botswana shoulders a substantial part of the burden. The good progress we are making would have been even better had it not been for the effects of stigma, discrimination and other inhibitions. Unless the costs of treatment and drugs further come down significantly, it will be difficult to sustain the costs of the various programmes without compromising sustainable development.

Needless to say, HIV/Aids are reversing some of the achievements we had made. And high levels of mortality and morbidity have an adverse effect on labour productivity. This has accentuated the shortages of skilled and professional human resources. This is particularly so for health personnel which is causing a severe strain to our health facilities.

The fabric of our society and culture is being tested to the limit by the care for the sick and infected as well as the increasing number of orphans and the effect this has on rates of savings. Registered orphans in 2004 numbered 47,925. The fight against HIV/Aids is central to poverty reduction, employment creation as well as sustained improvements in living standards. I would like to believe that institutions such as the Institute for Development Studies can find a way of contributing to our efforts to overcome the HIV and Aids pandemic. This is truly a human tragedy that requires the undivided attention of all of humanity.

As I already pointed out earlier, Botswana is susceptible to severe and frequent droughts. At the present time, the capital, Gaborone, is under water restrictions because the dam that feeds it is about 25% full, enough supply for just seven or so months. Finding reliable water sources for agricultural development and human consumption is a major development challenge for Botswana.

I wish to conclude by observing that economic management in a given country has to respond to the particular circumstances on the ground. Good policies, strategies and management cannot simply be transplanted from one economic regime to another. Without appropriate policies, the exploitation of valuable natural resources is no guarantee for success. In my view, key prerequisites for success include the following:

- The need for national priorities and well defined and agreed coordinated development processes right from the grassroots levels.
- Inclusiveness in the development process, i.e. development policies must not favour particular individuals or sectors at the expense of the rest of society. All must share in the fruits of development.
- Government must recognise the important role of other development stakeholders and establish fora for regular consultations.
- There is a need to develop trust among key stakeholders, by acknowledging mistakes and taking corrective action on key matters. Disagreements must be well managed so that they do not degenerate into irreconcilable differences over protracted periods of time.

Botswana's development experience may not be perfect, but many independent development analysts have concluded that the lives of the vast majority of Batswana have been significantly improved by government policies and programmes. The Botswana economy has been transformed from a backwater economy to a progressive and forward-looking economy in just over three-and-a-half decades, but I say this, fully cognisant of the fact that many challenges lie ahead.

There's something odd about it: In an era of unprecedented concern for universal human rights, doubts still linger about whether the basic needs of working men and women qualify as "fights." A disaster at a toy factory on the outskirts of Bangkok ought to help erase those doubts. When a sudden fire last May destroyed the Kader-owned facility, some 188 Thai workers lost their lives because their fight to a reasonably safe workplace had been grossly violated. The four-story factory was a death trap- it had no fire alarm, no sprinkler system, no fire hoses, and no fire escape; some regular exits were locked or blocked. Besides the fatalities, 379 other workers were injured.

Even as Thai officials were investigating the cause of the fire and promising to increase safety inspections of the country's many new factories, The Economist of London offered its historical perspective on the tragedy. "The early stages of industrialization are often rough," it explained. "Britain and America were able to afford better laws and safer workplaces as they got richer." This kind of analysis, often deployed to put a gloss of inevitability on even the most indefensible abuses of human fights, can sound plausible to the uninformed. But in this case it clearly doesn't fit the facts. The Kader factory, owned by some of the wealthiest Asians in the region, mass-produces stuffed dolls (Bart Simpson, Cabbage Patch, and others) for highly profitable U.S. retail outlets selling to the richest consumers in the world.

The enterprise has been well integrated into a thriving global economy, one that differs radically from the historical model on which The Economist builds its rationale. Despite Kader's economic success, its workers have long been victimized by the company's low-wage policy. According to sources within the company, Kader has avoided paying many of its workers even Thailand's $5-a-day minimum wages by classifying them as "temporary" on renewable contracts. The English-language

Bangkok daily, The Nation, which does not share the detached Economist outlook, pointed out a significant aspect of the tragedy: "The bodies pulled out of the wreckage [at Kader] were mostly young and female. Some of them may have been underage. At least two were heavily pregnant. What a waste."

The "waste" multiplied in Bangkok two months later when ten female workers, nine of them teen-agers, died in a garment factory fire from which they could not escape because of locked doors and barred windows. Similar disastrous fires have in recent years occurred in Bangladesh, China, Hong Kong, Indonesia, and Malaysia. In Bangladesh's capital city of Dhaka, for example, three twelve-year-old girls died in a 1990 garment factory fire that killed twenty-five persons and injured about two hundred, the great majority of them young women. Disregard for safety is only one of the significant issues affecting the rights of workers in poor countries. Often in violation of their own laws, many third-world governments permit and even foster abuses, such as child labor (girls as young as seven and eight in Bangladesh), forced labor (notably in China, on a mass scale), bonded labor (especially for carpets in India), wide-scale discrimination and violence against women, and suppression (by violence, if necessary) of any worker efforts to form their own independent organizations.

A century ago Pope Leo XIII condemned the Western industrializing world for debasing the labor of human beings to the level of a thing, a commodity. He blamed the "cal1ousness of employers and the greed of unrestrained competition" for the rampant exploitation of working men. Today, with competition unleashed on a global scale, working women have become the commodities of newly industrialized nations. Goods now travel farther than ever; trade and investment reach out further than ever. But personal responsibility does not. At the U.S. end, we- -customers, store owners, importers, investors, and all the others- handle the finished products, concerned only about price and quality. It is easier to be callous when the people working for us are Asians on the other side of the world. After the Kader fire, a U.S. trade association officer quickly distanced his industry from the disaster by emphasizing that the Kader workers were not on the payrolls of the U.S. companies.

It's true that fewer and fewer American businesses are directly involved with labor in foreign countries. They own a dwindling proportion of the plants in the export industries of developing countries, even though the United States is often the largest market for their output. Instead of producing the goods, U.S. companies increasingly act as distributors and marketers. Nike and Reebok, for example, have a few American quality control managers in Indonesian factories producing athletic shoes, but the factories, Asian-owned, work simply as suppliers under contract. Levi Strauss & Co., another large U.S. company that mass markets foreign-made goods, has about six hundred suppliers under contract in fifty countries around the world.

Contracting-out gives the U.S. companies a number of advantages. It makes their operations highly mobile, by allowing them enormous flexibility to choose among competing suppliers within a country, within a region, or even beyond, and to make and unmake contracts based on the lowest cost for a certain level of quality. Suppliers and countries compete against one another to offer labor at the lowest possible price. Local factories squeezed by competitive pressure, cut corners. This can mean no pay for overtime work, no days off even on holidays, no sick pay, and no first-aid for injuries, no decent toilets, and no fire escapes. The most vulnerable under this global squeeze are uncounted millions of young women at sewing machines, behind microscopes, and along assembly lines in third-world factories.

Back in 1988, the Kadet multinational offered a memorable example of the behavior often bred by transnational mobility. To meet the big holiday demand for Ghostbusters, Mickey Mouse dolls, and Big Hauler trains, a Kader factory in the province of China bordering Hong Kong was requiring its young women workers to work fourteen hours a day, seven days a week. Troubled by such abuses, Chinese government officials objected, but, as a Kadet executive in Hong Kong, Andy Lee, said to a Business Week reporter, "We told them, this is the toy biz. If you don't allow us to do things our way, we'll close down our Chinese factories and move to Thailand." Kader didn't have to move; it did things "our way" both in China and in Thailand.

A few U.S. corporations that rely heavily on third-world imports are beginning to appreciate that they cannot operate that way. Levi Strauss & Co. took the lead in 1992 by adopting a sophisticated, two-tier human rights "code of conduct." One tier, its "terms of engagement for business partners," addresses a wide range of issues that are "substantially controllable" by suppliers. Important examples: no employment of children under fourteen, no use of prison or forced labor, no long working hours (over sixty hours a week), no "corporal punishment or other forms of mental or physical coercion." Recognizing that some problems are beyond the control of suppliers, Levi Strauss's code has another tier called "guidelines for country selection." Under one of those guidelines ("we should not initiate or renew contractual relations in countries where there are pervasive violations of basic human rights"), Levi Strauss has stopped doing business in Burma and is phasing out its operations in the People's Republic of China.

The breadth of the Levi Strauss code is exceptional. Organized U.S. business has so far strongly resisted proposals to give its blessing even to less sweeping codes such as the "Human Rights Production Standards" adopted by Reebok earlier this year, which covers much the same ground as the Levi Strauss code but is silent about doing business in entire countries known for pervasive violations of human fights. The codes are disturbing because they add a dimension beyond the profit motive to doing business abroad.

Moreover, worker rights codes depart from the dominant macroeconomic approach of economists, most of whom concentrate on growth in national output and per capita income, as though these describe the total economic reality. Per capita income averages say nothing about how income is distributed. The Far Eastern Economic Review reported last year: "A significant shift in the distribution of income and wealth in Hong Kong seems to have taken place over the past few years. Review research suggests that the majority of people have gained little from the advances in per capita GDP over that period. Instead, the gains have gone primarily to owners of capital and secondarily to acquisition of assets by the government."

By creating new jobs in the third world, trade should enable poor countries to get off the treadmill of underdevelopment without undermining the standard of living in the developed world. Instead, trade is primarily benefiting the elites, in both developing and developed countries, largely because the international labor market is a jungle. There are no binding international rules safeguarding the fights of workers. Policymakers, liberal and conservative alike, aggressively promote and enforce international agreements to protect the rights of investors and owners of intellectual property fights. But international rules to protect the fights of workers? That's heresy.

Not to everyone, however. The economic theories indoctrinated in graduate schools are facing some real-world challenges. In Asia hundreds of new nongovernmental organizations (NGOs) now speak out for the fights of ordinary people, including workers. Though still neophytes, these Asian NGOs are numerous and like-minded enough that they sometimes dare to oppose the development and labor policies of their own governments. In the United States the TV networks, chiefly through their popular "newsmagazine" shows, have turned their cameras on the harsh labor realities, including the devastating Kader fire. Illustrated stories about hundreds of thousands of preteen Asian and North African children making carpets for Western living rooms have been perennial features in many leading world newspapers for some years. Now, despite the sensitivities of advertising departments, commercial TV is exposing such scandals, even revealing the brand names of companies involved.

These audio-visual stories have a much greater impact on public opinion than headlines and photos appearing on the front pages of the New York Times and the Washington Post. Meanwhile, a few economists and policymakers are trying to inject some reality into the profession's ratified perspective. Laura d' Andtea Tyson, the new head of the Council of Economic Advisers [CEA], is one such ground-breaker. In the current issue of The American Prospect, economist James K. Galbraith writes that Tyson is not a "model builder" working from economic theory but "a nuanced observer of the world as it actually is, a collector and weigher of evidence, a student of details." So far the Clinton administration has shown a mixed record on international worker fights. The appointment of Robert Reich as secretary of labor is on the plus side. The big minus is its failure to add a meaningful worker rights "side agreement" to the North American Free Trade Agreement, which devotes more than sixty pages to protecting the rights of investors and intellectual property owners.

Opportunities to translate into reality the campaign slogan of putting "people first" are still at hand. The Office of the U.S. Trade Representative, headed by Mickey Kantor, has before it petitions charging serious worker rights violations in Thailand and nineteen other countries and urging cancellation of the extraordinary privileges that businesses, U.S. and foreign, get for shipping imports from those countries into the U.S. Thanks to those privileges, granted under the so-called Generalized System of Preferences (GSP), importers benefit from what amounts to a government subsidy saving them tens of millions each year in U.S. import duties. In the case of Thailand, U.S. and foreign businessmen in 1992 saved uncounted millions by being freed of U.S. duties on dolls and other imports worth $1.8 billion (yes, billions).

The intended purpose of these privileges is to promote healthy economic development in poor countries, and so under U.S. law countries with GSP status are supposed to meet certain criteria, among them enforcement of basic worker rights such as banning child labor and meeting minimal health and safety standards. Although Thailand has been in the dock since 1987 for violating those rights, the U.S. government has so far always found it "in compliance." Such decisions have naturally led many developing countries and companies operating in them to believe that the worker rights aspects of U.S. law mean nothing. One important worker-rights step that the Clinton administration could take this year is to show that there is finally a price to pay-loss of the GSP freebies for ignoring U.S. law.

Even equipped with the constitutional power to regulate international trade, however, the U.S. government can't, and shouldn't, carry the burden alone. Since private commerce now surges across most latitudes and longitudes, international businesses could assume some responsibility to police themselves, following the example set by Levi Strauss. Pressure from consumers and shareholders would help. Women's clubs, church groups, and others could develop contacts with Asia's struggling NGOs. If good people do nothing, it will be a green light for continuing the kind of callous irresponsibility that on the afternoon of May 10, 1993, brought a fiery death to 188 Thai workers, most of them women in their teens and early twenties.

There is no doubt that Seattle was a major up for the left. Massive and militant demonstrations stopped business as usual. Media attention was widespread and managed to convey the protesters' serious sense of purpose and their critique of capital's model of globalization. The unity demonstrated in the now-famous turtle-teamster lovefest symbolized the healing of a breach between the ecological and anti-imperialist concerns of young people and an end to the narrow business unionism and Gold-War collaboration of the Meany-Kirkland years in the labor movement. A new left is emerging on campuses and in the streets among young people and renewed trade-union militancy is more visible. The outrage at the loss of democratic control to global-state economic institutions has prompted a vital and promising internationalism.

The events in Seattle confront progressives with two interconnected questions. First, what can we do to make the World Trade Organization (WTO), the International Monetary Fund (IMF), and the other institutions of global governance democratically accountable? Second, how can we strengthen internationalist consciousness and build working-class solidarity? At the most general level, there need be no conflict between the answers to these questions. However, it is important to understand that, while the WTO and the IMF are undemocratic tools of transnational capital, so too are the governments that appoint the leaders of these institutions. The real issue is the class nature of both the international institutions and the states represented in them. Care must be taken, too, to recognize the tremendous co-optive power of capital.

For example, the United Nations (UN), which has become a sort of institutional home for the thinking of those opposed to transnational capital and in favor of more socially and ecological ly balanced development, often acts as a safety valve for capital. That is, capital dominates the WTO and the IMF, and these organizations serve capital's designs, while capital confines its opponents to nonbinding resolutions and good intentions. In Seattle, the critique of accumulation reached a new level of mass consciousness and breathed life into alternative visions. The "street heat" put muscle behind the challenge to labor exploitation, environmental degradation, and poverty we may be seeing a shift of historical importance. Yet social change is a slow process and we need to assess the impact of Seattle and the increased social activism with both an optimism of the spirit and a more critical intellect.

We should look first at the connection between the institutions of global governance and the leading sectors of capital and then at elite designs in this post-Seattle period, focusing briefly on this year's meeting of the World Global Forum in Davos, Switzerland; turn to the long-term perspective of globalist policy makers; note issues surrounding labor regulation and sustainable development; and end with a closer look at the significance of the WTO decision on sea turtles and the future of progressive struggle. The contours of class struggle are changing. Seattle and the response to it is a helpful lens through which to examine some important aspects of those changes.

While new forms of governance are being imposed by the WTO, the IMF, and other global-state economic institutions, these organizations hardly initiate the rules. Rather, before any of these organizations meet, the United States makes proposals which are discussed within the QUAD- a group composed of the United States, the European Union (EU), Japan, and Canada- which convenes separately and, in secrecy, makes key decisions without the participation of the other members of the world community. The QUAD is not recognized in any of their charters, but it acts as an executive committee that determines their direction. In Seattle, the vast majority of WTO members waited outside the exclusive Green Room meetings, as they were called, for the QUAD to reach decisions that would then be discussed by the body.

It was clear to the other delegates that they were essentially excluded from real decision-making. Thanks to the tens of thousands of demonstrators in the streets outside, delegates were encouraged to say no to the QUAD's demands. It was the most assertive participation from the developing world at any such gathering. Behind the officials representing the QUAD are the corporations they serve. Personnel move back and forth between lobbyists for and leadership of giant corporations, the biggest banks, and the leading legal firms, and what is called public service. Corporate groups such as the Business Roundtable in the United States, the European Roundtable of Industrialists in Europe, the Business Council on National Issues in Canada, and the Keidanren in Japan consult closely with the officials who go first to QUAD meetings and then to the general gatherings that the broad membership of the noncore states attend.

Through this process, the desires of the dominant sectors of the capitalist class are first negotiated and then imposed on weaker capitals and the workers of the world. While these institutions are all undemocratic and erode people's sovereign authority to govern them, in a real sense so are the governments that have created them. Greater democratic control is prevented at all levels by this corporate-government collusion and the power of money to buy politicians and exclude other voices from the councils where the deals are made. The structural roots of this collusion lie in the nature of a system that allows one class to dominate others, a political order in which corporations with sales larger than the Gross Domestic Product (GDP) of most countries are considered individuals with the same legal rights as other "citizens," and in which formal equality masks the unequal power to command government.

It is therefore not only the unjust rules and practices of the IMF and the WTO that need to be addressed, but the class relationships that circumscribe government decision-making more broadly. The democratic deficit at the global level reflects these economic and political relations of dominance. The role of governments, courts, and police powers in defending property rights rather than people's needs may look different to many citizens of the core because we are not used to thinking in such structural terms or, indeed, to being treated this way. Citizens and workers in the QUAD have been, relatively speaking, the beneficiaries of the uneven development and imperialist relations inherent in the way the world system has operated. In an era of economic restructuring and globalization, however, a harsher face of capitalism has presented itself to the core.

Without downplaying the enormous differences that still remain between workers in the core and those on the periphery, first-world workers have more and more in common with third-world workers. Hopefully, these changes in objective conditions will make it easier for the world's workers to unite. Capital's powers are further increased by the sharp divisions of nationality, ethnicity, gender, and religion among workers, as well as by the fact that capital has allies among certain professional and technical workers. Capital also has considerable control over the media and the political establishment, which benefit from globalization.

However, the workings of the market system now make capital vulnerable in new ways. For many corporations, the most important asset is their image. Nike's and Disney's profits, for example, flow from consumers' willingness to buy- and enthusiasm for- their branded products. As information about how they (mis) treat their workers and the environment is brought to light (through public campaigns, consumer boycotts, strike support, and court challenges) , a critique of exploitation, consumerism, and a wider anti-corporate consciousness grows. These campaigns demand accountability and democratic control over transnationals. They suggest that a different kind of multilateral agreement on investment, trade, and finance is possible.

This winter in Davos, Switzerland, the closest thing the world has to an executive committee of the ruling class and its key agents met, as they do annually, at the World Economic Forum. It cost 22,500 dollars to come to the meeting- on top of the fifteen thousand dollar annual dues paid by the one thousand companies whose CEOs attend Forum events. (Of course, it's all tax deductible.) There was a different spirit in the air this year, as the world elite faced the unhappy prospect of demonstrators coming to their isolated retreat, disturbing their deliberations, and bringing with them Seattle-style "no justice, no peace" street heat. As a result, the Forum wanted "constructive dialogue." Not only was AFL-CIO chief John Sweeney invited to speak but the human rights group Amnesty International and the environmental-action organization Greenpeace was also welcomed.

Of course, this (perhaps temporary) commitment to dialogue is newfound. The whole point of Davos is for the movers and shakers to get far away from everyone else to reach consensus. It was only the threat of worldwide rebellion to their domination that led them to stress unfamiliar words and concepts. Having previously excluded the dissenters' concerns as irrelevant to the U.S. free-trade agenda, U.S. Trade Representative Charlene Barshefsky now struck a very different note at the meeting, saying, "We cannot isolate economics as distinct from the environment and labor." Ambassador Barshefsky said this even though that was the very reason the QUAD had structured the rules of the WTO the way it had. After Seattle, she was ready to concede, "That's a distinction that's artificial."

President Clinton referred to Mr. Sweeney by name three times in his own remarks, more than he mentioned anyone else, and said, "People who favor freer trade have no choice now but to open the door to these new voices. The more we deny this the more we fuel the fires of protectionism, not put them out." Whether flattery and more "feel your pain" rhetoric will be enough to blunt labor militancy remains to be seen. UN Secretary General Kofi Annan was a guest at the World Economic Forum as well. He was there to urge the corporate elite to "give a human face to the global market." He saw his task as urging social harmony and warning of the costs economic volatility could bring. He spoke of the need to compensate the victims.

Otherwise all those "isms" of the age of globalization-protectionism, fanaticism, populism, ethnic chauvinism and terrorism- would overwhelm the smooth operation of an open world market. He offered a partnership between the UN and the corporations, making it clear that he understood who would be junior partner. "I made the point that the everyday work of the United Nations- whether in peacekeeping, setting technical standards, protecting intellectual property, or providing much-needed assistance to developing countries- helps to expand opportunities for business around the world." Without "your resources," he told the capitalists assembled in Davos, the objectives of the UN would "remain elusive."

One of the effects of U.S. refusal to pay its UN dues has been to encourage the UN to cast around for alternative sources of funds, including corporate sponsorship. Some of the NGOs not offered a seat at the table have suggested a compact between the UN and civil society with regard to the UN's relation with the private sector. They propose a legal framework to govern the behavior of multinational corporations (MNCs) to protect ecosystems, human health, labor standards, and human rights.

The assistance the UN might offer corporations to improve their human rights and environmental behavior will not, they said pointedly, "be considered a 'partnership.'" Perhaps they envisioned health clinics in Myanmar with plaques thanking the UN and Socal and advertisements that celebrate the schools built for the Ogoni in Nigeria by Shell being featured during TV programs- thanks to a grant from the generous transnational attempting to rehabilitate its reputation. The NGOs urged that any money the UN accepted from corpo rate sponsors be used for programs that did not have a direct connection to the commercial projects of that company.

The movement should make as much noise as it can clarify the issues involved. Things are moving quite quickly; what seemed like radical demands only a few months ago have been embraced, at least rhetorically, by government policy-makers. The demand for debt forgiveness for the poorest, most heavily indebted countries and the regulation of offshore tax havens (where banking secrecy laws have permitted money-laundering by drug cartels and corrupt politicians and well-connected tax-evaders and other crooks) are part of mainstream reform proposals these days. The World Bank consults in a highly visible fashion with NGOs, which has significantly defused antagonisms towards that organization. There is widespread discussion of restructuring the IMF and reducing its role in running the economies of debtor nations.

The strength of the popular movements and the anger of many developing economies exhibited in Seattle has led to substantial public-relations efforts by the corporations and some fast footwork by politicians trying to spin a more sympathetic posture. Some movement "leaders" have offered to collaborate in exchange for a seat at the table. Will their participation as insiders make a positive difference for working people and the environment? Or will these efforts succeed only in disarming the movement and reducing the militancy of the elements that are considered responsible negotiating partners? There is always a tension between inside and outside progressive strategies. Our own political clarity becomes increasingly important if this new wave of radical activism is to develop.

At Davos, Mexican President Ernesto Zedillo told the World Economic Forum that, "What most people fail to realize is that the low salaries and poor working conditions to which most workers are subject is their only alternative to extreme rural poverty." Workers are always told this: "You have two choices: take the wages we offer, or fend for yourself without access to our capital. You are free to choose." About the same time Zedillo was wowing them in Davos, John Stackhouse, writing in the Toronto Globe and Mail (December 2, 1999), was reporting from Mexico that many of the workers struggling to make ends meet in the maquiladoras "do not blame the World Trade Organization or even the free-trade agreement that had enriched the Mexican economy.

They fault their own government for crushing union movements and letting companies skirt basic national and international laws." The workers seem to see that there is a third choice between accepting what the ruling class is willing to give them and quietly going off to starve, and that it is always one's own ruling class that must be dealt with first. Workers in the third world worry when the leading capitalist states are suddenly interested in labor rights and environmental standards in their countries. It is not that the trade unions and popular movements do not want improved conditions. Rather, they see the apparent discovery of universal human values and standards by Western governments as a ploy to advance the interests of their own corporations. As Sanjay Mangala Gopal, the co-coordinator of the National Alliance of People's Movements in India says, "We will define our own way of development and we are capable of doing it. Who are you to teach us about child labor or anything else?"

Gopal is right to be outraged. The now-righteous United States has not signed the International Covenant on Economic, Social, and Cultural Rights, the Convention on the Rights of the Child, or the Convention on the Elimination of Discrimination Against Women. It also explicitly exempts international workers from the Fair Labor Standards Act, excusing itself and its transnationals from accountability for labor-rights violations of workers abroad. Of the more than 180 International Labor Organization (ILO) conventions, the United States has ratified only twelve. Yet the United States tells poor nations that they must submit to rules imposed by international governance institutions over which they have little control.

For the progressive movement, the points raised by Gopal are complicated. For example, the ILO core labor standards are protection of the right of free association; protection of the right to organize and bargain collectively; the abolition of forced labor and child labor; the equal remuneration for men and women for equal work; and the establishment of a policy of nondiscrimination. Of course, these standards should be adopted worldwide and enforced by national courts. But their adoption, which will be applauded by liberals as some sort of ultimate victory, must not serve to disorient the left.

Their adoption will not mean much in practice unless there are strong social movements in place locally to enforce them every day at the point of production and constant international pressure on transnational corporations by solidarity movements. To believe that the WTO and the IMF, which could, in theory, enforce labor standards, will do so is wishful thinking, as is the belief that the national governments of the advanced capitalist nations will use their considerable powers to insure that corporations to obey such standards in every country. The issue of child labor is an example of the complexities faced by progressives. About 70 percent of the 250 million children between the ages of five and fourteen who work are unpaid family workers, and mostly live in rural areas.

Only 5 percent are estimated to be employed in export-related production (though there they sometimes represent a substantial proportion of labor employed). Land reform and other family assistance could do much to ease child labor by reducing the poverty that makes education an unlikely alternative. Similarly, job creation for adults at livable wages in the cities would be the best "family values" policy, in rich countries as well as poor ones. If child labor is not a make-or-break issue for transnational corporations, since it involves a relatively small part of their overall employment (where adult labor is so cheap why employ children?), it is nevertheless possible to define child labor in ways that will raise consciousness and garner strong support in third-world countries.

Child-labor practices include trafficking in children, forced or compulsory labor (including debt bondage and serfdom), the use or offering of children for prostitution or pornographic performances, and the employment of children in the drug trade and other illegal activities. These practices jeopardize children's health and safety and are opposed by local labor-advocacy groups and trade unions. Our support for these groups would make a difference. This is a job for solidarity movements and not for Western governments, which are driven by the interests of their corporations and care about labor standards only when pushed by politically strong, progressive movements or when t hat interest serves their own ends. They are the wrong instrument to control and enforce progressive labor standards in other countries.

Indeed, the governments, and especially the United States government, have been busy undermining health, safety, and environmental protections at home. Even where independent, outside monitors exist, there are problems. These monitors are often private, for-profit companies that exploit their own employees, the actual factory inspectors. Their profitability might depend on them giving abusive corporations clean bills of health. Finally, it is important to acknowledge that concern in the West for widespread labor abuse is primarily the result of fear of competition. Exploitation "there" erodes living standards and intensifies work for workers "here."

This issue will only become more important. The global workforce doubled in size between 1965 and 1995. As David Coates writes: "Globalization in its modern form is a process based less on the proliferation of computers than on the proliferation of proletarians. The growth in the size of the world's proletariat and the change in its geographical centers of gravity- and not simply the enhanced mobility of capital- are among the defining features of the current phase of global capitalism."

U.S. Secretary of the Treasury Lawrence Summers spoke this past February to the Senate Committee on Foreign Relations. After explaining how the international financial institutions (IFIs) promote vital humanitarian objectives, he got down to his more central argument that these IFIs promote liberalized markets, strengthen the rights of property, and provide the right environment for private investment. He underlined the national and class interests involved: "The United States has 4.5 percent of the world's population, 22 percent of its income. In a very real sense, the future growth in our standard of living will depend a great deal on the growth of our export markets. And that, in turn, will depend a great deal on whether the kinds of development strategies that the IFIs support are successful."

As opposed to the true believers in the free market, represented by the International Financial Institution Financial Advisory Commission (established by the Congressional Republican leadership under the monetarist Allan Meltzer and intent on trimming the wings of the IFIs and leaving things to the market), Summers represents the perspective of the corporatist internationalists, who want to continue to use the IFIs to force dependent economies to restructure in ways that are conducive to U.S. capital's interests. As Summers explains, every dollar the United States contributes to the multilateral development banks leverages to more than forty-five dollars in official lending to countries where three-quarters of the world's population lives. Given U.S. influence over the conditions these institutions put on lending, this would seem a bargain.

He offers the example of Indonesia, the world's fourth most populous economy, which in its most recent Letter of Intent pledged to "maintain a liberal trade regime, avoid introducing any new trade barriers, remove remaining distortionary elements in the trade structure, eliminate during the program period all exemptions to import tariffs, and remove all existing nontariff barriers." A weakened, debt-ridden Indonesia was forced to give international capital what it wanted, an economy foreign capital could enter on its own terms without government restrictions.

Secretary Summers explained to the committee the corporate internationalists' long-term thinking on the labor supply and market needs of the transnationals. "Mr. Chairman," he said, "debt relief for the poorest countries is a global moral imperative. It is also a global economic imperative, at a time when nearly all of the growth in the world's labor force and productivity will be in the developing countries- and their success in a new global economy is going to be important to the success of us all." These countries are the location of the global factory and markets of the twenty-first century.

What Summers' remarks signify is a refocusing of elite tactics- both a response to critics and the strength of the progressive movements on the one hand and a sure understanding of the long-term interests of capital on the other. Now that the Cold War has waned, capital no longer needs to accept the rent-seeking of local elites and military rulers who rip off foreign capital even as they exploit their own people in ways that limit the long-term growth prospects of their economies. During the Cold War they were necessary, but in an era of globalization, they typically are not. Indeed, their domination can be counterproductive.

None of this means that police-state tactics will not continue to be used as needed or that military interventions are a thing of the past. However, in recognition of new realities, there has been a shift to a kinder, gentler model, as exemplified by the IMF in 1999. It replaced its Enhanced Structural Adjustment Facility with the Poverty Reduction and Growth Facility and required countries seeking debt relief and new concessional loans to not only establish a solid track record of reform but also produce a "forward-looking Poverty Reduction Strategy Paper." The World Bank has said that it will do its part in assisting these countries to define national poverty reduction goals, such as reducing infant mortality and malnutrition.

One would feel better about U.S. efforts to push the IFIs in this direction if our country adopted such priorities at home. The suspicion has to be that these are new controls with which to manipulate dependent economies. But just as national elites in the United States in the 1960s accepted the need to modernize race relations in the U.S. South, so too have they now seen the need to promote governance in poor nations by a Western-trained technocratic elite oriented toward market efficiency (combined with some showcase poverty programs) to defuse radical demands. There are positive aspects of these actions.

The local ruling classes, which have oppressed national workers in places like Indonesia and Nigeria, are on the defensive as the global-state governance institutions force a respect for the rule of law and allow competition from lower-cost producers. This is the modernization process Marx applauded. But if workers are to benefit from this universalizing of the market, they must organize all the workers of the world in class-conscious movements to claim what is their right. Otherwise the social disorganization and harsh realities of single-minded market-driven development will continue to put off meeting human needs in favor of a long run to which many will have been sacrificed and that will exist only as an ever-receding mirage for most working people.

This brings us to the leaders and members of the Teamsters Union who have become active in anti-WTO activities. They have done so in significant measure because, under the North American Free Trade Agreement (NAFTA), Mexican truck drivers are allowed to carry cargo to final destinations inside the United States. Thanks to President Clinton's newfound interest in highway safety and his serendipitous discovery that Mexican inspections are not adequate to insure it, he has banned Mexican trucks from coming across the border- at least until after the November election. At that point, Teamster president Jimmy Hoffa, Jr. and his "take back the power" campaign will have begun to wear thin. Hopefully, trade unionists and their allies will come to see that only the organization of those who drive and compete with the current union members will work as a strategy to protect union benefits.

Similarly, labor's campaign to keep China out of the WTO will not change what happens inside China nearly as much as the Chinese working class organizing independent trade unions will. It is clear that the Chinese ruling elite, which include the privileged children of top party officials, are capitalist roaders who attract foreign capital by suppressing free-trade unionism and denying other political freedoms. I do not think that it is xenophobic to point this out, nor should we deny the impact of China's policies and those of other repressive Asian regimes on workers elsewhere. Because of the Republican right wing's (and some sectors of U.S. capital's) support for the campaign to demonize China and the "yellow peril," many on the left have argued that it is wrong to support efforts to keep China out of the WTO and to pressure China to improve its human rights practices. The United States, they argue, has supported worse states and never made such a campaign against them.

What is certain is that China's admittance or non-admittance to the WTO is largely beside the point, from the perspective of working-class struggle. Blocking China's membership in the WTO- if that were possible- would do little to help workers inside or outside China. Nor would admitting China to WTO membership help its workers. The China Labour Bulletin- a Hong Kong bimonthly founded by Han Dong-fang, the Chinese electrician jailed without trial for twenty-two months for antigovernment and pro-working-class activity- points Out that wage arrears, unemployment, and poverty "are the norm, not the exception" in China. It declares that, "It is [the] experience of 20 years of reform that does not give much cause for optimism about China's WTO entry.

The proposal to set up a WTO working group on the effects of globalization on labor standards is also unlikely to have the Chinese government rushing to ratify and implement the UN conventions it has already signed that are supposed to guarantee freedom of association and other human rights. It is hard to see how membership will improve our situation." WTO membership for China would help foreign capital in China, allowing it to exert additional pressure on the government to protect its interests at the expense of Chinese workers, while promoting a kind of comprador elite in China- insofar as Chinese elites would increasingly be converted into junior partners in the more systematic international exploitation of their own workers. This is why corporate America is pressing for closer ties to China.

International labor conditions/coalitions obviously were not the only issues in Seattle. Protestors in colorful turtle outfits also called attention to the role of the WTO in dismantling environmental protections. Sea turtles are one of nature's wonders. They can live up to eighty years and the largest can weigh 1400 pounds. Currently 125,000 of them are killed each year- hauled up as unwanted by catch by shrimpers and other fishermen. At least four of the existing species face extinction. In response to this threat, a grid trapdoor was developed. Installed inside trawling nets, it allows shrimp to pass to the back of the net while directing sea turtles and other large unintentionally caught objects out of the net.

Under the authority of the Endangered Species Act, the Department of Commerce promulgated regulations requiring U.S. shrimp trawlers to use these devices. Congress placed a limitation on the importation of shrimp from nations which have not taken adequate measures to protect sea turtles. India, Malaysia, Pakistan, and Thailand complained first to the General

Agreement on Tarriffs and Trade (GAIT) and then to its successor, the WTO, on the grounds that the United States was forcing its environmental ideals on others and violating the rules of the free-trade regime. The WTO panel agreed.

The WTO requirement that "like goods be treated as equal" means that since shrimp harvested using turtle-excluding devices cannot be distinguished from shrimp caught in traditional mechanical nets, there can be no discriminating against the latter in favor of the former. This reification of commodities (in which the social relations of exploitation and extraction of "natural resources" become invisible) appears in other decisions as well. Soccer balls sewn by children look like those made under safe and fair conditions by adult employees- making the exploitation of children invisible at the level of market exchange. The rule's purpose is to turn what are social relations into an exchange of things from which all traces of moral specificity can be hidden as a matter of international treaty- reinforcing the reification of commodities with reification as legal principle. Many, perhaps most, of us- in our role as consumers- reject such logic. That is why corporations need the WTO to overrule our ability to const rain their behavior.

The case is complicated but- although the panel report contains hundreds of pages of closely printed text, appendices, and annexes- its conclusion is simple: market values trump all else.

The purpose of the agreement is free trade and nothing can stand in the way of this overriding goal. The United States claimed support for its actions in the Convention on International Trade in Endangered Species and the UN Convention on the Law of the Sea, which require governments to ensure that living resources are not endangered by overexploitation, and from the WTO agreement itself, which seems to allow exceptions from unfettered trade in such instances as well.

The panel rejected the U.S. case, saying that under GATT and the WTO, "the central focus of the agreement remains the promotion of economic development through trade." NGOs wishing to file amicus briefs were told by the panel they had no right to participate, that this was "incompatible with the provisions of the DSU [Dispute Settlement Understanding] as currently applied." The United States also lost on appeal to the Appellate Body, although the rulings there reflected the impact of the environmental movement's angry and effective response to t he WTO. It is an important decision because the Body rejected the logic of the panel and, in theory, opened the door to more progressive interpretation of the rules.

The Appellate Body said that environmental measures could potentially be compatible with WTO rules. However, while the ruling opened the way for a country to take strong measures to protect shared global resources like sea turtles, it established such stringent conditions that it could declare that U.S. law did not meet them. Debates in the law journals continue over the significance of the ruling. My own view is that popular pressure will decide the issue. The WTO surely wants to follow the corporation's preferences. It is the task of the movement to insure that they cannot get away with this.

Elites understand that they rule not only through the capacities they have to use force on recalcitrants, but through ideological hegemony, the acceptance that there is no alternative. They say that even if their system is not perfect, it is the best that is possible. The new movement is successfully conveying that this is an unjust, harmful system that needs to be stopped; that it is only the opposition of a counter-hegemonic set of ideas about how society can and should be managed, and self-organization by popular movements, that can save the planet from the devastating policies of a system based on greed and protect and enhance the lives and working conditions of the vast majority of those now sacrificed to this greed. It is not possible to tell what the outcome will be as such critiques deepen and understanding and activism spread. Seattle will undoubtedly be remembered as a turning point in a global struggle.

This past April, demonstrations in Washington, DC, at the annual joint meeting of the IMF and the World Bank called attention to the way these international agencies have contributed to economic crisis and to the ways that their imposition of austere solutions on the nations in crisis have exacerbated human misery. The World Bank has identified over one hundred major episodes of bank insolvency in ninety developing countries and transitional economies (former socialist nations) from the late 1970s to 1994.

There have been more since 1994- in Mexico, in East Asia, and in Russia, to name only the most spectacular. In more than two-thirds of the countries for which data are available, the direct economic loss suffered was more than 3 percent of GDP, about the total increase in an average country's output in a good year. In the early 1980s, Argentina lost the equivalent of more than half of its GDP and Chile more than 40 percent. One might think that such costs would call into question the financial liberalization demanded as part of the Washington Consensus and the cause of much of the problem, but such notions have only begun to penetrate these institutions, and only after intense protest and criticism.

Financial liberalization and crisis have been good for transnational capital, making it easier for financial imperialism to penetrate and control developing economies. The austerity required to pay for the damages is absorbed by local populations, which suffer unemployment, lost government services, and higher prices resulting from forced currency devaluations. The IMF plays the "bad cop," making its performance criteria high growth and low inflation, while ignoring the accompanying increases in unemployment and poverty. It declares a nation like South Korea a success when output rebounds, even though unemployment remains at triple the pre-crisis level.

The World Bank plays the "good cop," feeling the pain of the poor and extending some finances to address a bit of the suffering unleashed by neoliberal policies. It offers a spoonful of sugar to help the bitter medicine go down. The struggle for economic justice in the twenty-first century will be international. As the drive by transnational corporations an d transnational finance to impose their rule over the working people of the world comes to be seen for what it is, some old ways of thinking will come back into vogue. Perhaps it is not unreasonable to expect that sooner or later, some new bumper stickers will boldly say, "Workers of the World, Unite."

Bibliography

Noeleen Heyzer. *Daughters in Industry: Work, Skills, and Consciousness of Women Workers in Asia.* Kuala Lumpur: Asian and Pacific Development Centre, 1988.

David Wigg ; foreword by H.E. Dame R. Nita Barrow. *In a Class of Their Own: A Look at the Campaign against Female Illiteracy.* Washington, D.C.: World Bank, c1994.

My Rights, Who Control[S]? : A Report of the Regional Consultation, Asia Pacific Women's Issues, Law and Development ... Kuala Lumpur: Asia Pacific Forum on Women Law & Development, 1989.

Kate Young. *Serving Two Masters: Third World Women in Development.* Ahmedabad: Allied Publishers, 1989.

Betty Jamie Chung, Ng Shui Meng. *The Status of Women in Law: A Comparison of Four Asian Countries.* Singapore: Institute of Southeast Asian Studies, 1977.

San Juan. *Women Empowering Women: Proceedings of the Human Rights Conference On The Trafficking Of Asian Women,* April 2-4, .../ Metro Manila : Coalition Against Trafficking in Women-Asia, 1993.

Barbara E. Ward. *Women in the New Asia; The Changing Social Roles of Men and Women in South and South-East Asia.* Paris: UNESCO, 1963.

Rekha Dayal. *Women in Health and Development in South-East Asia.* New Delhi: World Health Organization, Regional Office for South-East Asia, 1985.

Lynne Brydon and Sylvia Chant. *Women in the Third World: Gender Issues in Rural and Urban Areas.* New Brunswick, NJ : Rutgers University, 1989.

Penny van Esterik. *Women of Southeast Asia.* De Kalb, IL: Northern Illinois University, Center for Southeast Asian Studies, c1996.

Yayori Matsui. *Women's Asia.* London; Atlantic Highlands, N.J. : Zed Books, c1989.

Committee on Women's Studies in Asia. *Women's Studies, Women's Lives: Theory and Practice in South and Southeast Asia.* New Delhi: Kali for Women, c1994.

R. Lund and S. M. Panda. Asian Financial Crisis, Women's Work and Forced Migration. *Norsk Geografisk Tidsskrift, v. 54:3, 2000, p. 128-133.*

Darunee Tantiwiramanond. Changing Gender Relations in Southeast Asia and the Contribution of Women's Organizations. *Southeast Asia Studies Bulletin, Oct 1997, p.18.*

Richard Leete. The Continuing Flight from Marriage and Parenthood among the Overseas Chinese in East and Southeast Asia: Dimensions and Implications. *Population and Development Review, v. 20:4, Dec 1994, p. 811 (19 pages).*

Barbara Watson Andaya. From Temporary Wife to Prostitute: Sexuality and Economic Change in Early Modern Southeast Asia. *Journal of Women's History, v. 9:4, Win 1998, p. 11 (24 pages).*

Wazir Jahan Karim. *Gender Studies in Southeast Asia. Southeast Asian Journal of Social Science, v. 21:1, 1993, p. 98-113.*

Gavin W Jones. Modernization and Divorce: Contrasting Trends in Islamic Southeast Asia and the West. *Population and Development Review, v. 23:1, March 1997, p. 95 (20 pages).*

Parvati Raghuram and Irene Hardill. Netgitiating a Market: A Case Study of an Asian Woman in Business. *Women's Studies International Fourm, v. 21:5, Sept 10, 1998, p. 475-483.*

Purification V. Quisumbing The Position of Women Under Labor Laws in ASEAN. *Philippine Journal of Industrial Relations, v. 8:2 & v. 9:1, 1986-1987, p. 138-144.*

Robert Weissman. Repression to Cooptation: Challenges for Women Workers in Southeast Asia. *Multinational Monitor, v. 14:11, Nov 1993, 20 pages.*

Spinder Dhaliwal. Silent Contributors, Asian Female Entrepreneurs and Women in Business. *Women's Studies International Forum, v. 21:5, Sept 10, 1998, p. 463-474.*

Judith Nagata & Janet W. Salaff. Strategies for Survival: Lives of Southeast Asian Women. *Southeast Asian Journal of Social Science, v. 24:1, 1996.*

Barbara Watson Andaya. Women and Economic Change: The Pepper Trade in Pre-Modern Southeast Asia [On Sumatra]. *Journal of the Economic and Social History of the Orient, v. 38:2, May 1995, p. 165-190.*

C. Shan Beyrer. Women and Girls and the Sex Industry in Southeast Asia; Political Causes and Human Rights Implications. *Social Science & Medicine, August 2001, v. 53:4, p. 543-550.*

Laura Sanchez. Women's Power and the Gendered Division of Domestic Labor in the Third World. *Gender and Society, v.7:3, 1993, p.434-59.*

Jan Jindy Pettman.Women on the Move: Globalization and Labor Migration from South and Southeast Asian States. *Global Society, v. 12, Sept 1998, p. 389-403.*

Jurgette Hondulado. Women Workers in Southeast Asia: Issues, Demands and Participation in Trade Unions. *Philippine Journal of Industrial Relations, v. 8:2 & v. 9:1, 1986-1987, p. 161-172.*

Tania Murray Li. Working Separately but Eating Together: Personhood, Property, and Power Inconjugal Relations. *American Ethnologist, v. 25:4, Nov 1998 p. 675-676.*

Index